Old Manse Edition

THE COMPLETE WRITINGS OF NATHANIEL HAWTHORNE

WITH PORTRAITS, ILLUSTRATIONS, AND FACSIMILES

IN TWENTY–TWO VOLUMES

VOLUME XXII

Ross Turner

A Roman Vista

THE WRITINGS OF

Nathaniel Hawthorne

HOUGHTON MIFFLIN COMPANY

NOTES OF TRAVEL

BY

NATHANIEL HAWTHORNE

IN FOUR VOLUMES

VOLUME IV

BOSTON AND NEW YORK

HOUGHTON MIFFLIN COMPANY

The Riverside Press Cambridge

LIST OF ILLUSTRATIONS

NOTES OF TRAVEL

IV

PERUGIA, *May* 28, 1858. — As I said last night, we left Foligno betimes in the morning, which was bleak, chill, and very threatening, there being very little blue sky anywhere, and the clouds lying heavily on some of the mountain ridges. The wind blew sharply, right in Una's face and mine, as we occupied the coupé, so that there must have been a great deal of the north in it. We drove through a wide plain — the Umbrian valley, I suppose — and soon passed the old town of Spello, just touching its skirts, and wondering how people, who had this rich and convenient plain from which to choose a site, could think of covering a huge island of rock with their dwellings, — for Spello tumbled its crooked and narrow streets down a steep descent, and cannot well have a yard of even space within its walls. It is said to contain some rare treasures of ancient pictorial art.

I do not remember much that we saw on our route. The plains and the lower hillsides seemed fruitful of everything that belongs to

Italy, especially the olive and the vine. As usual, there were a great many shrines, and frequently a cross, by the wayside. Hitherto it had been merely a plain wooden cross ; but now almost every cross was hung with various instruments, represented in wood, apparently symbols of the crucifixion of our Saviour, — the spear, the sponge, the crown of thorns, the hammer, a pair of pincers, and always St. Peter's cock, made a prominent figure, generally perched on the summit of the cross.

From our first start this morning we had seen mists in various quarters, betokening that there was rain in those spots, and now it began to spatter in our own faces, although within the wide extent of our prospect we could see the sunshine falling on portions of the valley. A rainbow, too, shone out, and remained so long visible that it appeared to have made a permanent stain in the sky.

By and by we reached Assisi, which is magnificently situated for pictorial purposes, with a gray castle above it, and a gray wall around it, itself on a mountain, and looking over the great plain which we had been traversing, and through which lay our onward way. We drove through the Piazza Grande to an ancient house a little beyond, where a hospitable old lady receives travellers for a consideration, without exactly keeping an inn.

In the piazza we saw the beautiful front of a temple of Minerva, consisting of several marble pillars, fluted, and with rich capitals supporting a pediment. It was as fine as anything I had seen at Rome, and is now, of course, converted into a Catholic church.

I ought to have said that, instead of driving straight to the old lady's, we alighted at the door of a church near the city gate, and went in to inspect some melancholy frescos, and thence clambered up a narrow street to the Cathedral, which has a Gothic front, old enough, but not very impressive. I really remember not a single object that we saw within, but am pretty certain that the interior had been stuccoed and whitewashed. The ecclesiastics of old time did an excellent thing in covering the interiors of their churches with brilliant frescos, thus filling the holy places with saints and angels, and almost with the presence of the Divinity. The modern ecclesiastics do the next best thing in obliterating the wretched remnants of what has had its day and done its office. These frescos might be looked upon as the symbol of the living spirit that made Catholicism a true religion, and glorified it as long as it did live ; now the glory and beauty have departed from one and the other.

My wife, Una, and Miss Shepard now set out with a cicerone to visit the great Franciscan con-

3

vent, in the church of which are preserved some miraculous specimens, in fresco and in oils, of early Italian art; but as I had no mind to suffer any further in this way, I stayed behind with Julian and Rose, who were equally weary of these things.

After they were gone we took a ramble through the city, but were almost swept away by the violence of the wind, which struggled with me for my hat, and whirled Rose before it like a feather. The people in the public square seemed much diverted at our predicament, being, I suppose, accustomed to these rude blasts in their mountain home. However, the wind blew in momentary gusts, and then became more placable till another fit of fury came, and passed as suddenly as before. We walked out of the same gate through which we had entered, — an ancient gate, but recently stuccoed and whitewashed, in wretched contrast to the gray, venerable wall through which it affords ingress, — and I stood gazing at the magnificent prospect of the wide valley beneath. It was so vast that there appeared to be all varieties of weather in it at the same instant; fields of sunshine, tracts of storm, — here the coming tempest, there the departing one. It was a picture of the world on a vast canvas, for there was rural life and city life within the great expanse, and the whole set in a frame of mountains, — the

nearest bold and distinct, with the rocky ledges
showing through their sides, the distant ones
blue and dim, — so far stretched this broad
valley.

When I had looked long enough, — no, not
long enough, for it would take a great while to
read that page, — we returned within the gate,
and we clambered up, past the Cathedral, and
into the narrow streets above it.   The aspect of
everything was immeasurably old; a thousand
years would be but a middle age for one of those
houses, built so massively with huge stones and
solid arches, that I do not see how they are ever
to tumble down, or to be less fit for human
habitation than they are now.   The streets crept
between them, and beneath arched passages, and
up and down steps of stone or ancient brick, for
it would be altogether impossible for a carriage
to ascend above the Grand Piazza, though possibly a donkey or a chairman's mule might find
foothold.   The city seems like a stony growth
out of the hillside, or a fossilized city, — so old
and singular it is, without enough life and juici-
ness in it to be susceptible of decay.   An earthquake is the only chance of its ever being ruined,
beyond its present ruin.   Nothing is more
strange than to think that this now dead city —
dead, as regards the purposes for which men live
nowadays — was, centuries ago, the seat and
birthplace almost of art, the only art in which

the beautiful part of the human mind then developed itself. How came that flower to grow among these wild mountains? I do not conceive, however, that the people of Assisi were ever much more enlightened or cultivated on the side of art than they are at present. The ecclesiastics were then the only patrons; and the flower grew here because there was a great ecclesiastical garden in which it was sheltered and fostered. But it is very curious to think of Assisi, a school of art within, and mountain and wilderness without.

My wife and the rest of the party returned from the convent before noon, delighted with what they had seen, as I was delighted not to have seen it. We ate our *déjeuner*, and resumed our journey, passing beneath the great convent, after emerging from the gate opposite to that of our entrance. The edifice made a very good spectacle, being of great extent, and standing on a double row of high and narrow arches, on which it is built up from the declivity of the hill.

We soon reached the Church of St. Mary of the Angels, which is a modern structure, and very spacious, built in place of one destroyed by an earthquake. It is a fine church, opening out a magnificent space in its nave and aisles; and beneath the great dome stands the small old chapel, with its rude stone walls, in which

6

St. Francis founded his order. This chapel and
the dome appear to have been the only portions
of the ancient church that were not destroyed
by the earthquake.   The dwelling of St. Francis is said to be also preserved within the church ;
but we did not see it, unless it were a little dark
closet into which we squeezed to see some frescos by La Spagna.   It had an old wooden door,
of which Una picked off a little bit of a chip, to
serve as a relic.   There is a fresco in the church,
on the pediment of the chapel, by Overbeck,
representing the Assumption of the Virgin.   It
did not strike me as wonderfully fine.   The
other pictures, of which there were many, were
modern, and of no great merit.

We pursued our way, and came, by and by,
to the foot of the high hill on which stands
Perugia, and which is so long and steep that
Gaetano took a yoke of oxen to aid his horses
in the ascent.   We all, except my wife, walked
a part of the way up, and I myself, with Julian
for my companion, kept on even to the city
gate, — a distance, I should think, of two or
three miles at least.   The lower part of the road
was on the edge of the hill, with a narrow valley
on our left ; and as the sun had now broken
out, its verdure and fertility, its foliage and cultivation, shone forth in miraculous beauty, as
green as England, as bright as only Italy.   Perugia appeared above us, crowning a mighty

7

hill, the most picturesque of cities; and the higher we ascended, the more the view opened before us, as we looked back on the course that we had traversed, and saw the wide valley, sweeping down and spreading out, bounded afar by mountains, and sleeping in sun and shadow. No language nor any art of the pencil can give an idea of the scene. When God expressed himself in the landscape to mankind, He did not intend that it should be translated into any tongue save his own immediate one. Julian meanwhile, whose heart is now wholly in snail shells, was rummaging for them among the stones and hedges by the roadside; yet, doubtless, enjoyed the prospect more than he knew. The coach lagged far behind us, and when it came up, we entered the gate, where a soldier appeared, and demanded my passport. We drove to the Grand Hôtel de France, which is near the gate, and two fine little boys ran beside the carriage, well dressed and well looking enough to have been a gentleman's sons, but claiming Gaetano for their father. He is an inhabitant of Perugia, and has therefore reached his own home, though we are still little more than midway to our journey's end.

Our hotel proves, thus far, to be the best that we have yet met with. We are only in the outskirts of Perugia; the bulk of the city, where the most interesting churches and the public

8

edifices are situated, being far above us on the hill. My wife, Una, Miss Shepard, and Rose streamed forth immediately, and saw a church; but Julian, who hates them, and I, remained behind; and, for my part, I added several pages to this volume of scribble.

This morning was as bright as morning could be, even in Italy, and in this transparent mountain atmosphere. We at first declined the services of a cicerone, and went out in the hopes of finding our way to whatever we wished to see, by our own instincts. This proved to be a mistaken hope, however; and we wandered about the upper city, much persecuted by a shabby old man who wished to guide us; so, at last, Miss Shepard went back in quest of the cicerone at the hotel, and, meanwhile, we climbed to the summit of the hill of Perugia, and, leaning over a wall, looked forth upon a most magnificent view of mountain and valley, terminating in some peaks, lofty and dim, which surely must be the Apennines. There again a young man accosted us, offering to guide us to the Cambio, or Exchange; and as this was one of the places which we especially wished to see, we accepted his services. By the bye, I ought to have mentioned that we had already entered a church (San Luigi, I believe), the interior of which we found very impressive, dim with the light of stained and painted windows, insomuch that it at first seemed almost dark, and we could only see the bright twinkling of the tapers at the shrines; but, after a few minutes, we discerned the tall octagonal pillars of the nave, marble, and supporting a beautiful roof of crossed arches. The church was neither Gothic nor classic, but a mixture of both, and most likely barbarous; yet it had a grand effect in its tinted twilight, and convinced me more than ever how desirable it is that religious edifices should have painted windows.

The door of the Cambio proved to be one that we had passed several times, while seeking for it, and was very near the church just mentioned, which fronts on one side of the same piazza. We were received by an old gentleman, who appeared to be a public officer, and found ourselves in a small room, wainscoted with beautifully carved oak, roofed with a coved ceiling, painted with symbols of the planets, and arabesqued in rich designs by Raphael, and lined with splendid frescos of subjects, scriptural and historical, by Perugino. When the room was in its first glory, I can conceive that the world had not elsewhere to show, within so small a space, such magnificence and beauty as were then displayed here. Even now, I enjoyed (to the best of my belief, for we can never feel sure that we are not bamboozling ourselves in such matters) some real pleasure in what I saw; and especially seemed to feel, after all these ages, the old painter's devout sentiment still breathing forth from the religious pictures, the work of a hand that had so long been dust.

When we had looked long at these, the old gentleman led us into a chapel, of the same size as the former room, and built in the same fashion, wainscoted likewise with old oak. The walls were also frescoed, entirely frescoed, and retained more of their original brightness than those we had already seen, although the pictures were the production of a somewhat inferior hand, a pupil of Perugino. They seemed to be very striking, however, not the less so, that one of them provoked an unseasonable smile. It was the Decapitation of John the Baptist; and this holy personage was represented as still on his knees, with his hands clasped in prayer, although the executioner was already depositing the head in a charger, and the blood was spouting from the headless trunk, directly, as it were, into the face of the spectator.

While we were in the outer room, the cicerone who first offered his services at the hotel had come in ; so we paid our chance guide, and expected him to take his leave. It is characteristic of this idle country, however, that if you once speak to a person, or connect yourself with him by the slightest possible tie, you will hardly get rid of him by anything short of main force. He still lingered in the room, and was still there when I came away; for, having had as many pictures as I could digest, I left my wife and Una with the cicerone, and set out on a ramble with Julian. We plunged from the upper city down through some of the strangest passages that ever were called streets; some of them, indeed, being arched all over, and, going down into the unknown darkness, looked like caverns; and we followed one of them doubtfully, till it opened out upon the light. The houses on each side were divided only by a pace or two, and communicated with one another, here and there, by arched passages. They looked very ancient, and may have been inhabited by Etruscan princes, judging from the massiveness of some of the foundation stones. The present inhabitants, nevertheless, are by no means princely, — shabby men, and the careworn wives and mothers of the people, — one of whom was guiding a child in leading-strings through these antique alleys, where hundreds of generations have trod before those little feet. Finally, we came out through a gateway, the same gateway at which we entered last night.

I ought to have mentioned, in the narrative of yesterday, that we crossed the Tiber shortly before reaching Perugia, already a broad and rapid stream, and already distinguished by the same turbid and mud-puddly quality of water that we see in it at Rome. I think it will never

be so disagreeable to me hereafter, now that I
find this turbidness to be its native color, and
not (like that of the Thames) accruing from city
sewers or any impurities of the lowlands.

As I now remember, the small Chapel of
Santa Maria degli Angeli seems to have been
originally the house of St. Francis.

May 29. — This morning we visited the
Church of the Dominicans, where we saw some
quaint pictures by Fra Angelico, with a good
deal of religious sincerity in them ; also a picture
of St. Columbo, by Perugino, which unquestionably is very good. To confess the truth, I
took more interest in a fair Gothic monument,
in white marble, of Pope Benedict XII., representing him reclining under a canopy, while two
angels draw aside the curtain, the canopy being supported by twisted columns, richly ornamented. I like this overflow and gratuity of
device, with which Gothic sculpture works out
its designs, after seeing so much of the simplicity of classic art in marble.

We then tried to find the Church of San Pietro in Martire, but without success, although
every person of whom we inquired immediately
attached himself or herself to us, and could
hardly be got rid of by any efforts on our part.
Nobody seemed to know the church we wished
for, but all directed us to another Church of

San Pietro, which contains nothing of interest; whereas the right church is supposed to contain a celebrated picture by Perugino.

Finally, we ascended the hill and the city proper of Perugia (for our hotel is in one of the suburbs), and Julian and I set out on a ramble about the city. It was market day, and the principal piazza, with the neighboring streets, was crowded with people. . . .

The best part of Perugia, that in which the grand piazzas and the principal public edifices stand, seems to be a nearly level plateau on the summit of the hill; but it is of no very great extent, and the streets rapidly run downward on either side. Julian and I followed one of these descending streets, and were led a long way by it, till we at last emerged from one of the gates of the city, and had another view of the mountains and valleys, the fertile and sunny wilderness in which this ancient civilization stands.

On the right of the gate there was a rude country path, partly overgrown with grass, bordered by a hedge on one side, and on the other by the gray city wall, at the base of which the track kept onward. We followed it, hoping that it would lead us to some other gate by which we might reënter the city; but it soon grew so indistinct and broken, that it was evidently on the point of melting into somebody's olive orchard or wheat fields or vineyards, all of which lay on the other side of the hedge; and a kindly old woman of whom I inquired told me (if I rightly understood her Italian) that I should find no further passage in that direction. So we turned back, much broiled in the hot sun, and only now and then relieved by the shadow of an angle or a tower.

A lame beggar-man sat by the gate, and as we passed him Julian gave him two baiocchi (which he himself had begged of me to buy an orange with), and was loaded with the pauper's prayers and benedictions as we entered the city. A great many blessings can be bought for very little money anywhere in Italy; and whether they avail anything or no, it is pleasant to see that the beggars have gratitude enough to bestow them in such abundance.

Of all beggars I think a little fellow, who rode beside our carriage on a stick, his bare feet scampering merrily, while he managed his steed with one hand, and held out the other for charity, howling piteously the while, amused me most.

PASSIGNANO, *May* 29. — We left Perugia at about three o'clock to-day, and went down a pretty steep descent; but I have no particular recollection of the road till it again began to descend, before reaching the village of Mugione. We all, except my wife, walked up the long hill, while the vettura was dragged after us with the aid of a yoke of oxen. Arriving first at the village, I leaned over the wall to admire the beautiful *paese* (" le bel piano," as a peasant called it, who made acquaintance with me) that lay at the foot of the hill, so level, so bounded within moderate limits by a frame of hills and ridges, that it looked like a green lake. In fact, I think it was once a real lake, which made its escape from its bed, as I have known some lakes to have done in America.

Passing through and beyond the village, I saw, on a height above the road, a half-ruinous tower, with great cracks running down its walls, halfway from top to bottom. Some little children had mounted the hill with us, begging all the way ; they were recruited with additional numbers in the village ; and here, beneath the ruinous tower, a madman, as it seemed, assaulted us, and ran almost under the carriage wheels, in his earnestness to get a baioccho. Ridding ourselves of these annoyances, we drove on, and, between five and six o'clock came in sight of the Lake of Thrasymene, obtaining our first view of it, I think, in its longest extent. There were high hills, and one mountain with its head in the clouds, visible on the farther shore, and on the horizon beyond it ; but the nearer banks were long ridges, and hills of only moderate height. The declining

sun threw a broad sheen of brightness over the
surface of the lake, so that we could not well
see it for excess of light ; but had a vision of
headlands and islands floating about in a flood
of gold, and blue, airy heights bounding it afar.
When we first drew near the lake, there was
but a narrow tract, covered with vines and
olives, between it and the hill that rose on the
other side. As we advanced, the tract grew
wider, and was very fertile, as was the hillside,
with wheat fields, and vines, and olives, especially the latter, which, symbol of peace as it is,
seemed to find something congenial to it in the
soil stained long ago with blood. Farther onward, the space between the lake and hill grew
still narrower, the road skirting along almost
close to the waterside ; and when we reached
the town of Passignano there was but room
enough for its dirty and ugly street to stretch
along the shore. I have seldom beheld a lovelier scene than that of the lake and the landscape around it ; never an uglier one than that
of this idle and decaying village, where we were
immediately surrounded by beggars of all ages,
and by men vociferously proposing to row us
out upon the lake. We declined their offers
of a boat, for the evening was very fresh and
cool, insomuch that I should have liked an
outside garment, — a temperature that I had
not anticipated, so near the beginning of June,

17

in sunny Italy.   Instead of a row, we took a
walk through the village, hoping to come upon
the shore of the lake in some secluded spot;
but an incredible number of beggar children,
both boys and girls, but more of the latter,
rushed out of every door, and went along with
us, all howling their miserable petitions at the
same moment.   The village street is long, and
our escort waxed more numerous at every step,
till Miss Shepard actually counted forty of
these little reprobates, and more were doubtless added afterwards.   At first, no doubt, they
begged in earnest hope of getting some baiocchi; but, by and by, perceiving that we had determined not to give them anything, they made
a joke of the matter, and began to laugh and to
babble, and turn heels over head, still keeping
about us, like a swarm of flies, and now and
then begging again with all their might.   There
were as few pretty faces as I ever saw among
the same number of children; and they were
as ragged and dirty little imps as any in the
world, and, moreover, tainted the air with a
very disagreeable odor from their rags and dirt;
rugged and healthy enough, nevertheless, and
sufficiently intelligent; certainly bold and per-
severing too; so that it is hard to say what
they needed to fit them for success in life.   Yet
they begin as beggars, and no doubt will end
so, as all their parents and grandparents do;

for, in our walk through the village, every old woman and many younger ones held out their hands for alms, as if they had all been famished. Yet these people kept their houses over their heads ; had firesides in winter, I suppose, and food out of their little gardens every day ; pigs to kill, chickens, olives, wine, and a great many things to make life comfortable.   The children, desperately as they begged, looked in good bodily case, and happy enough ; but, certainly, there was a look of earnest misery in the faces of some of the old women, either genuine or exceedingly well acted.

I could not bear the persecution, and went into our hotel, determining not to venture out again till our departure ; at least not in the day-light.   My wife, and the rest of the family, how-ever, continued their walk, and at length were relieved from their little pests by three police-men (the very images of those in Rome, in their blue, long-skirted coats, cocked chapeaux-bras, white shoulder-belts, and swords), who boxed their ears, and dispersed them.   Meanwhile, they had quite driven away all sentimental effu-sion (of which I felt more, really, than I ex-pected) about the Lake of Thrasymene.

The inn of Passignano promised little from its outward appearance ; a tall, dark old house, with a stone staircase leading us up from one sombre story to another, into a brick-paved dining-room, with our sleeping chambers on each side. There was a fireplace of tremendous depth and height, fit to receive big forest-logs, and with a queer, double pair of ancient and-irons, capable of sustaining them; and in a handful of ashes lay a small stick of olive wood, — a specimen, I suppose, of the sort of fuel which had made the chimney black in the course of a good many years. There must have been much shivering and misery of cold around this fireplace. However, we needed no fire now, and there was promise of good cheer in the spectacle of a man cleaning some lake fish for our dinner, while the poor things flounced and wriggled under the knife.

The dinner made its appearance, after a long while, and was most plentiful, . . . so that, having measured our appetite in anticipation of a paucity of food, we had to make more room for such overflowing abundance.

When dinner was over, it was already dusk, and before retiring I opened the window, and looked out on Lake Thrasymene, the margin of which lies just on the other side of the narrow village street. The moon was a day or two past the full, just a little clipped on the edge, but gave light enough to show the lake and its nearer shores almost as distinctly as by day; and, there being a ripple on the surface of the water, it made a sheen of silver over a wide space.

Arezzo, *May* 30. — We started at six o'clock, and left the one ugly street of Passignano before many of the beggars were awake. Immediately in the vicinity of the village, there is very little space between the lake in front and the ridge of hills in the rear; but the plain widened as we drove onward, so that the lake was scarcely to be seen, or often quite hidden among the intervening trees, although we could still discern the summits of the mountains that rise far beyond its shores. The country was fertile, presenting, on each side of the road, vines trained on fig-trees; wheat fields and olives, in greater abundance than any other product. On our right, with a considerable width of plain between, was the bending ridge of hills that shut in the Roman army, by its close approach to the lake at Passignano. In perhaps half an hour's drive, we reached the little bridge that throws its arch over the Sanguinetto, and alighted there. The stream has but about a yard's width of water; and its whole course, between the hills and the lake, might well have been reddened and swollen with the blood of the multitude of slain Romans. Its name put me in mind of the Bloody Brook at Deerfield, where a company of Massachusetts men were massacred by the Indians.

The Sanguinetto flows over a bed of pebbles; and Julian crept under the bridge, and got one of them for a memorial; while Una, Miss Shepard, and Rose plucked some olive twigs and oak leaves, and made them into wreaths together, — symbols of victory and peace. The tower, which is traditionally named after Hannibal, is seen on a height that makes part of the line of enclosing hills. It is a large, old castle, apparently of the Middle Ages, with a square front, and a battlemented sweep of wall. The town of Torres (its name, I think), where Hannibal's main army is supposed to have lain while the Romans came through the pass, was in full view; and I could understand the plan of the battle better than any system of military operations which I have hitherto tried to fathom. Both last night and to-day, I found myself stirred more sensibly than I expected by the influences of this scene. The old battlefield is still fertile in thoughts and emotions, though it is so many ages since the blood spilt there has ceased to make the grass and flowers grow more luxuriantly. I doubt whether I should feel so much on the field of Saratoga or Monmouth; but these old classic battlefields belong to the whole world, and each man feels as if his own forefathers fought them. Mine, by the bye, if they fought them at all, must have been on the side of Hannibal; for, certainly, I sympathized with him, and exulted in the defeat of the Romans on their own soil. They excite much the same emotion of general hostility that the English do. Byron has written some very fine stanzas on the battlefield, — not so good as others that he has written on classical scenes and subjects, yet wonderfully impressing his own perception of the subject on the reader. Whenever he has to deal with a statue, a ruin, a battlefield, he pounces upon the topic like a vulture, and tears out its heart in a twinkling, so that there is nothing more to be said.

If I mistake not, our passport was examined by the papal officers at the last custom-house in the pontifical territory, before we traversed the path through which the Roman army marched to its destruction. Lake Thrasymene, of which we took our last view, is not deep set among the hills, but is bordered by long ridges, with loftier mountains receding into the distance. It is not to be compared to Windermere or Loch Lomond for beauty, nor with Lake Champlain and many a smaller lake in my own country, none of which, I hope, will ever become so historically interesting as this famous spot. A few miles onward our passport was countersigned at the Tuscan custom-house, and our luggage permitted to pass without examination on payment

23

of a fee of nine or ten pauls, besides two pauls to the porters. There appears to be no concealment on the part of the officials in thus waiving the exercise of their duty, and I rather imagine that the thing is recognized and permitted by their superiors. At all events, it is very convenient for the traveller.

We saw Cortona, sitting, like so many other cities in this region, on its hill, and arrived about noon at Arezzo, which also stretches up a high hillside, and is surrounded, as they all are, by its walls or the remains of one, with a fortified gate across every entrance.

I remember one little village, somewhere in the neighborhood of the Clitumnus, which we entered by one gateway, and, in the course of two minutes at the utmost, left by the opposite one, so diminutive was this walled town. Everything hereabouts bears traces of times when war was the prevalent condition, and peace only a rare gleam of sunshine.

At Arezzo we have put up at the Hôtel Royal, which has the appearance of a grand old house, and proves to be a tolerable inn enough. After lunch, we wandered forth to see the town, which did not greatly interest me after Perugia, being much more modern and less picturesque in its aspect. We went to the Cathedral, — a Gothic edifice, but not of striking exterior. As the doors were closed, and not to be opened till

24

three o'clock, we seated ourselves under the
trees, on a high, grassy space, surrounded and
intersected with gravel walks, — a public promenade, in short, near the Cathedral; and after
resting ourselves here we went in search of Petrarch's house, which Murray mentions as being
in this neighborhood. We inquired of several
people, who knew nothing about the matter;
one woman misdirected us, out of mere fun, I
believe, for she afterwards met us and asked how
we had succeeded. But finally, through ——'s
enterprise and perseverance, we found the spot,
not a stone's throw from where we had been
sitting.

Petrarch's house stands below the promenade
which I have just mentioned, and within hearing of the reverberations between the strokes of
the Cathedral bell. It is two stories high, covered with a light-colored stucco, and has not the
slightest appearance of antiquity, no more than
many a modern and modest dwelling-house in
an American city. Its only remarkable feature
is a pointed arch of stone, let into the plastered
wall, and forming a framework for the doorway.
I set my foot on the doorsteps, ascended them,
and Miss Shepard and Julian gathered some
weeds or blades of grass that grew in the chinks
between the steps. There is a long inscription
on a slab of marble set in the front of the house,
as is the fashion in Arezzo when a house has

25

been the birthplace or residence of a distinguished man.

Right opposite Petrarch's birth-house — and it must have been the well whence the water was drawn that first bathed him — is a well which Boccaccio has introduced into one of his stories. It is surrounded with a stone curb, octagonal in shape, and evidently as ancient as Boccaccio's time. It has a wooden cover, through which is a square opening, and looking down I saw my own face in the water far beneath.

There is no familiar object connected with daily life so interesting as a well; and this well of old Arezzo, whence Petrarch had drank, around which he had played in his boyhood, and which Boccaccio has made famous, really interested me more than the Cathedral. It lies right under the pavement of the street, under the sunshine, without any shade of trees about it, or any grass, except a little that grows in the crevices of its stones; but the shape of its stonework would make it a pretty object in an engraving. As I lingered round it, I thought of my own town-pump in old Salem, and wondered whether my townspeople would ever point it out to strangers, and whether the stranger would gaze at it with any degree of such interest as I felt in Boccaccio's well. O, certainly not; but yet I made that humble town-pump the most celebrated structure in the good

26

town.   A thousand and a thousand people had pumped there, merely to water oxen or fill their tea-kettles ; but when once I grasped the handle, a rill gushed forth that meandered as far as England, as far as India, besides tasting pleasantly in every town and village of our own country.   I like to think of this, so long after I did it, and so far from home, and am not without hope of some kindly local remembrance on this score.

Petrarch's house is not a separate and insulated building, but stands in contiguity and connection with other houses on each side ; and all, when I saw them, as well as the whole street, extending down the slope of the hill, had the bright and sunny aspect of a modern town.

As the Cathedral was not yet open, and as Julian and I had not so much patience as my wife, we left her and Miss Shepard, and set out to return to the hotel.   We lost our way, however, and finally had to return to the Cathedral, to take a fresh start ; and as the door was now open we went in.   We found the Cathedral very stately with its great arches, and darkly magnificent with the dim rich light coming through its painted windows, some of which are reckoned the most beautiful that the whole world has to show.   The hues are far more brilliant than those of any painted glass I saw in

England, and a great wheel window looks like a constellation of many-colored gems. The old English glass gets so smoky and dull with dust, that its pristine beauty cannot any longer be even imagined; nor did I imagine it till I saw these Italian windows. We saw nothing of my wife and Miss Shepard; but found afterwards that they had been much annoyed by the attentions of a priest who wished to show them the Cathedral, till they finally told him that they had no money with them, when he left them without another word. The attendants in churches seem to be quite as venal as most other Italians, and, for the sake of their little profit, they do not hesitate to interfere with the great purposes for which their churches were built and decorated; hanging curtains, for instance, before all the celebrated pictures, or hiding them away in the sacristy, so that they cannot be seen without a fee.

Returning to the hotel, we looked out of the window, and, in the street beneath, there was a very busy scene, it being Sunday, and the whole population, apparently, being astir, — promenading up and down the smooth flag-stones, which made the breadth of the street one sidewalk, or at their windows, or sitting before their doors.

The vivacity of the population in these parts is very striking, after the gravity and lassitude

of Rome; and the air was made cheerful with
the talk and laughter of hundreds of voices. I
think the women are prettier than the Roman
maids and matrons, who, as I think I have said
before, have chosen to be very uncomely since
the rape of their ancestresses, by way of wreak-
ing a terrible spite and revenge.

I have nothing more to say of Arezzo, except
that, finding the ordinary wine very bad, as black
as ink, and tasting as if it had tar and vinegar
in it, we called for a bottle of Monte Pulciano,
and were exceedingly gladdened and mollified
thereby.

INCISA. — We left Arezzo early on Monday
morning, the sun throwing the long shadows
of the trees across the road, which at first, after
we had descended the hill, lay over a plain. As
the morning advanced, or as we advanced, the
country grew more hilly. We saw many bits
of rustic life, — such as old women tending
pigs or sheep by the roadside, and spinning
with a distaff; women sewing under trees or
at their own doors; children leading goats, tied
by the horns, while they browse; sturdy, sunburnt creatures, in petticoats, but otherwise
manlike, at work side by side with male laborers in the fields. The broad-brimmed, high-
crowned hat of Tuscan straw is the customary
female headdress, and is as unbecoming as can

possibly be imagined, and of little use, one
would suppose, as a shelter from the sun, the
brim continually blowing upward from the face.
Some of the elder women wore black felt hats,
likewise broad-brimmed; and the men wore
felt hats also, shaped a good deal like a mush-
room, with hardly any brim at all. The scenes
in the villages through which we passed were
very lively and characteristic, all the population
seeming to be out of doors : some at the butch-
er's shop, others at the well; a tailor sewing in
the open air, with a young priest sitting sociably beside him; children at play; women mend-
ing clothes, embroidering, spinning with the distaff at their own doorsteps; many idlers, letting
the pleasant morning pass in the sweet-do-
nothing; all assembling in the street, as in the
common room of one large household, and thus
brought close together, and made familiar with
one another, as they can never be in a different
system of society. As usual, along the road, we
passed multitudes of shrines, where the Virgin
was painted in fresco, or sometimes represented
in bas-reliefs, within niches, or under more spacious arches. It would be a good idea to place
a comfortable and shady seat beneath all these
wayside shrines, where the wayfarer might rest
himself, and thank the Virgin for her hospitality; nor can I believe that it would offend her,
any more than other incense, if he were to re-

gale himself, even in such consecrated spots, with the fragrance of a pipe or cigar.

In the wire-work screen, before many of the shrines, hung offerings of roses and other flowers, some wilted and withered, some fresh with that morning's dew, some that never bloomed and never faded, — being artificial. I wonder that they do not plant rose-trees and all kinds of fragrant and flowering shrubs under the shrines, and twine and wreathe them all around, so that the Virgin may dwell within a bower of perpetual freshness, — at least put flower-pots, with living plants, into the niche. There are many things in the customs of these people that might be made very beautiful, if the sense of beauty were as much alive now as it must have been when these customs were first imagined and adopted.

I must not forget, among these little descriptive items, the spectacle of women and girls bearing huge bundles of twigs and shrubs, or grass, with scarlet poppies and blue flowers intermixed ; the bundles sometimes so huge as almost to hide the woman's figure from head to heel, so that she looked like a locomotive mass of verdure and flowers ; sometimes reaching only halfway down her back, so as to show the crooked knife slung behind, with which she had been reaping this strange harvest sheaf. A Pre-Raphaelite painter — the one, for instance, who painted the heap of autumnal leaves which we saw at the Manchester Exhibition — would find an admirable subject in one of these girls, stepping with a free, erect, and graceful carriage, her burden on her head ; and the miscellaneous herbage and flowers would give him all the scope he could desire for minute and various delineation of nature.

The country houses which we passed had sometimes open galleries, or arcades, on the second story and above, where the inhabitants might perform their domestic labor in the shade and in the air. The houses were often ancient, and most picturesquely time-stained, the plaster dropping in spots from the old brickwork ; others were tinted of pleasant and cheerful hues ; some were frescoed with designs in arabesques, or with imaginary windows ; some had escutcheons of arms painted on the front. Wherever there was a pigeon house, a flight of doves were represented as flying into the holes, doubtless for the invitation and encouragement of the real birds.

Once or twice I saw a bush stuck up before the door of what seemed to be a wine shop. If so, it is the ancient custom, so long disused in England, and alluded to in the proverb, "Good wine needs no bush." Several times we saw grass spread to dry on the road, covering half the track, and concluded it to have

been cut by the roadside for the winter forage
of his ass by some poor peasant, or peasant's
wife, who had no grassland, except the margin
of the public way.

A beautiful feature of the scene to-day, as
the preceding day, were the vines growing on
fig-trees (?),[1] and often wreathed in rich fes-
toons from one tree to another, by and by to
be hung with clusters of purple grapes.   I suspect the vine is a pleasanter object of sight
under this mode of culture than it can be in
countries where it produces a more precious
wine, and therefore is trained more artificially.
Nothing can be more picturesque than the spectacle of an old grapevine, with almost a trunk
of its own, clinging round its tree, imprisoning
within its strong embrace the friend that supported its tender infancy, converting the tree
wholly to its own selfish ends, as seemingly
flexible natures are apt to do, stretching out its
innumerable arms on every bough, and allow-
ing hardly a leaf to sprout except its own.   I
must not yet quit this hasty sketch, without
throwing in, both in the early morning, and later
in the forenoon, the mist that dreamed among
the hills, and which, now that I have called it
mist, I feel almost more inclined to call light,
being so quietly cheerful with the sunshine

[1] This interrogation mark must mean that Mr. Hawthorne was not
sure they were fig-trees. — S. H.

33

through it.   Put in, now and then, a castle on
a hilltop ; a rough ravine, a smiling valley ; a
mountain stream, with a far wider bed than it
at present needs, and a stone bridge across it,
with ancient and massive arches, — and I shall
say no more, except that all these particulars,
and many better ones which escape me, made
up a very pleasant whole.

At about noon we drove into the village of
Incisa, and alighted at the albergo where we
were to lunch.   It was a gloomy old house, as
much like my idea of an Etruscan tomb as
anything else that I can compare it to.   We
passed into a wide and lofty entrance-hall,
paved with stone, and vaulted with a roof of
intersecting arches, supported by heavy columns
of stuccoed brick, the whole as sombre and
dingy as can well be.   This entrance-hall is not
merely the passageway into the inn, but is likewise the carriage house, into which our vettura
is wheeled ; and it has, on one side, the stable,
odorous with the litter of horses and cattle, and
on the other the kitchen and a common sitting-
room.   A narrow stone staircase leads from it
to the dining-room, and chambers above, which
are paved with brick, and adorned with rude
frescos instead of paper hangings.   We look
out of the windows, and step into a little iron-
railed balcony, before the principal window, and
observe the scene in the village street.   The

street is narrow, and nothing can exceed the tall, grim ugliness of the village houses, many of them four stories high, contiguous all along, and paved quite across; so that nature is as completely shut out from the precincts of this little town as from the heart of the widest city. The walls of the houses are plastered, gray, dilapidated; the windows small, some of them drearily closed with wooden shutters, others flung wide open, and with women's heads protruding; others merely frescoed, for a show of light and air. It would be a hideous street to look at in a rainy day, or when no human life pervaded it. Now it has vivacity enough to keep it cheerful. People lounge round the door of the albergo, and watch the horses as they drink from a stone trough, which is built against the wall of the house, and filled with the unseen gush of a spring.

At first there is a shade entirely across the street, and all the within-doors of the village empties itself there, and keeps up a babblement that seems quite disproportioned even to the multitude of tongues that make it. So many words are not spoken in a New England village in a whole year as here in this single day. People talk about nothing as if they were terribly in earnest, and laugh at nothing as if it were an excellent joke.

As the hot noon sunshine encroaches on our

side of the street, it grows a little more quiet. The loungers now confine themselves to the shady margin (growing narrower and narrower) of the other side, where, directly opposite the albergo, there are two cafés and a wine shop, "vendeta di pane, vino, ed altri generi," all in a row with benches before them. The benchers joke with the women passing by, and are joked with back again. The sun still eats away the shadow inch by inch, beating down with such intensity that finally everybody disappears except a few passers-by.

Doubtless the village snatches this half-hour for its siesta. There is a song, however, inside one of the cafés, with a burden in which several voices join. A girl goes through the street, sheltered under her great bundle of freshly cut grass. By and by the song ceases, and two young peasants come out of the café, a little affected by liquor, in their shirt-sleeves and bare feet, with their trousers tucked up. They resume their song in the street, and dance along, one's arm around his fellow's neck, his own waist grasped by the other's arm. They whirl one another quite round about, and come down upon their feet. Meeting a village maid coming quietly along, they dance up and intercept her for a moment, but give way to her sobriety of aspect. They pass on, and the shadow soon begins to spread from one side of the street, which presently fills again, and becomes once more, for its size, the noisiest place I ever knew.

We had quite a tolerable dinner at this ugly inn, where many preceding travellers had written their condemnatory judgments, as well as a few their favorable ones, in pencil, on the walls of the dining-room.

At setting off [from Incisa], we were surrounded by beggars as usual, the most interesting of whom were a little blind boy and his mother, who had besieged us with gentle pertinacity during our whole stay there. There was likewise a man with a maimed hand, and other hurts or deformities ; also, an old woman, who, I suspect, only pretended to be blind, keeping her eyes tightly squeezed together, but directing her hand very accurately where the copper shower was expected to fall. Besides these, there were a good many sturdy little rascals, vociferating in proportion as they needed nothing. It was touching, however, to see several persons — themselves beggars for aught I know — assisting to hold up the little blind boy's tremulous hand, so that he, at all events, might not lack the pittance which we had to give. Our dole was but a poor one, after all, consisting of what Roman coppers we had brought into Tuscany with us ; and as we drove off, some of the boys ran shouting and whining after us in the hot sunshine, nor stopped till we reached the summit of the hill, which rises immediately from the village street. We heard Gaetano once say a good thing to a swarm of beggar children, who were infesting us, " Are your fathers all dead ? " — a proverbial expression, I suppose. The pertinacity of beggars does not, I think, excite the indignation of an Italian, as it is apt to do that of Englishmen or Americans. The Italians probably sympathize more, though they give less. Gaetano is very gentle in his modes of repelling them, and, indeed, never interferes at all, as long as there is a prospect of their getting anything.

Immediately after leaving Incisa, we saw the Arno, already a considerable river, rushing between deep banks, with the greenish hue of a duck pond diffused through its water. Nevertheless, though the first impression was not altogether agreeable, we soon became reconciled to this hue, and ceased to think it an indication of impurity ; for, in spite of it, the river is still, to a certain degree, transparent, and is, at any rate, a mountain stream, and comes uncontaminated from its source. The pure, transparent brown of the New England rivers is the most beautiful color ; but I am content that it should be peculiar to them.

Our afternoon's drive was through scenery less striking than some which we had traversed, but still picturesque and beautiful. We saw deep valleys and ravines, with streams at the bottom; long, wooded hillsides, rising far and high, and dotted with white dwellings, well towards the summits. By and by we had a distant glimpse of Florence, showing its great dome and some of its towers out of a sidelong valley, as if we were between two great waves of the tumultuous sea of hills; while, far beyond, rose in the distance the blue peaks of three or four of the Apennines, just on the remote horizon. There being a haziness in the atmosphere, however, Florence was little more distinct to us than the Celestial City was to Christian and Hopeful, when they spied at it from the Delectable Mountains.

Keeping steadfastly onward, we ascended a winding road, and passed a grand villa, standing very high, and surrounded with extensive grounds. It must be the residence of some great noble; and it has an avenue of poplars or aspens, very light and gay, and fit for the passage of the bridal procession, when the proprietor or his heir brings home his bride; while, in another direction from the same front of the palace, stretches an avenue or grove of cypresses, very long, and exceedingly black and dismal, like a train of gigantic mourners. I have seen few things more striking, in the way of trees, than this grove of cypresses.

From this point we descended, and drove along an ugly, dusty avenue, with a high brick wall on one side or both, till we reached the gate of Florence, into which we were admitted with as little trouble as custom-house officers, soldiers, and policemen can possibly give. They did not examine our luggage, and even declined a fee, as we had already paid one at the frontier custom-house. Thank Heaven and the Grand Duke!

As we hoped that the Casa del Bello had been taken for us, we drove thither in the first place, but found that the bargain had not been concluded. As the house and studio of Mr. Powers were just on the opposite side of the street, I went to it, but found him too much engrossed to see me at the moment; so I returned to the vettura, and we told Gaetano to carry us to a hotel. He established us at the Albergo della Fontana, a good and comfortable house. . . . Mr. Powers called in the evening, —a plain personage, characterized by strong simplicity and warm kindliness, with an impending brow, and large eyes, which kindle as he speaks. He is gray, and slightly bald, but does not seem elderly, nor past his prime. I accept him at once as an honest and trustworthy man, and shall not vary from this judgment. Through his good offices, the next day, we engaged the Casa del Bello, at a rent of fifty dollars a month, and I shall take another opportunity (my fingers and head being tired now) to write about the house, and Mr. Powers, and what appertains to him, and about the beautiful city of Florence. At present, I shall only say further, that this journey from Rome has been one of the brightest and most uncareful interludes of my life; we have all enjoyed it exceedingly, and I am happy that our children have it to look back upon.

June 4. — At our visit to Powers's studio on Tuesday, we saw a marble copy of the fisher boy holding a shell to his ear, and the bust of Proserpine, and two or three other ideal busts; various casts of most of the ideal statues and portrait busts which he has executed. He talks very freely about his works, and is no exception to the rule that an artist is not apt to speak in a very laudatory style of a brother artist. He showed us a bust of Mr. Sparks, by Persico, — a lifeless and thoughtless thing enough, to be sure, — and compared it with a very good one of the same gentleman by himself; but his chiefest scorn was bestowed on a wretched and ridiculous image of Mr. King, of Alabama, by Clarke Mills, of which he said he had been employed to make several copies for Southern gentlemen. The consciousness of power is plainly to be seen, and the assertion of it by no means withheld, in his simple and natural character; nor does it give me an idea of vanity on his part to see and hear it. He appears to consider himself neglected by his country, — by the government of it, at least, — and talks with indignation of the byways and political intrigue which, he thinks, win the rewards that ought to be bestowed exclusively on merit. An appropriation of twenty-five thousand dollars was made, some years ago, for a work of sculpture by him, to be placed in the Capitol; but the intermediate measures necessary to render it effective have been delayed; while the above-mentioned Clarke Mills— certainly the greatest bungler that ever botched a block of marble — has received an order for an equestrian statue of Washington. Not that Mr. Powers is made bitter or sour by these wrongs, as he considers them; he talks of them with the frankness of his disposition when the topic comes in his way, and is pleasant, kindly, and sunny when he has done with it.

His long absence from our country has made him think worse of us than we deserve; and it is an effect of what I myself am sensible, in my shorter exile: the most piercing shriek, the wildest yell, and all the ugly sounds of popular turmoil, inseparable from the life of a republic, being a million times more audible than the peaceful hum of prosperity and content which is going on all the while.

He talks of going home, but says that he has been talking of it every year since he first came to Italy ; and between his pleasant life of congenial labor and his idea of moral deterioration in America, I think it doubtful whether he ever crosses the sea again. Like most exiles of twenty years, he has lost his native country without finding another; but then it is as well to recognize the truth, — that an individual country is by no means essential to one's comfort.

Powers took us into the farthest room, I believe, of his very extensive studio, and showed us a statue of Washington that has much dignity and stateliness. He expressed, however, great contempt for the coat and breeches, and masonic emblems, in which he had been required to drape the figure. What would he do with Washington, the most decorous and respectable personage that ever went ceremoniously through the realities of life ? Did anybody ever see Washington nude ? It is inconceivable. He had no nakedness, but I imagine he was born with his clothes on, and his hair powdered, and made a stately bow on his first appearance in the world. His costume, at all events, was a part of his character, and must be dealt with by whatever sculptor undertakes to represent him. I wonder that so very sensible a man as Powers should not see the necessity of accepting drapery, and the very drapery of the day, if he will keep his art alive. It is his business to idealize the tailor's actual work. But he seems to be especially fond of nudity, none of his ideal statues, so far as I know them, having so much as a rag of clothes. His statue of California, lately finished, and as naked as Venus, seemed to me a very good work; not an actual woman, capable of exciting passion, but evidently a little out of the category of human nature. In one hand she holds a divining rod. "She says to the emigrants," observed Powers, "' Here is the gold, if you choose to take it.'" But in her face, and in her eyes, very finely expressed, there is a look of latent mischief, rather grave than playful, yet somewhat impish or sprite-like; and, in the other hand, behind her back, she holds a bunch of thorns. Powers calls her eyes Indian. The statue is true to the present fact and history of California, and includes the age-long truth as respects the "auri sacra fames." . . .

When we had looked sufficiently at the sculpture, Powers proposed that we should now go across the street and see the Casa del Bello. We did so in a body, Powers in his dressing-gown and slippers, and his wife and daughters without assuming any street costume.

The Casa del Bello is a palace of three pianos, the topmost of which is occupied by the Countess of St. George, an English lady, and two lower pianos are to be let, and we looked at both. The upper one would have suited me well enough; but the lower has a terrace, with a rustic summer-house over it, and is connected with a garden, where there are arbors and a willow-tree, and a little wilderness of shrubbery and roses, with a fountain in the midst. It has likewise an immense suite of rooms, round the four sides of a small court, spacious, lofty, with frescoed ceilings and rich hangings, and abundantly furnished with armchairs, sofas, marble tables, and great looking-glasses. Not that these last are a great temptation, but in our wandering life I wished to be perfectly comfortable myself, and to make my family so, for just this summer, and so I have taken the lower piano, the price being only fifty dollars per month (entirely furnished, even to silver and linen). Certainly this is something like the paradise of cheapness we were told of, and which we vainly sought in Rome. . . .

To me has been assigned the pleasantest room for my study; and when I like I can overflow into the summer-house or an arbor, and sit there dreaming of a story. The weather is delightful,

too warm to walk, but perfectly fit to do nothing in, in the coolness of these great rooms.
Every day I shall write a little, perhaps, — and
probably take a brief nap somewhere between
breakfast and tea, — but go to see pictures and
statues occasionally, and so assuage and mollify
myself a little after that uncongenial life of the
consulate, and before going back to my own
hard and dusty New England.

After concluding the arrangement for the
Casa del Bello, we stood talking a little while
with Powers and his wife and daughter before
the door of the house, for they seem so far to
have adopted the habits of the Florentines as to
feel themselves at home on the shady side of the
street.   The out-of-door life and free communication with the pavement, habitual apparently
among the middle classes, reminds me of the
plays of Molière and other old dramatists, in
which the street or the square becomes a sort
of common parlor, where most of the talk and
scenic business of the people is carried on.

June 5. — For two or three mornings after
breakfast I have rambled a little about the city
till the shade grew narrow beneath the walls of
the houses, and the heat made it uncomfortable
to be in motion.   To-day I went over the Ponte
Carraja, and thence into and through the heart
of the city, looking into several churches, in all

46

of which I found people taking advantage of the cool breadth of these sacred interiors to refresh themselves and say their prayers. Florence at first struck me as having the aspect of a very new city in comparison with Rome; but, on closer acquaintance, I find that many of the buildings are antique and massive, though still the clear atmosphere, the bright sunshine, the light, cheerful hues of the stucco, and — as much as anything else, perhaps — the vivacious character of the human life in the streets, take away the sense of its being an ancient city. The streets are delightful to walk in after so many penitential pilgrimages as I have made over those little square, uneven blocks of the Roman pavement, which wear out the boots and torment the soul. I absolutely walk on the smooth flags of Florence for the mere pleasure of walking, and live in its atmosphere for the mere pleasure of living; and, warm as the weather is getting to be, I never feel that inclination to sink down in a heap and never stir again, which was my dull torment and misery as long as I stayed in Rome. I hardly think there can be a place in the world where life is more delicious for its own simple sake than here.

I went to-day into the Baptistery, which stands near the Duomo, and, like that, is covered externally with slabs of black and white marble, now grown brown and yellow with age. The edifice is octagonal, and on entering, one immediately thinks of the Pantheon, — the whole space within being free from side to side, with a dome above; but it differs from the severe simplicity of the former edifice, being elaborately ornamented with marble and frescos, and lacking that great eye in the roof that looks so nobly and reverently heavenward from the Pantheon. I did little more than pass through the Baptistery, glancing at the famous bronze doors, some perfect and admirable casts of which I had already seen at the Crystal Palace.

The entrance of the Duomo being just across the piazza, I went in there after leaving the Baptistery, and was struck anew — for this is the third or fourth visit — with the dim grandeur of the interior, lighted as it is almost exclusively by painted windows, which seem to me worth all the variegated marbles and rich cabinet-work of St. Peter's. The Florentine Cathedral has a spacious and lofty nave, and side-aisles divided from it by pillars; but there are no chapels along the aisles, so that there is far more breadth and freedom of interior, in proportion to the actual space, than is usual in churches. It is woeful to think how the vast capaciousness within St. Peter's is thrown away, and made to seem smaller than it is by every possible device, as if on purpose. The pillars and walls of this Duomo are of a uniform brownish, neutral tint; the pave-

ment, a mosaic work of marble; the ceiling of
the dome itself is covered with frescos, which,
being very imperfectly lighted, it is impossible
to trace out. Indeed, it is but a twilight region
that is enclosed within the firmament of this
great dome, which is actually larger than that of
St. Peter's, though not lifted so high from the
pavement. But looking at the painted windows,
I little cared what dimness there might be elsewhere ; for certainly the art of man has never
contrived any other beauty and glory at all to be
compared to this.

The dome sits, as it were, upon three smaller
domes, — smaller, but still great, — beneath
which are three vast niches, forming the transepts of the Cathedral and the tribune behind
the high altar. All round these hollow, dome-
covered arches or niches are high and narrow
windows crowded with saints, angels, and all
manner of blessed shapes, that turn the common daylight into a miracle of richness and
splendor as it passes through their heavenly substance. And just beneath the swell of the great
central dome is a wreath of circular windows
quite round it, as brilliant as the tall and narrow ones below. It is a pity anybody should
die without seeing an antique painted window,
with the bright Italian sunshine glowing through
it. This is " the dim, religious light " that Milton speaks of; but I doubt whether he saw these

windows when he was in Italy, or any but those
faded or dusty and dingy ones of the English
cathedrals, else he would have illuminated that
word "dim" with some epithet that should not
chase away the dimness, yet should make it shine
like a million of rubies, sapphires, emeralds, and
topazes, — bright in themselves, but dim with
tenderness and reverence, because God himself
was shining through them. I hate what I have
said.

All the time that I was in the Cathedral the
space around the high altar, which stands exactly
under the dome, was occupied by priests or acolytes in white garments, chanting a religious
service.

. After coming out, I took a view of the edifice from a corner of the street nearest to the
dome, where it and the smaller domes can be
seen at once. It is greatly more satisfactory
than St. Peter's in any view I ever had of it, —
striking in its outline, with a mystery, yet not
a bewilderment, in its masses and curves and
angles, and wrought out with a richness of detail that gives the eyes new arches, new galleries,
new niches, new pinnacles, new beauties, great
and small, to play with when wearied with the
vast whole. The hue, black and white marbles,
like the Baptistery, turned also yellow and
brown, is greatly preferable to the buff traver-
tine of St. Peter's.

From the Duomo it is but a moderate street's length to the Piazza del Gran Duca, the principal square of Florence. It is a very interesting place, and has on one side the old Governmental Palace, — the Palazzo Vecchio, — where many scenes of historic interest have been enacted; for example, conspirators have been hanged from its windows, or precipitated from them upon the pavement of the square below.

It is a pity that we cannot take as much interest in the history of these Italian Republics as in that of England, for the former is much the more picturesque and fuller of curious incident. The sobriety of the Anglo-Saxon race — in connection, too, with their moral sense — keeps them from doing a great many things that would enliven the page of history; and their events seem to come in great masses, shoved along by the agency of many persons, rather than to result from individual will and character. A hundred plots for a tragedy might be found in Florentine history for one in English.

At one corner of the Palazzo Vecchio is a bronze equestrian statue of Cosmo de' Medici, the first Grand Duke, very stately and majestic; there are other marble statues — one of David, by Michel Angelo — at each side of the palace door; and entering the court I found a rich antique arcade within, surrounded by marble pillars, most elaborately carved, supporting arches that were covered with faded frescos. I went no farther, but stepped across a little space of the square to the Loggia di Lanzi, which is broad and noble, of three vast arches, at the end of which, I take it, is a part of the Palazzo Uffizi fronting on the piazza. I should call it a portico if it stood before the palace door; but it seems to have been constructed merely for itself, and as a shelter for the people from sun and rain, and to contain some fine specimens of sculpture, as well antique as of more modern times. Benvenuto Cellini's Perseus stands here; but it did not strike me so much as the cast of it in the Crystal Palace.

A good many people were under these great arches; some of whom were reclining, half or quite asleep, on the marble seats that are built against the back of the loggia. A group was reading an edict of the Grand Duke, which appeared to have been just posted on a board, at the farther end of it; and I was surprised at the interest which they ventured to manifest, and the freedom with which they seemed to discuss it. A soldier was on guard, and doubtless there were spies enough to carry every word that was said to the ear of absolute authority. Glancing myself at the edict, however, I found it referred only to the furtherance of a project, got up among the citizens themselves, for bring-

ing water into the city ; and on such topics, I
suppose, there is freedom of discussion.

June 7. — Saturday evening we walked, with
Una and Julian, into the city, and looked at
the exterior of the Duomo with new admiration.
Since my former view of it, I have noticed —
which, strangely enough, did not strike me before — that the façade is but a great, bare, ugly
space, roughly plastered over, with the brickwork peeping through it in spots, and a faint,
almost invisible fresco of colors upon it. This
front was once nearly finished with an incrusta-
tion of black and white marble, like the rest
of the edifice ; but one of the city magistrates,
Benedetto Uguacione, demolished it three hundred years ago, with the idea of building it again
in better style. He failed to do so, and ever
since the magnificence of the great church has
been marred by this unsightly roughness of
what should have been its richest part ; nor is
there, I suppose, any hope that it will ever be
finished now.

The campanile, or bell-tower, stands within
a few paces of the Cathedral, but entirely dis-
connected from it, rising to a height of nearly
three hundred feet, a square tower of light marbles, now discolored by time. It is impossible
to give an idea of the richness of effect produced
by its elaborate finish ; the whole surface of the

four sides, from top to bottom, being decorated with all manner of statuesque and architectural sculpture. It is like a toy of ivory, which some ingenious and pious monk might have spent his lifetime in adorning with scriptural designs and figures of saints; and when it was finished, seeing it so beautiful, he prayed that it might be miraculously magnified from the size of one foot to that of three hundred. This idea somewhat satisfies me, as conveying an impression how gigantesque the campanile is in its mass and height, and how minute and varied in its detail. Surely these mediæval works have an advantage over the classic. They combine the telescope and the microscope.

The city was all alive in the summer evening, and the streets humming with voices. Before the doors of the cafés were tables, at which people were taking refreshment, and it went to my heart to see a bottle of English ale, some of which was poured foaming into a glass; at least it had exactly the amber hue and the foam of English bitter ale; but perhaps it may have been merely a Florentine imitation.

As we returned home over the Arno, crossing the Ponte di Santa Trinita, we were struck by the beautiful scene of the broad, calm river, with the palaces along its shores repeated in it, on either side, and the neighboring bridges, too, just as perfect in the tide beneath as in the air

The Campanile, Florence

above, — a city of dream and shadow so close to the actual one. God has a meaning, no doubt, in putting this spiritual symbol continually beside us.

Along the river, on both sides, as far as we could see, there was a row of brilliant lamps, which, in the far distance, looked like a cornice of golden light ; and this also shone as brightly in the river's depths. The hues of the evening, in the quarter where the sun had gone down, were very soft and beautiful, though not so gorgeous as thousands that I have seen in America. But I believe I must fairly confess that the Italian sky, in the daytime, is bluer and brighter than our own, and that the atmosphere has a quality of showing objects to better advantage. It is more than mere daylight ; the magic of moonlight is somehow mixed up with it, although it is so transparent a medium of light.

Last evening Mr. Powers called to see us, and sat down to talk in a friendly and familiar way. I do not know a man of more facile intercourse, nor with whom one so easily gets rid of ceremony. His conversation, too, is interesting. He talked, to begin with, about Italian food, as poultry, mutton, beef, and their lack of savoriness as compared with our own ; and mentioned an exquisite dish of vegetables which they prepare from squash or pumpkin blossoms; likewise another dish, which it will be well for us to remember when we get back to the Wayside, where we are overrun with acacias. It consists of the acacia blossoms, in a certain stage of their development, fried in olive oil. I shall get the receipt from Mrs. Powers, and mean to deserve well of my country by first trying it, and then making it known; only I doubt whether American lard, or even butter, will produce the dish quite so delicately as fresh Florence oil.

Meanwhile, I like Powers all the better, because he does not put his life wholly into marble. We had much talk, nevertheless, on matters of sculpture, for he drank a cup of tea with us, and stayed a good while.

He passed a condemnatory sentence on classic busts in general, saying that they were conventional, and not to be depended upon as true representations of the persons. He particularly excepted none but the bust of Caracalla; and, indeed, everybody that has seen this bust must feel the justice of the exception, and so be the more inclined to accept his opinion about the rest. There are not more than half a dozen — that of Cato the Censor among the others — in regard to which I should like to ask his judgment individually. He seems to think the faculty of making a bust an extremely rare one. Canova put his own likeness into all the

busts he made.   Greenough could not make a
good one ; nor Crawford, nor Gibson.   Mr.
Hart, he observed, — an American sculptor,
now a resident in Florence, — is the best man
of the day for making busts.   Of course, it is
to be presumed that he excepts himself ; but I
would not do Powers the great injustice to imply that there is the slightest professional jealousy in his estimate of what others have done,
or are now doing, in his own art.   If he saw a
better man than himself, he would recognize
him at once, and tell the world of him ; but he
knows well enough that, in this line, there is no
better, and probably none so good.   It would
not accord with the simplicity of his character
to blink a fact that stands so broadly before
him.

We asked him what he thought of Mr. Gibson's practice of coloring his statues, and he
quietly and slyly said that he himself had made
wax figures in his earlier days, but had left off
making them now.   In short, he objected to
the practice wholly, and said that a letter of his
on the subject had been published in the London Athenæum, and had given great offence to
some of Mr. Gibson's friends.   It appeared to
me, however, that his arguments did not apply
quite fairly to the case, for he seems to think
Gibson aims at producing an illusion of life in
the statue, whereas I think his object is merely

to give warmth and softness to the snowy marble, and so bring it a little nearer to our hearts and sympathies. Even so far, nevertheless, I doubt whether the practice is defensible, and I was glad to see that Powers scorned, at all events, the argument drawn from the use of color by the antique sculptors, on which Gibson relies so much. It might almost be implied, from the contemptuous way in which Powers spoke of color, that he considers it an impertinence on the face of visible nature, and would rather the world had been made without it; for he said that everything in intellect or feeling can be expressed as perfectly, or more so, by the sculptor in colorless marble, as by the painter with all the resources of his palette. I asked him whether he could model the face of Beatrice Cenci from Guido's picture so as to retain the subtle expression, and he said he could, for that the expression depended entirely on the drawing, " the picture being a badly colored thing." I inquired whether he could model a blush, and he said " Yes ;" and that he had once proposed to an artist to express a blush in marble, if he would express it in picture. On consideration, I believe one to be as impossible as the other ; the life and reality of the blush being in its tremulousness, coming and going. It is lost in a settled red just as much as in a settled paleness, and neither the sculptor nor painter can do more than represent the circumstances of attitude and expression that accompany the blush. There was a great deal of truth in what Powers said about this matter of color, and in one of our interminable New England winters it ought to comfort us to think how little necessity there is for any hue but that of the snow.

Mr. Powers, nevertheless, had brought us a bunch of beautiful roses, and seemed as capable of appreciating their delicate blush as we were. The best thing he said against the use of color in marble was to the effect that the whiteness removed the object represented into a sort of spiritual region, and so gave chaste permission to those nudities which would otherwise suggest immodesty. I have myself felt the truth of this in a certain sense of shame as I looked at Gibson's tinted Venus.

He took his leave at about eight o'clock, being to make a call on the Bryants, who are at the Hôtel de New York, and also on Mrs. Browning at Casa Guidi.

June 8. — I went this morning to the Uffizi gallery. The entrance is from the great court of the palace, which communicates with Lung' Arno at one end, and with the Grand Ducal Piazza at the other. The gallery is in the upper story of the palace, and in the vestibule are some busts of the princes and cardinals of the Medici family, — none of them beautiful, one or two so ugly as to be ludicrous, especially one who is all but buried in his own wig. I at first travelled slowly through the whole extent of this long, long gallery, which occupies the entire length of the palace on both sides of the court, and is full of sculpture and pictures. The latter, being opposite to the light, are not seen to the best advantage ; but it is the most perfect collection, in a chronological series, that I have seen, — comprehending specimens of all the masters since painting began to be an art. Here are Giotto, and Cimabue, and Botticelli, and Fra Angelico, and Filippo Lippi, and a hundred others, who have haunted me in churches and galleries ever since I have been in Italy, and who ought to interest me a great deal more than they do. Occasionally to-day I was sensible of a certain degree of emotion in looking at an old picture ; as, for example, by a large, dark, ugly picture of Christ bearing the cross and sinking beneath it, when, somehow or other, a sense of his agony and the fearful wrong that mankind did (and does) its Redeemer, and the scorn of his enemies, and the sorrow of those who loved him, came knocking at my heart and got entrance there. Once more I deem it a pity that Protestantism should have entirely laid aside this mode of appealing to the religious sentiment.

I chiefly paid attention to the sculpture, and was interested in a long series of busts of the emperors and the members of their families, and some of the great men of Rome. There is a bust of Pompey the Great, bearing not the slightest resemblance to that vulgar and unintellectual one in the gallery of the Capitol, altogether a different cast of countenance. I could not judge whether it resembled the face of the statue, having seen the latter so imperfectly in the duskiness of the hall of the Spada Palace. These, I presume, are the busts which Mr. Powers condemns, from internal evidence, as unreliable and conventional. He may be right,— and is far more likely, of course, to be right than I am,— yet there certainly seems to be character in these marble faces, and they differ as much among themselves as the same number of living faces might. The bust of Caracalla, however, which Powers excepted from his censure, certainly does give stronger assurance of its being an individual and faithful portrait than any other in the series. All the busts of Caracalla — of which I have seen many — give the same evidence of their truth ; and I should like to know what it was in this abominable emperor that made him insist upon having his actual likeness perpetuated, with all the ugliness of its animal and moral character. I rather respect him for it, and still more the sculptor, whose hand, methinks, must have trembled as he wrought the bust. Generally these wicked old fellows, and their wicked wives and daughters, are not so hideous as we might expect. Messalina, for instance, has small and pretty features, though with rather a sensual development of the lower part of the face. The busts, it seemed to me, are usually superior as works of art to those in the Capitol, and either better preserved or more thoroughly restored. The bust of Nero might almost be called handsome here, though bearing his likeness unmistakably.

I wish some competent person would undertake to analyze and develop his character, and how and by what necessity — with all his elegant tastes, his love of the beautiful, his artist nature — he grew to be such a monster. Nero has never yet had justice done him, nor have any of the wicked emperors ; not that I suppose them to have been any less monstrous than history represents them; but there must surely have been something in their position and circumstances to render the terrible moral disease which seized upon them so generally almost inevitable. A wise and profound man, tender and reverent of the human soul, and capable of appreciating it in its height and depth, has a great field here for the exercise of his powers. It has struck me, in reading the history of the Italian republics, that many of the tyrants, who sprung up after the destruction of their liberties, resembled the worst of the Roman emperors. The subject of Nero and his brethren has often perplexed me with vain desires to come at the truth.

There were many beautiful specimens of antique, ideal sculpture all along the gallery, — Apollos, Bacchuses, Venuses, Mercurys, Fauns, — with the general character of all of which I was familiar enough to recognize them at a glance. The mystery and wonder of the gallery, however, the Venus di Medici, I could nowhere see, and indeed was almost afraid to see it; for I somewhat apprehended the extinction of another of those lights that shine along a man's pathway, and go out in a snuff the instant he comes within eyeshot of the fulfilment of his hopes. My European experience has extinguished many such. I was pretty well contented, therefore, not to find the famous statue in the whole of my long journey from end to end of the gallery, which terminates on the opposite side of the court from that where it commences. The ceiling, by the bye, through the entire length, is covered with frescos, and the floor paved with a composition of stone smooth and polished like marble. The final piece of sculpture, at the end of the gallery, is

a copy of the Laocoön, considered very fine.
I know not why, but it did not impress me with
the sense of mighty and terrible repose — a repose growing out of the infinitude of trouble
— that I had felt in the original.

Parallel with the gallery, on both sides of
the palace court, there runs a series of rooms
devoted chiefly to pictures, although statues and
bas-reliefs are likewise contained in some of
them.   I remember an unfinished bas-relief by
Michel Angelo of a Holy Family, which I
touched with my finger, because it seemed as if
he might have been at work upon it only an
hour ago. The pictures I did little more than
glance at, till I had almost completed again the
circuit of the gallery, through this series of parallel rooms, and then I came upon a collection
of French and Dutch and Flemish masters, all of
which interested me more than the Italian generally. There was a beautiful picture by Claude,
almost as good as those in the British National
Gallery, and very like in subject ; the sun near
the horizon, of course, and throwing its line of
light over the ripple of water, with ships at the
strand, and one or two palaces of stately architecture on the shore.   Landscapes by Rembrandt ; fat Graces and other plump nudities by
Rubens ; brass pans and earthen pots and her-
rings by Teniers and other Dutchmen ; none
by Gerard Dow, I think, but several by Mieris ;

all of which were like bread and beef and ale, after having been fed too long on made dishes. This is really a wonderful collection of pictures ; and from first to last — from Giotto to the men of yesterday — they are in admirable condition, and may be appreciated for all the merit that they ever possessed.

I could not quite believe that I was not to find the Venus di Medici ; and still, as I passed from one room to another, my breath rose and fell a little, with the half-hope, half-fear, that she might stand before me. Really, I did not know that I cared so much about Venus, or any possible woman of marble. At last, when I had come from among the Dutchmen, I believe, and was looking at some works of Italian artists, chiefly Florentines, I caught a glimpse of her through the door of the next room. It is the best room of the series, octagonal in shape, and hung with red damask, and the light comes down from a row of windows, passing quite round, beneath an octagonal dome. The Venus stands somewhat aside from the centre of the room, and is surrounded by an iron railing, a pace or two from her pedestal in front, and less behind. I think she might safely be left to the reverence her womanhood would win, without any other protection. She is very beautiful, very satisfactory ; and has a fresh and new charm about her unreached by any cast or copy.

The hue of the marble is just so much mellowed by time, as to do for her all that Gibson tries, or ought to try to do for his statues by color, softening her, warming her almost imperceptibly, making her an inmate of the heart, as well as a spiritual existence. I felt a kind of tenderness for her; an affection, not as if she were one woman, but all womanhood in one. Her modest attitude, which, before I saw her, I had not liked, deeming that it might be an artificial shame, is partly what unmakes her as the heathen goddess, and softens her into woman. There is a slight degree of alarm, too, in her face; not that she really thinks anybody is looking at her, yet the idea has flitted through her mind, and startled her a little. Her face is so beautiful and intellectual, that it is not dazzled out of sight by her form. Methinks this was a triumph for the sculptor to achieve. I may as well stop here. It is of no use to throw heaps of words upon her; for they all fall away, and leave her standing in chaste and naked grace, as untouched as when I began.

She has suffered terribly by the mishaps of her long existence in the marble. Each of her legs has been broken into two or three fragments, her arms have been severed, her body has been broken quite across at the waist, her head has been snapped off at the neck. Furthermore, there have been grievous wounds and

66

losses of substance in various tender parts of
her person.   But on account of the skill with
which the statue has been restored, and also
because the idea is perfect and indestructible,
all these injuries do not in the least impair
the effect, even when you see where the dis-
severed fragments have been reunited.   She is
just as whole as when she left the hands of
the sculptor.   I am glad to have seen this
Venus, and to have found her so tender and so
chaste.   On the wall of the room, and to be
taken in at the same glance, is a painted Venus
by Titian, reclining on a couch, naked and
lustful.

The room of the Venus seems to be the
treasure place of the whole Uffizzi Palace, containing more pictures by famous masters than
are to be found in all the rest of the gallery.
There were several by Raphael, and the room
was crowded with the easels of artists.   I did
not look half enough at anything, but merely
took a preliminary taste, as a prophecy of enjoyment to come.

As we were at dinner to-day, at half past
three, there was a ring at the door, and a minute after our servant brought a card.   It was
Mr. Robert Browning's, and on it was written
in pencil an invitation for us to go to see them
this evening.   He had left the card and gone
away; but very soon the bell rang again, and he

had come back, having forgotten to give his address. This time he came in; and he shook hands with all of us, children and grown people, and was very vivacious and agreeable. He looked younger and even handsomer than when I saw him in London, two years ago, and his gray hairs seemed fewer than those that had then strayed into his youthful head. He talked a wonderful quantity in a little time, and told us — among other things that we should never have dreamed of — that Italian people will not cheat you, if you construe them generously, and put them upon their honor.

Mr. Browning was very kind and warm in his expressions of pleasure at seeing us; and, on our part, we were all very glad to meet him. He must be an exceedingly likeable man. . . . They are to leave Florence very soon, and are going to Normandy, I think he said, for the rest of the summer.

The Venus di Medici has a dimple in her chin.

June 9. — We went last evening, at eight o'clock, to see the Brownings; and, after some search and inquiry, we found the Casa Guidi, which is a palace in a street not very far from our own. It being dusk, I could not see the exterior, which, if I remember, Browning has celebrated in song; at all events, Mrs. Brown-

ing has called one of her poems Casa Guidi
Windows.

The street is a narrow one; but on entering
the palace we found a spacious staircase and
ample accommodations of vestibule and hall,
the latter opening on a balcony, where we could
hear the chanting of priests in a church close by.
Browning told us that this was the first church
where an oratorio had ever been performed. He
came into the anteroom to greet us, as did his
little boy, Robert, whom they call Pennini for
fondness. The latter cognomen is a diminutive of Apennino, which was bestowed upon
him at his first advent into the world because
he was so very small, there being a statue in
Florence of colossal size called Apennino. I
never saw such a boy as this before; so slender,
fragile, and spirit-like, — not as if he were actually in ill health, but as if he had little or nothing to do with human flesh and blood. His
face is very pretty and most intelligent, and exceedingly like his mother's. He is nine years
old, and seems at once less childlike and less
manly than would befit that age. I should
not quite like to be the father of such a boy,
and should fear to stake so much interest and
affection on him as he cannot fail to inspire. I
wonder what is to become of him, — whether
he will ever grow to be a man, — whether it is
desirable that he should. His parents ought

to turn their whole attention to making him robust and earthly, and to giving him a thicker scabbard to sheathe his spirit in. He was born in Florence, and prides himself on being a Florentine, and is indeed as un-English a production as if he were native of another planet.

Mrs. Browning met us at the door of the drawing-room, and greeted us most kindly,— a pale, small person, scarcely embodied at all; at any rate, only substantial enough to put forth her slender fingers to be grasped, and to speak with a shrill, yet sweet, tenuity of voice. Really, I do not see how Mr. Browning can suppose that he has an earthly wife any more than an earthly child ; both are of the elfin race, and will flit away from him some day when he least thinks of it. She is a good and kind fairy, however, and sweetly disposed towards the human race, although only remotely akin to it. It is wonderful to see how small she is, how pale her cheek, how bright and dark her eyes. There is not such another figure in the world ; and her black ringlets cluster down into her neck, and make her face look the whiter by their sable profusion. I could not form any judgment about her age ; it may range anywhere within the limits of human life or elfin life. When I met her in London at Lord Houghton's breakfast-table, she did not impress me so singularly ;

for the morning light is more prosaic than the
dim illumination of their great tapestried drawing-room ; and, besides, sitting next to her,
she did not have occasion to raise her voice in
speaking, and I was not sensible what a slender
voice she has.   It is marvellous to me how so
extraordinary, so acute, so sensitive a creature
can impress us, as she does, with the certainty
of her benevolence.   It seems to me there were
a million chances to one that she would have
been a miracle of acidity and bitterness.

We were not the only guests.   Mr. and Mrs.
E——, Americans, recently from the East, and
on intimate terms with the Brownings, arrived
after us ; also Miss F. H——, an English literary lady, whom I have met several times in
Liverpool ; and lastly came the white head and
palmer-like beard of Mr. Bryant with his
daughter.   Mr. Browning was very efficient in
keeping up conversation with everybody, and
seemed to be in all parts of the room and in
every group at the same moment ; a most vivid
and quick-thoughted person, logical and com-
mon-sensible, as, I presume, poets generally are
in their daily talk.   Mr. Bryant, as usual, was
homely and plain of manner, with an old-fashioned dignity, nevertheless, and a remarkable
deference and gentleness of tone in addressing
Mrs. Browning.   I doubt, however, whether he

has any high appreciation either of her poetry or her husband's, and it is my impression that they care as little about his.

We had some tea and some strawberries, and passed a pleasant evening. There was no very noteworthy conversation ; the most interesting topic being that disagreeable and now wearisome one of spiritual communications, as regards which Mrs. Browning is a believer, and her husband an infidel. Mr. Bryant appeared not to have made up his mind on the matter, but told a story of a successful communication between Cooper the novelist and his sister, who had been dead fifty years. Browning and his wife had both been present at a spiritual session held by Mr. Home, and had seen and felt the unearthly hands, one of which had placed a laurel wreath on Mrs. Browning's head. Browning, however, avowed his belief that these hands were affixed to the feet of Mr. Home, who lay extended in his chair, with his legs stretched far under the table. The marvellousness of the fact, as I have read of it, and heard it from other eye-witnesses, melted strangely away in his hearty gripe, and at the sharp touch of his logic ; while his wife, ever and anon, put in a little gentle word of expostulation.

I am rather surprised that Browning's conversation should be so clear, and so much to the purpose at the moment, since his poetry can seldom proceed far without running into the high grass of latent meanings and obscure allusions.

Mrs. Browning's health does not permit late hours, so we began to take leave at about ten o'clock. I heard her ask Mr. —— if he did not mean to revisit Europe, and heard him answer, not uncheerfully, taking hold of his white hair, " It is getting rather too late in the evening now." If any old age can be cheerful, I should think his might be ; so good a man, so cool, so calm, so bright, too, we may say. His life has been like the days that end in pleasant sunsets. He has a great loss, however, or what ought to be a great loss, — soon to be encountered in the death of his wife, who, I think, can hardly live to reach America. He is not eminently an affectionate man. I take him to be one who cannot get closely home to his sorrow, nor feel it so sensibly as he gladly would ; and, in consequence of that deficiency, the world lacks substance to him. It is partly the result, perhaps, of his not having sufficiently cultivated his emotional nature. His poetry shows it, and his personal intercourse, though kindly, does not stir one's blood in the least.

Little Pennini, during the evening, sometimes helped the guests to cake and strawberries ; joined in the conversation, when he had anything to say, or sat down upon a couch to enjoy his own meditations. He has long curling hair, and has not yet emerged from his frock and short hose. It is funny to think of putting him into trousers. His likeness to his mother is strange to behold.

June 10. — My wife and I went to the Pitti Palace to-day ; and first entered a court where, yesterday, she had seen a carpet of flowers, arranged for some great ceremony. It must have been a most beautiful sight, the pavement of the court being entirely covered by them, in a regular pattern of brilliant hues, so as really to be a living mosaic. This morning, however, the court had nothing but its usual stones, and the show of yesterday seemed so much the more inestimable as having been so evanescent. Around the walls of the court there were still some pieces of splendid tapestry which had made part of yesterday's magnificence. We went up the staircase, of regally broad and easy ascent, and made application to be admitted to see the grand ducal apartments. An attendant accordingly took the keys, and ushered us first into a great hall with a vaulted ceiling, and then through a series of noble rooms, with rich frescos above the mosaic floors, hung with damask, adorned with gilded chandeliers, and glowing, in short, with more gorgeousness than I could have imagined beforehand, or can now remember. In many of the rooms were those superb

antique cabinets which I admire more than any
other furniture ever invented; only these were
of unexampled art and glory, inlaid with precious stones, and with beautiful Florentine mosaics, both of flowers and landscapes, — each
cabinet worth a lifetime's toil to make it, and the
cost a whole palace to pay for it. Many of the
rooms were covered with arras, of landscapes,
hunting scenes, mythological subjects, or historical scenes, equal to pictures in truth of representation, and possessing an indescribable
richness that makes them preferable as a mere
adornment of princely halls and chambers.
Some of the rooms, as I have said, were laid
in mosaic of stone and marble, otherwise in
lovely patterns of various woods; others were
covered with carpets, delightful to tread upon,
and glowing like the living floor of flowers which
my wife saw yesterday. There were tables, too,
of Florentine mosaic, the mere materials of
which — lapis lazuli, malachite, pearl, and a
hundred other precious things — were worth a
fortune, and made a thousand times more valuable by the artistic skill of the manufacturer.
I toss together brilliant words by the handful,
and make a rude sort of patchwork, but can
record no adequate idea of what I saw in this
suite of rooms; and the taste, the subdued
splendor, so that it did not shine too high, but
was all tempered into an effect at once grand

and soft, — this was quite as remarkable as the gorgeous material.   I have seen a very dazzling effect produced in the principal cabin of an American clipper ship quite opposed to this in taste.

After making the circuit of the grand ducal apartments, we went into a door in the left wing of the palace, and ascended a narrow flight of stairs, — several tortuous flights indeed, — to the picture gallery.   It fills a great many stately halls, which themselves are well worth a visit for the architecture and frescos ; only these matters become commonplace after travelling through a mile or two of them.   The collection of pictures — as well for their number as for the celebrity and excellence of many of them — is the most interesting that I have seen, and I do not yet feel in a condition, nor perhaps ever shall, to speak of a single one.   It gladdened my very heart to find that they were not darkened out of sight, nor apparently at all injured by time, but were well kept and varnished, brilliantly framed, and, no doubt, restored by skilful touches if any of them needed it.   The artists and amateurs may say what they like ; for my part, I know no drearier feeling than that inspired by a ruined picture, — ruined, that is, by time, damp, or rough treatment, — and I would a thousand times rather an artist should do his best towards reviving it, than have it left in such a condition.   I do not believe, however, that these pictures have been sacrilegiously interfered with; at all events, I saw in the masterpieces no touch but what seemed worthy of the master-hand.

The most beautiful picture in the world, I am convinced, is Raphael's Madonna della Seggiola.   I was familiar with it in a hundred engravings and copies, and therefore it shone upon me as with a familiar beauty, though infinitely more divine than I had ever seen it before.   An artist was copying it, and producing certainly something very like a facsimile, yet leaving out, as a matter of course, that mysterious something that renders the picture a miracle.   It is my present opinion that the pictorial art is capable of something more like magic, more wonderful and inscrutable in its methods than poetry, or any other mode of developing the beautiful. But how does this accord with what I have been saying only a minute ago?   How then can the decayed picture of a great master ever be restored by the touches of an inferior hand? Doubtless it never can be restored; but let some devoted worshipper do his utmost, and the whole inherent spirit of the divine picture may pervade his restorations likewise.

I saw the Three Fates of Michel Angelo, which were also being copied, as were many other of the best pictures.   Miss Fanny Howorth, whom I met in the gallery, told me that, to copy the Madonna della Seggiola, application must be made five years beforehand, so many are the artists who aspire to copy it. Michel Angelo's Fates are three very grim and pitiless old women, who respectively spin, hold, and cut the thread of human destiny, all in a mood of sombre gloom, but with no more sympathy than if they had nothing to do with us. I remember seeing an etching of this when I was a child, and being struck, even then, with the terrible, stern, passionless severity, neither loving us nor hating us, that characterizes these ugly old women. If they were angry, or had the least spite against humankind, it would render them the more tolerable. They are a great work, containing and representing the very idea that makes a belief in fate such a cold torture to the human soul. God give me the sure belief in his Providence !

In a year's time, with the advantage of access to this magnificent gallery, I think I might come to have some little knowledge of pictures. At present I still know nothing; but am glad to find myself capable, at least, of loving one picture better than another. I cannot always "keep the heights I gain," however; and after admiring and being moved by a picture one day, it is within my experience to look at it the next as little moved as if it were a tavern sign. It is pretty much the same with statuary ; the same, too, with those pictured windows of the Duomo, which I described so rapturously a few days ago. I looked at them again the next morning, and thought they would have been hardly worthy of my eulogium, even had all the separate windows of the Cathedral combined their narrow lights into one grand, resplendent, many-colored arch at the eastern end.   It is a pity they are so narrow.   England has many a great chancel-window that, though dimmer in its hues, dusty, and perhaps made up of heterogeneous fragments, eclipses these by its spacious breadth.

From the gallery, I went into the Boboli Gardens, which are contiguous to the palace ; but found them too sunny for enjoyment.   They seem to consist partly of a wilderness ; but the portion into which I strayed was laid out with straight walks, lined with high box-hedges, along which there was only a narrow margin of shade. I saw an amphitheatre, with a wide sweep of marble seat around it, enclosing a grassy space, where, doubtless, the Medici may have witnessed splendid spectacles.

June 11. — I paid another visit to the Uffizi gallery this morning, and found that the Venus is one of the things the charm of which does not diminish on better acquaintance.   The world has not grown weary of her in all these ages ; and mortal man may look on her with new delight from infancy to old age, and keep the memory of her, I should imagine, as one of the treasures of spiritual existence hereafter. Surely, it makes me more ready to believe in the high destinies of the human race, to think that this beautiful form is but nature's plan for all womankind, and that the nearer the actual woman approaches it, the more natural she is. I do not, and cannot, think of her as a senseless image, but as a being that lives to gladden the world, incapable of decay and death ; as young and fair to-day as she was three thousand years ago, and still to be young and fair as long as a beautiful thought shall require physical embodiment. I wonder how any sculptor has had the impertinence to aim at any other presentation of female beauty. I mean no disrespect to Gibson or Powers, or a hundred other men who people the world with nudities, all of which are abortions as compared with her ; but I think the world would be all the richer if their Venuses, their Greek Slaves, their Eves, were burnt into quicklime, leaving us only this statue as our image of the beautiful. I observed to-day that the eyes of the statue are slightly hollowed out, in a peculiar way, so as to give them a look of depth and intelligence. She is a miracle. The sculptor must have wrought religiously, and have felt that something far beyond his own

skill was working through his hands. I mean
to leave off speaking of the Venus hereafter, in
utter despair of saying what I wish ; especially
as the contemplation of the statue will refine
and elevate my taste, and make it continually
more difficult to express my sense of its excellence, as the perception of it grows upon me.
If at any time I become less sensible of it, it will
be my deterioration, not any defect in the statue.

I looked at many of the pictures, and found
myself in a favorable mood for enjoying them.
It seems to me that a work of art is entitled to
credit for all that it makes us feel in our best
moments ; and we must judge of its merits by
the impression it then makes, and not by the
coldness and insensibility of our less genial
moods.

After leaving the Uffizi Palace, . . . I went
into the Museum of Natural History, near the
Pitti Palace. It is a very good collection of
almost everything that Nature has made, — or
exquisite copies of what she has made, — stones,
shells, vegetables, insects, fishes, animals, man ;
the greatest wonders of the museum being some
models in wax of all parts of the human frame.
It is good to have the wholeness and summed-
up beauty of woman in the memory, when looking at the details of her system as here displayed ;
for these last, to the natural eye, are by no means
beautiful. But they are what belong only to

our mortality. The beauty that makes them invisible is our immortal type, which we shall take away with us. Under glass cases, there were some singular and horribly truthful representations, in small wax figures, of a time of pestilence; the hasty burial, or tossing into one common sepulchre, of discolored corpses, — a very ugly piece of work, indeed. I think Murray says that these things were made for the Grand Duke Cosmo; and if so, they do him no credit, indicating something dark and morbid in his character.

June 13. — We called at the Powers's yesterday morning to leave Rose there for an hour or two to play with the children; and it being not yet quite time for the Pitti Palace, we stepped into the studio. Soon Mr. Powers made his appearance, in his dressing-gown and slippers and sculptor's cap, smoking a cigar. . . . He was very cordial and pleasant, as I have always found him, and began immediately to be communicative about his own works, or any other subject that came up. There were two casts of the Venus di Medici in the rooms, which he said were valuable in a commercial point of view, being genuine casts from the mould taken from the statue. He then gave us a quite unexpected but most interesting lecture on the Venus, demonstrating it, as he proceeded, by reference to the points which he criticised. The figure, he seemed to allow, was admirable, though I think he hardly classes it so high as his own Greek Slave or Eve; but the face, he began with saying, was that of an idiot. Then, leaning on the pedestal of the cast, he continued, "It is rather a bold thing to say, isn't it, that the sculptor of the Venus di Medici did not know what he was about?"

Truly, it appeared to me so; but Powers went on remorselessly, and showed, in the first place, that the eye was not like any eye that Nature ever made; and, indeed, being examined closely, and abstracted from the rest of the face, it has a very queer look, — less like a human eye than a half-worn buttonhole! Then he attacked the ear, which, he affirmed and demonstrated, was placed a good deal too low on the head, thereby giving an artificial and monstrous height to the portion of the head above it. The forehead met with no better treatment in his hands, and as to the mouth, it was altogether wrong, as well in its general make as in such niceties as the junction of the skin of the lips to the common skin around them. In a word, the poor face was battered all to pieces and utterly demolished; nor was it possible to doubt or question that it fell by its own demerits. All that could be urged in its defence — and even *that* I did not urge — being that this very face

had affected me, only the day before, with a
sense of higher beauty and intelligence than I
had ever then received from sculpture, and that
its expression seemed to accord with that of the
whole figure, as if it were the sweetest note of
the same music.   There must be something in
this ; the sculptor disregarded technicalities, and
the imitation of actual nature, the better to produce the effect which he really does produce,
in somewhat the same way as a painter works
his magical illusions by touches that have no
relation to the truth if looked at from the wrong
point of view.   But Powers considers it certain
that the antique sculptor had bestowed all his
care on the study of the human figure, and really
did not know how to make a face.   I myself
used to think that the face was a much less important thing with the Greeks, among whom the
entire beauty of the form was familiarly seen,
than with ourselves, who allow no other nudity.

After annihilating the poor visage, Powers
showed us his two busts of Proserpine and
Psyche, and continued his lecture by showing the
truth to nature with which these are modelled.
I freely acknowledge the fact ; there is no sort
of comparison to be made between the beauty,
intelligence, feeling, and accuracy of representation in these two faces and in that of the Venus
di Medici.   A light — the light of a soul proper
to each individual character — seems to shine

from the interior of the marble, and beam forth
from the features, chiefly from the eyes. Still in-
sisting upon the eye, and hitting the poor Venus
another and another and still another blow on
that unhappy feature, Mr. Powers turned up
and turned inward and turned outward his own
Titanic orb, — the biggest, by far, that ever I
saw in mortal head, — and made us see and
confess that there was nothing right in the
Venus and everything right in Psyche and Proserpine. To say the truth, their marble eyes
have life, and, placing yourself in the proper
position towards them, you can meet their
glances, and feel them mingle with your own.
Powers is a great man, and also a tender and delicate one, massive and rude of surface as he looks ;
and it is rather absurd to feel how he impressed
his auditor, for the time being, with his own evident idea that nobody else is worthy to touch
marble. Mr. B—— told me that Powers has
had many difficulties on professional grounds, as
I understood him, and with his brother artists.
No wonder ! He has said enough in my hearing
to put him at swords' points with sculptors of
every epoch and every degree between the two
inclusive extremes of Phidias and Clarke Mills.

He has a bust of the reigning Grand Duchess
of Tuscany, who sat to him for it. The bust
is that of a noble-looking lady ; and Powers
remarked that royal personages have a certain

look that distinguishes them from other people, and is seen in individuals of no lower rank. They all have it ; the Queen of England and Prince Albert have it ; and so likewise has every other Royalty, although the possession of this kingly look implies nothing whatever as respects kingly and commanding qualities. He said that none of our public men, whatever authority they may have held, or for whatever length of time, possess this look, but he added afterwards that Washington had it. Commanders of armies sometimes have it, but not in the degree that royal personages do. It is, as well as I could make out Powers's idea, a certain coldness of demeanor, and especially of eye, that surrounds them with an atmosphere through which the electricity of human brotherhood cannot pass. From their youth upward they are taught to feel themselves apart from the rest of mankind, and this manner becomes a second nature to them in consequence, and as a safeguard to their conventional dignity. They put themselves under glass, as it were (the illustration is my own), so that, though you see them, and see them looking no more noble and dignified than other mortals, nor so much so as many, still they keep themselves within a sort of sanctity, and repel you by an invisible barrier. Even if they invite you with a show of warmth and hospitality, you cannot get through.

I, too, recognize this look in the portraits of Washington ; in him, a mild, benevolent coldness and apartness, but indicating that formality which seems to have been deeper in him than in any other mortal, and which built up an actual fortification between himself and human sympathy.   I wish, for once, Washington could come out of his envelopment and show us what his real dimensions were.

Among other models of statues heretofore made, Powers showed us one of Melancholy, or rather of Contemplation, from Milton's Penseroso ; a female figure with uplifted face and rapt look, " communing with the skies." It is very fine, and goes deeply into Milton's thought; but, as far as the outward form and action are concerned, I remember seeing a rude engraving in my childhood that probably suggested the idea. It was prefixed to a cheap American edition of Milton's poems, and was probably as familiar to Powers as to myself.   It is very remarkable how difficult it seems to be to strike out a new attitude in sculpture; a new group or a new single figure.

One piece of sculpture Powers exhibited, however, which was very exquisite, and such as I never saw before.   Opening a desk, he took out something carefully enclosed between two layers of cotton wool, on removing which there appeared a little baby's hand most delicately repre-

sented in the whitest marble ; all the dimples
where the knuckles were to be, all the creases in
the plump flesh, every infantile wrinkle of the
soft skin, being lovingly recorded. " The critics
condemn minute representation," said Powers ;
" but you may look at this through a microscope and see if it injures the general effect."
Nature herself never made a prettier or truer
little hand. It was the hand of his daughter, —
" Luly's hand," Powers called it, — the same
that gave my own such a frank and friendly
grasp when I first met " Luly." The sculptor
made it only for himself and his wife ; but so
many people, he said, had insisted on having a
copy, that there are now forty scattered about
the world. At sixty years Luly ought to have
her hand sculptured again, and give it to her
grandchildren with the baby's hand of five
months old. The baby hand that had done nothing, and felt only its mother's kiss ; the old
lady's hand that had exchanged the love pressure, worn the marriage ring, closed dead eyes,
— done a lifetime's work, in short. The sentiment is rather obvious, but true nevertheless.

Before we went away, Powers took us into a
room apart — apparently the secretest room he
had — and showed us some tools and machinery,
all of his own contrivance and invention. " You
see I am a bit of a Yankee," he observed.

This machinery is chiefly to facilitate the pro-

cess of modelling his works, for — except in por-
trait-busts — he makes no clay model as other
sculptors do, but models directly in the plaster;
so that instead of being crumbled, like clay, the
original model remains a permanent possession.
He has also invented a certain open file, which
is of great use in finishing the surface of the
marble ; and likewise a machine for making these
files and for punching holes through iron, and
he demonstrated its efficiency by punching a
hole through an iron bar, with a force equivalent to ten thousand pounds, by the mere application of a part of his own weight.   These
inventions, he says, are his amusement, and the
bent of his nature towards sculpture must indeed
have been strong, to counteract, in an American, such a capacity for the contrivance of steam-
engines. . . .

I had no idea of filling so many pages of this
journal with the sayings and characteristics of
Mr. Powers ; but the man and his talk are fresh,
original, and full of bone and muscle, and I enjoy him much.

We now proceeded to the Pitti Palace, and
spent several hours pleasantly in its saloons of
pictures.   I never enjoyed pictures anywhere else
as I do in Florence. There is an admirable Judith in this gallery by Allori ; a face of great
beauty and depth, and her hand clutches the
head of Holofernes by the hair in a way that

startles the spectator. There are two peasant Madonnas by Murillo; simple women, yet with a thoughtful sense of some high mystery connected with the baby in their arms.

Raphael grows upon me; several other famous painters — Guido, for instance — are fading out of my mind. Salvator Rosa has two really wonderful landscapes, looking from the shore seaward; and Rubens too, likewise on a large scale, of mountain and plain. It is very idle and foolish to talk of pictures; yet, after poring over them and into them, it seems a pity to let all the thought excited by them pass into nothingness.

The copyists of pictures are very numerous, both in the Pitti and Uffizi galleries; and, unlike sculptors, they appear to be on the best of terms with one another, chatting sociably, exchanging friendly criticism, and giving their opinions as to the best mode of attaining the desired effects. Perhaps, as mere copyists, they escape the jealousy that might spring up between rival painters attempting to develop original ideas. Miss Howorth says that the business of copying pictures, especially those of Raphael, is a regular profession, and she thinks it exceedingly obstructive to the progress or existence of a modern school of painting, there being a regular demand and sure sale for all copies of the old masters, at prices proportioned to their merit; whereas the effort to be original insures nothing, except long neglect, at the beginning of a career, and probably ultimate failure, and the necessity of becoming a copyist at last. Some artists employ themselves from youth to age in nothing else but the copying of one single and selfsame picture by Raphael, and grow at last to be perfectly mechanical, making, I suppose, the same identical stroke of the brush in fifty successive pictures.

The weather is very hot now, — hotter in the sunshine, I think, than a midsummer day usually is in America, but with rather a greater possibility of being comfortable in the shade. The nights, too, are warm, and the bats fly forth at dusk, and the fireflies quite light up the green depths of our little garden. The atmosphere, or something else, causes a sort of alacrity in my mind and an affluence of ideas, such as they are; but it does not thereby make me the happier. I feel an impulse to be at work, but am kept idle by the sense of being unsettled with removals to be gone through, over and over again, before I can shut myself into a quiet room of my own, and turn the key. I need monotony, too, an eventless exterior life, before I can live in the world within.

June 15. — Yesterday we went to the Uffizi gallery, and, of course, I took the opportunity to look again at the Venus di Medici after

Powers's attack upon her face. Some of the defects he attributed to her I could not see in the statue; for instance, the ear appeared to be in accordance with his own rule, the lowest part of it being about in a straight line with the upper lip. The eyes must be given up, as not, when closely viewed, having the shape, the curve outwards, the formation of the lids, that eyes ought to have; but still, at a proper distance, they seemed to have intelligence in them beneath the shadow cast by the brow. I cannot help thinking that the sculptor intentionally made every feature what it is, and calculated them all with a view to the desired effect. Whatever rules may be transgressed, it is a noble and beautiful face, — more so, perhaps, than if all rules had been obeyed. I wish Powers would do his best to fit the Venus's figure (which he does not deny to be admirable) with a face which he would deem equally admirable and in accordance with the sentiment of the form.

We looked pretty thoroughly through the gallery, and I saw many pictures that impressed me; but among such a multitude, with only one poor mind to take note of them, the stamp of each new impression helps to obliterate a former one. I am sensible, however, that a process is going on, and has been ever since I came to Italy, that puts me in a state to see pictures with less toil and more pleasure, and makes me more fastidious, yet more sensible of beauty where I saw none before. It is the sign, I presume, of a taste still very defective, that I take singular pleasure in the elaborate imitations of Van Mieris, Gerard Dow, and other old Dutch wizards, who painted such brass pots that you can see your face in them, and such earthen pots that they will surely hold water; and who spent weeks and months in turning a foot or two of canvas into a perfect microscopic illusion of some homely scene. For my part, I wish Raphael had painted The Transfiguration in this style, at the same time preserving his breadth and grandeur of design; nor do I believe that there is any real impediment to the combination of the two styles, except that no possible space of human life could suffice to cover a quarter part of the canvas of The Transfiguration with such touches as Gerard Dow's. But one feels the vast scope of this wonderful art, when we think of two excellences so far apart as that of this last painter and Raphael. I pause a good while, too, before the Dutch paintings of fruit and flowers, where tulips and roses acquire an immortal bloom, and grapes have kept the freshest juice in them for two or three hundred years. Often, in these pictures, there is a bird's nest, every straw perfectly represented, and the stray feather or the down that the mother-bird plucked from her bosom, with the three or four small speckled eggs, that seem as if they might be yet warm. These pretty miracles have their use in assuring us that painters really can do something that takes hold of us in our most matter-of-fact moods ; whereas, the merits of the grander style of art may be beyond our ordinary appreciation, and leave us in doubt whether we have not befooled ourselves with a false admiration.

Until we learn to appreciate the cherubs and angels that Raphael scatters through the blessed air, in a picture of The Nativity, it is not amiss to look at a Dutch fly settling on a peach, or a humblebee burying himself in a flower.

It is another token of imperfect taste, no doubt, that queer pictures and absurd pictures remain in my memory, when better ones pass away by the score. There is a picture of Venus, combing her son Cupid's head with a small-tooth comb, and looking with maternal care among his curls ; this I shall not forget. Likewise, a picture of a broad, rubicund Judith, by Bardone, — a widow of fifty, of an easy, lymphatic, cheerful temperament, who has just killed Holofernes, and is as self-complaisant as if she had been carving a goose. What could possibly have stirred up this pudding of a woman (unless it were a pudding-stick) to do such a deed ! I looked with much pleasure at an ugly, old, fat, jolly Bacchus, astride on a barrel, by Rubens; the most natural and lifelike representation of a tipsy rotundity of flesh that it is possible to imagine. And sometimes, amid these sensual images, I caught the divine pensiveness of a Madonna's face, by Raphael, or the glory and majesty of the babe Jesus in her arms, with his Father shining through him. This is a sort of revelation, whenever it comes.

This morning, immediately after breakfast, I walked into the city, meaning to make myself better acquainted with its appearance, and to go into its various churches; but it soon grew so hot, that I turned homeward again. The interior of the Duomo was deliciously cool, to be sure, — cool and dim, after the white-hot sunshine; but an old women began to persecute me, so that I came away. A male beggar drove me out of another church; and I took refuge in the street, where the beggar and I would have been two cinders together, if we had stood long enough on the sunny sidewalk. After my five summers' experience of England, I may have forgotten what hot weather is; but it does appear to me that an American summer is not so fervent as this. Besides the direct rays, the white pavement throws a furnace heat up into one's face; the shady margin of the street is barely tolerable; but it is like going through the ordeal of fire to cross the broad bright glare of an open piazza. The narrow streets prove themselves a blessing at this season, except when the sun looks directly into them ; the broad eaves of the houses, too, make a selvage of shade, almost always. I do not know what becomes of the street merchants at the noontide of these hot days. They form a numerous class in Florence, displaying their wares — linen or cotton cloth, threads, combs, and all manner of haberdashery — on movable counters that are borne about on wheels. In the shady morning, you see a whole side of a street in a piazza occupied by them, all offering their merchandise at full cry. They dodge as they can from shade to shade ; but at last the sunshine floods the whole space, and they seem to have melted away, leaving not a rag of themselves or what they dealt in.

Cherries are very abundant now, and have been so ever since we came here, in the markets and all about the streets. They are of various kinds, some exceedingly large, insomuch that it is almost necessary to disregard the old proverb about making two bites of a cherry. Fresh figs are already spoken of, though I have seen none ; but I saw some peaches this morning, looking as if they might be ripe.

June 16. — Mr. and Mrs. Powers called to see us last evening. Mr. Powers, as usual, was full of talk, and gave utterance to a good many instructive and entertaining ideas.

As one instance of the little influence the religion of the Italians has upon their morals, he told a story of one of his servants, who desired leave to set up a small shrine of the Virgin in their room — a cheap print, or bas-relief, or image, such as are sold everywhere at the shops — and to burn a lamp before it; she engaging, of course, to supply the oil at her own expense. By and by her oil-flask appeared to possess a miraculous property of replenishing itself, and Mr. Powers took measures to ascertain where the oil came from. It turned out that the servant had all the time been stealing the oil from them, and keeping up her daily sacrifice and worship to the Virgin by this constant theft.

His talk soon turned upon sculpture, and he spoke once more of the difficulty imposed upon an artist by the necessity of clothing portrait statues in the modern costume. I find that he does not approve either of nudity or of the Roman toga for a modern statue; neither does he think it right to shirk the difficulty — as Chantrey did in the case of Washington — by enveloping him in a cloak; but acknowledges the propriety of taking the actual costume of the age and doing his best with it. He himself did so with his own Washington, and also with a

97

statue that he made of Daniel Webster. I suggested that though this costume might not
appear ridiculous to us now, yet, two or three
centuries hence, it would create, to the people
of that day, an impossibility of seeing the real
man through the absurdity of his envelopment,
after it shall have entirely grown out of fashion
and remembrance; and Webster would seem
as absurd to them then as he would to us now
in the masquerade of some by-gone day. It
might be well, therefore, to adopt some conventional costume, never actual, but always
graceful and noble. Besides, Webster, for example, had other costumes than that which he
wore in public, and perhaps it was in those that
he lived his most real life; his dressing-gown,
his drapery of the night, the dress that he wore
on his fishing excursions; in these other costumes he spent three fourths of his time, and
most probably was thus arrayed when he conceived the great thoughts that afterwards, in
some formal and outside mood, he gave forth
to the public. I scarcely think I was right, but
am not sure of the contrary. At any rate, I
know that I should have felt much more sure
that I knew the real Webster, if I had seen him
in any of the above-mentioned dresses, than
either in his swallow-tailed coat or frock.

Talking of a taste for painting and sculpture,
Powers observed that it was something very

different and quite apart from the moral sense, and that it was often, perhaps generally, possessed by unprincipled men of ability and cultivation. I have had this perception myself. A genuine love of painting and sculpture, and perhaps of music, seems often to have distinguished men capable of every social crime, and to have formed a fine and hard enamel over their characters. Perhaps it is because such tastes are artificial, the product of cultivation, and, when highly developed, imply a great remove from natural simplicity.

This morning I went with Una to the Uffizi gallery, and again looked with more or less attention at almost every picture and statue. I saw a little picture of the golden age, by Zucchero, in which the charms of youths and virgins are depicted with a freedom that this iron age can hardly bear to look at. The cabinet of gems happened to be open for the admission of a privileged party, and we likewise went in and saw a brilliant collection of goldsmiths' work, among which, no doubt, were specimens from such hands as Benvenuto Cellini's. Little busts with diamond eyes; boxes of gems; cups carved out of precious material; crystal vases, beautifully chased and engraved, and sparkling with jewels; great pearls, in the midst of rubies; opals, rich with all manner of lovely lights. I remember Benvenuto Cellini, in his memoirs, speaks of manufacturing such playthings as these.

I observed another characteristic of the summer streets of Florence to-day; tables, movable to and fro, on wheels, and set out with cool iced drinks and cordials.

June 17. — My wife and I went, this morning, to the Academy of Fine Arts, and, on our way thither, went into the Duomo, where we found a deliciously cool twilight, through which shone the mild gleam of the painted windows. I cannot but think it a pity that St. Peter's is not lighted by such windows as these, although I by no means saw the glory in them now that I have spoken of in a record of my former visit. We found out the monument of Giotto, a tablet, and portrait in bas-relief, on the walk near the entrance of the Cathedral, on the right hand; also, a representation, in fresco, of a knight on horseback, the memorial of one John Hawkwood, close by the door, to the left. The priests were chanting a service of some kind or other in the choir, terribly inharmonious and out of tune. . . .

On reaching the Academy, the soldier or policeman at the entrance directed us into the large hall, the walls of which were covered on both sides with pictures, arranged as nearly as possible in a progressive series, with reference to the

date of the painters ; so that here the origin and
procession of the art may be traced through the
course of, at least, two hundred years. Giotto,
Cimabue, and others of unfamiliar names to
me, are among the earliest; and, except as
curiosities, I should never desire to look once
at them, nor think of looking twice. They
seem to have been executed with great care
and conscientiousness, and the heads are often
wrought out with minuteness and fidelity, and
have so much expression that they tell their
own story clearly enough; but it seems not to
have been the painter's aim to effect a lifelike
illusion, the background and accessories being
conventional. The trees are no more like real
trees than the feather of a pen, and there is no
perspective, the figure of the picture being shadowed forth on a surface of burnished gold. The
effect, when these pictures, some of them very
large, were new and freshly gilded, must have
been exceedingly brilliant, and much resembling,
on an immensely larger scale, the rich illuminations in an old monkish missal. In fact, we
have not now, in pictorial ornament, anything
at all comparable to what their splendor must
have been. I was most struck with a picture,
by Fabriana Gentile, of the Adoration of the
Magi, where the faces and figures have a great
deal of life and action, and even grace, and where
the jewelled crowns, the rich embroidered robes,

and cloth of gold, and all the magnificence of the three kings, are represented with the vividness of the real thing; a gold sword-hilt, for instance, or a pair of gold spurs, being actually embossed on the picture. The effect is very powerful, and though produced in what modern painters would pronounce an unjustifiable way, there is yet pictorial art enough to reconcile it to the spectator's mind. Certainly, the people of the Middle Ages knew better than ourselves what is magnificence, and how to produce it; and what a glorious work must that have been, both in its mere sheen of burnished gold, and in its illuminating art, which shines thus through the gloom of perhaps four centuries!

Fra Angelico is a man much admired by those who have a taste for Pre-Raphaelite painters; and, though I take little or no pleasure in his works, I can see that there is great delicacy of execution in his heads, and that generally he produces such a Christ, and such a Virgin, and such saints, as he could not have foreseen, except in a pure and holy imagination, nor have wrought out without saying a prayer between every two touches of his brush. I might come to like him in time, if I thought it worth while; but it is enough to have an outside perception of his kind and degree of merit, and so to let him pass into the garret of oblivion, where many things as good, or better, are

piled away, that our own age may not stumble
over them. Perugino is the first painter whose
works seem really worth preserving for the
genuine merit that is in them, apart from any
quaintness and curiosity of an ancient and new-
born art. Probably his religion was more genuine than Raphael's, and therefore the Virgin
often revealed herself to him in a loftier and
sweeter face of divine womanhood than all the
genius of Raphael could produce. There is a
Crucifixion by him in this gallery, which made
me partly feel as if I were a far-off spectator, —
no, I did not mean a Crucifixion, but a picture
of Christ dead, lying, with a calm, sweet face, on
his mother's knees ["a Pietà"].

The most inadequate and utterly absurd picture here, or in any other gallery, is a head of
the Eternal Father, by Carlo Dolce; it looks
like a feeble saint, on the eve of martyrdom,
and very doubtful how he shall be able to bear
it; very finely and prettily painted, nevertheless.

After getting through the principal gallery
we went into a smaller room, in which are contained a great many small specimens of the old
Tuscan artists, among whom Fra Angelico
makes the principal figure. These pictures are
all on wood, and seem to have been taken from
the shrines and altars of ancient churches; they
are predellas and triptychs, or pictures on three

folding tablets, shaped quaintly, in Gothic peaks or arches, and still gleaming with backgrounds of antique gold. The wood is much worm-eaten, and the colors have often faded, or changed, from what the old artists meant them to be; a bright angel darkening into what looks quite as much like the Devil. In one of Fra Angelico's pictures, — a representation of the Last Judgment, — he has tried his saintly hand at making devils indeed, and showing them busily at work, tormenting the poor, damned souls in fifty ghastly ways. Above sits Jesus, with the throng of blessed saints around him, and a flow of tender and powerful love in his own face, that ought to suffice to redeem all the damned, and convert the very fiends, and quench the fires of hell. At any rate, Fra Angelico had a higher conception of his Saviour than Michel Angelo.

June 19. — This forenoon we have been to the Church of St. Lorenzo, which stands on the site of an ancient basilica, and was itself built more than four centuries ago. The façade is still an ugly height of rough brickwork, as is the case with the Duomo, and, I think, some other churches in Florence; the design of giving them an elaborate and beautiful finish having been delayed from cycle to cycle, till at length the day for spending mines of wealth on churches is gone by. The interior had a nave with a flat

roof, divided from the side-aisles by Corinthian
pillars, and, at the farther end, a raised space
around the high altar. The pavement is a mosaic of squares of black and white marble, the
squares meeting one another cornerwise; the
pillars, pilasters, and other architectural material is dark brown or grayish stone; and the
general effect is very sombre, especially as the
church is somewhat dimly lighted, and as the
shrines along the aisles, and the statues, and
the monuments of whatever kind, look dingy
with time and neglect. The nave is thickly set
with wooden seats, brown and worn. What
pictures there are, in the shrines and chapels,
are dark and faded. On the whole, the edifice
has a shabby aspect. On each side of the high
altar, elevated on four pillars of beautiful marble, is what looks like a great sarcophagus of
bronze. They are, in fact, pulpits, and are
ornamented with mediæval bas-reliefs, representing scenes in the life of our Saviour. Murray says that the resting-place of the first Cosmo
de' Medici, the old banker, who so managed his
wealth as to get the posthumous title of "father
of his country," and to make his posterity its
reigning princes, is in front of the high altar,
marked by red and green porphyry and marble,
inlaid into the pavement. We looked, but
could not see it there.

There were worshippers at some of the

shrines, and persons sitting here and there along the nave, and in the aisles, wrapt in devotional thought, doubtless, and sheltering themselves here from the white sunshine of the piazzas. In the vicinity of the choir and the high altar workmen were busy repairing the church, or perhaps only making arrangements for celebrating the great festival of St. John.

On the left hand of the choir is what is called the old sacristy, with the peculiarities or notabilities of which I am not acquainted. On the right hand is the new sacristy, otherwise called the Capella dei Deposité, or Chapel of the Buried, built by Michel Angelo, to contain two monuments of the Medici family. The interior is of somewhat severe and classic architecture, the walls and pilasters being of dark stone, and surmounted by a dome, beneath which is a row of windows, quite round the building, throwing their light down far beneath, upon niches of white marble. These niches are ranged entirely around the chapel, and might have sufficed to contain more than all the Medici monuments that the world would ever care to have. Only two of these niches are filled, however. In one of them sits Giuliano de' Medici, sculptured by Michel Angelo, — a figure of dignity, which would, perhaps, be very striking in any other presence than that of the statue which occupies the corresponding niche. At the feet of Giu-

liano recline two allegorical statues, Day and
Night, whose meaning there I do not know, and
perhaps Michel Angelo knew as little. As the
great sculptor's statues are apt to do, they fling
their limbs abroad with adventurous freedom.
Below the corresponding niche, on the opposite side of the chapel, recline two similar statues, representing Morning and Evening, sufficiently like Day and Night to be their brother
and sister; all, in truth, having sprung from
the same father. . . .

But the statue that sits above these two latter
allegories, Morning and Evening, is like no
other that ever came from a sculptor's hand. It
is the one work worthy of Michel Angelo's reputation, and grand enough to vindicate for him
all the genius that the world gave him credit
for. And yet it seems a simple thing enough
to think of or to execute; merely a sitting figure, the face partly overshadowed by a helmet,
one hand supporting the chin, the other resting
on the thigh. But after looking at it a little
while, the spectator ceases to think of it as a
marble statue; it comes to life, and you see that
the princely figure is brooding over some great
design, which, when he has arranged in his own
mind, the world will be fain to execute for him.
No such grandeur and majesty has elsewhere
been put into human shape. It is all a miracle; the deep repose, and the deep life within

it. It is as much a miracle to have achieved this as to make a statue that would rise up and walk. The face, when one gazes earnestly into it, beneath the shadow of its helmet, is seen to be calmly sombre ; a mood which, I think, is generally that of the rulers of mankind, except in moments of vivid action. This statue is one of the things which I look at with highest enjoyment, but also with grief and impatience, because I feel that I do not come at all which it involves, and that by and by I must go away and leave it forever. How wonderful ! To take a block of marble, and convert it wholly into thought, and to do it through all the obstructions and impediments of drapery ; for there is nothing nude in this statue but the face and hands. The vest is the costume of Michel Angelo's century. This is what I always thought a sculptor of true genius should be able to do, — to show the man, of whatever epoch, nobly and heroically, through the costume which he might actually have worn.

The statue sits within a square niche of white marble, and completely fills it. It seems to me a pity that it should be thus confined. At the Crystal Palace, if I remember, the effect is improved by a free surrounding space. Its naturalness is as if it came out of the marble of its own accord, with all its grandeur hanging heavily about it and sat down there beneath its weight.

I cannot describe it. It is like trying to stop the ghost of Hamlet's father by crossing spears before it.

Communicating with the sacristy is the Medicean Chapel, which was built more than two centuries ago, for the reception of the Holy Sepulchre; arrangements having been made about that time to steal this most sacred relic from the Turks. The design failing, the chapel was converted by Cosmo II. into a place of sepulture for the princes of his family. It is a very grand and solemn edifice, octagonal in shape, with a lofty dome, within which is a series of brilliant frescos, painted not more than thirty years ago. These pictures are the only portion of the adornment of the chapel which interferes with the sombre beauty of the general effect; for though the walls are incrusted, from pavement to dome, with marbles of inestimable cost, and it is a Florentine mosaic on a grander scale than was ever executed elsewhere, the result is not gaudy, as in many of the Roman chapels, but a dark and melancholy richness. The architecture strikes me as extremely fine; each alternate side of the octagon being an arch, rising as high as the cornice of the lofty dome, and forming the frame of a vast niche. All the dead princes, no doubt, according to the general design, were to have been honored with statues within this stately mausoleum; but only two

— those of Ferdinand I. and Cosmo II. — seem to have been placed here. They were a bad breed, and few of them deserved any better monument than a dunghill; and yet they have this grand chapel for the family at large, and yonder grand statue for one of its most worthless members. I am glad of it; and as for the statue, Michel Angelo wrought it through the efficacy of a kingly idea, which had no reference to the individual whose name it bears.

In the piazza, adjoining the church, is a statue of the first Cosmo, the old banker, in Roman costume, seated, and looking like a man fit to hold authority. No, I mistake; the statue is of John de' Medici, the father of Cosmo, and himself no banker, but a soldier.

June 21. — Yesterday, after dinner, we went with the two eldest children to the Boboli Gardens. . . . We entered by a gate nearer to our house than that by the Pitti Palace, and found ourselves almost immediately among embowered walks of box and shrubbery, and little wildernesses of trees, with here and there a seat under an arbor, and a marble statue, gray with ancient weather-stains. The site of the garden is a very uneven surface, and the paths go upward and downward, and ascend, at their ultimate point, to a base of what appears to be a

fortress, commanding the city. A good many
of the Florentines were rambling about the gardens, like ourselves : little parties of school-
boys, fathers and mothers, with their youthful
progeny ; young men in couples, looking closely
into every female face; lovers, with a maid or
two attendant on the young lady. All appeared
to enjoy themselves, especially the children,
dancing on the esplanades, or rolling down the
slopes of the hills ; and the loving pairs, whom
it was rather embarrassing to come upon unexpectedly, sitting together on the stone seat of an
arbor, with clasped hands, a passionate solemnity
in the young man's face, and a downcast pleasure
in the lady's. Policemen, in cocked hats and epaulets, cross-belts and swords, were scattered about
the grounds, but interfered with nobody, though
they seemed to keep an eye on all. A sentinel
stood in the hot sunshine, looking down over
the garden from the ramparts of the fortress.

For my part, in this foreign country, I have
no objection to policemen or any other minister
of authority ; though I remember, in America,
I had an innate antipathy to constables, and always sided with the mob against law. This was
very wrong and foolish, considering that I was
one of the sovereigns ; but a sovereign, or any
number of sovereigns, or the twenty-millionth
part of a sovereign, does not love to find him-

self, as an American must, included within the delegated authority of his own servants.

There is a sheet of water somewhere in the Boboli Gardens, inhabited by swans; but this we did not see. We found a smaller pond, however, set in marble, and surrounded by a parapet, and alive with a multitude of fish. There were minnows by the thousand, and a good many gold-fish; and Julian, who had brought some bread to feed the swans, threw in handfuls of crumbs for the benefit of these finny people. They seemed to be accustomed to such courtesies on the part of visitors; and immediately the surface of the water was blackened, at the spot where each crumb fell, with shoals of minnows, thrusting one another even above the surface in their eagerness to snatch it. Within the depths of the pond, the yellowish-green water — its hue being precisely that of the Arno — would be reddened duskily with the larger bulk of two or three gold-fishes, who finally poked their great snouts up among the minnows, but generally missed the crumb. Beneath the circular margin of the pond there are little arches, into the shelter of which the fish retire, when the noonday sun burns straight down into their dark waters. We went on through the garden paths, shadowed quite across by the high walls of box, and reached an esplanade, whence we had a good view of Florence,

with the bare brown ridges on the northern side
of the Arno, and glimpses of the river itself,
flowing like a street, between two rows of palaces.   A great way off, too, we saw some of the
cloudlike peaks of the Apennines, and, above
them, the clouds into which the sun was descending, looking quite as substantial as the
distant mountains.   The city did not present
a particularly splendid aspect, though its great
Duomo was seen in the middle distance, sitting
in its circle of little domes, with the tall campanile close by, and within one or two hundred
yards of it, the high, cumbrous bulk of the
Palazzo Vecchio, with its lofty, machicolated,
and battlemented tower, very picturesque, yet
looking exceedingly like a martin-box on a
pole.   There were other domes and towers and
spires, and here and there the distinct shape of
an edifice; but the general picture was of a contiguity of red, earthen roofs, filling a not very
broad or extensive valley, among dry and ridgy
hills, with a river gleam lightening up the landscape a little.   Una took out her pencil and tablets, and began to sketch the tower of the Palazzo
Vecchio; in doing which she immediately became an object of curiosity to some little boys
and larger people, who failed not, under such
pretences as taking a grasshopper off her dress,
or no pretence at all, to come and look over her
shoulder.   There is a kind of familiarity among

these Florentines, which is not meant to be discourteous, and ought to be taken in good part.

We continued to ramble through the gardens, in quest of a good spot from which to see the sunset, and at length found a stone bench, on the slope of a hill, whence the entire cloud and sun scenery was fully presented to us. At the foot of the hill were statues, and among them a Pegasus, with wings outspread; and, a little beyond, the garden front of the Pitti Palace, which looks a little less like a state prison here than as it fronts the street. Girls and children, and young men and old, were taking their pleasure in our neighborhood; and, just before us, a lady stood talking with her maid. By and by we discovered her to be Miss Howorth. There was a misty light streaming down on the hither side of the ridge of hills, that was rather peculiar; but the most remarkable thing was the shape into which the clouds gathered themselves after the disappearance of the sun. It was like a tree, with a broad and heavy mass of foliage, spreading high upward on the sky, and a dark and well-defined trunk, which rooted itself on the verge of the horizon.

This morning we went to the Pitti Palace. The air was very sultry, and the pavements, already heated with the sun, made the space between the buildings seem like a close room. The earth, I think, is too much stoned out of the streets of an Italian city, — paved, like those of Florence, quite across, with broad flag-stones, to the line where the stones of the houses on each side are piled up. Thunder rumbled over our heads, however, and the clouds were so dark that we scarcely hoped to reach the palace without feeling the first drops of the shower. The air still darkened and darkened, so that by the time we arrived at the suite of picture rooms the pictures seemed all to be changed to Rembrandts; the shadows as black as midnight, with only some highly illuminated portions gleaming out. The obscurity of the atmosphere made us sensible how splendid is the adornment of these saloons. For the gilded cornices shone out, as did the gilding of the arches and wreathed circles that divide the ceiling into compartments, within which the frescos are painted, and whence the figures looked dimly down, like gods out of a mysterious sky. The white marble sculptures also gleamed from their height, where winged cupids or cherubs gambolled aloft in bas-reliefs; or allegoric shapes reclined along the cornices, hardly noticed, when the daylight comes brightly into the window. On the walls, all the rich picture frames glimmered in gold, as did the framework of the chairs, and the heavy gilded pedestals of the marble, alabaster, and mosaic tables. These are very magnificent saloons; and since I have begun to speak of their splendor, I may as well add that the doors are framed in polished, richly veined marble, and the walls hung with scarlet damask.

It was useless to try to see the pictures. All the artists engaged in copying laid aside their brushes; and we looked out into the square before the palace, where a mighty wind sprang up, and quickly raised a prodigious cloud of dust. It hid the opposite side of the street, and was carried, in a great dusky whirl, higher than the roofs of the houses, higher than the top of the Pitti Palace itself. The thunder muttered and grumbled, the lightning now and then flashed, and a few raindrops pattered against the windows; but, for a long time, the shower held off. At last it came down in a stream, and lightened the air to such a degree that we could see some of the pictures, especially those of Rubens, and the illuminated parts of Salvator Rosa's, and, best of all, Titian's Magdalen, the one with golden hair clustering round her naked body. The golden hair, indeed, seemed to throw out a glory of its own. This Magdalen is very coarse and sensual, with only an impudent assumption of penitence and religious sentiment, scarcely so deep as the eyelids; but it is a splendid picture, nevertheless, with those naked, lifelike arms, and the hands that press the rich locks about her, and so carefully permit those voluptuous breasts to be seen. She a penitent!

She would shake off all pretence to it as easily as she would shake aside that clustering hair. . . . Titian must have been a very good-for-nothing old man.

I looked again at Michel Angelo's Fates to-day ; but cannot satisfactorily make out what he meant by them. One of them — she who holds the distaff — has her mouth open, as if uttering a cry, and might be fancied to look somewhat irate. The second, who holds the thread, has a pensive air, but is still, I think, pitiless at heart. The third sister looks closely and coldly into the eyes of the second, meanwhile cutting the thread with a pair of shears. Michel Angelo, if I may presume to say so, wished to vary the expression of these three sisters, and give each a different one, but did not see precisely how, in-asmuch as all the fatal Three are united, heart and soul, in one purpose. It is a very impres-sive group. But, as regards the interpretation of this, or of any other profound picture, there are likely to be as many interpretations as there are spectators. It is very curious to read criti-cisms upon pictures, and upon the same face in a picture, and by men of taste and feeling, and to find what different conclusions they arrive at. Each man interprets the hieroglyphic in his own way ; and the painter, perhaps, had a mean-ing which none of them have reached ; or pos-sibly he put forth a riddle without himself

knowing the solution. There is such a necessity, at all events, of helping the painter out
with the spectator's own resources of feeling and
imagination, that you can never be sure how
much of the picture you have yourself made.
There is no doubt that the public is, to a certain extent, right and sure of its ground, when
it declares, through a series of ages, that a certain picture is a great work. It is so; a great
symbol, proceeding out of a great mind ; but if
it means one thing, it seems to mean a thousand, and, often, opposite things.

June 27. — I have had a heavy cold and fever
almost throughout the past week, and have
thereby lost the great Florentine festivity, the
feast of St. John, which took place on Thursday
last, with the fireworks and illuminations the
evening before, and the races and court ceremonies on the day itself. However, unless
it were more characteristic and peculiar than
the Carnival, I have not missed anything very
valuable.

Mr. Powers called to see me one evening,
and poured out, as usual, a stream of talk, both
racy and oracular in its character. Speaking of
human eyes, he observed that they did not depend for their expression upon color, nor upon
any light of the soul beaming through them,
nor any glow of the eyeball, nor upon anything

but the form and action of the surrounding muscles. He illustrates it by saying, that if the eye of a wolf, or of whatever fiercest animal, could be placed in another setting, it would be found capable of the utmost gentleness of expression. "You yourself," said he, "have a very bright and sharp look sometimes; but it is not in the eye itself." His own eyes, as I could have sworn, were glowing all the time he spoke; and, remembering how many times I have seemed to see eyes glow, and blaze, and flash, and sparkle, and melt, and soften; and how all poetry is illuminated with the light of ladies' eyes; and how many people have been smitten by the lightning of an eye, whether in love or anger, it was difficult to allow that all this subtlest and keenest fire is illusive, not even phosphorescent, and that any other jelly in the same socket would serve as well as the brightest eye. Nevertheless, he must be right; of course he must, and I am rather ashamed ever to have thought otherwise. Where should the light come from? Has a man a flame inside of his head? Does his spirit manifest itself in the semblance of flame? The moment we think of it, the absurdity becomes evident. I am not quite sure, however, that the outer surface of the eye may not reflect more light in some states of feeling than in others; the state of the health, certainly, has an influence of this kind.

I asked Powers what he thought of Michel Angelo's statue of Lorenzo de' Medici. He allowed that its effect was very grand and mysterious; but added that it owed this to a trick, — the effect being produced by the arrangement of the hood, as he called it, or helmet, which throws the upper part of the face into shadow. The niche in which it sits has, I suppose, its part to perform in throwing a still deeper shadow. It is very possible that Michel Angelo may have calculated upon this effect of sombre shadow, and legitimately, I think; but it really is not worthy of Mr. Powers to say that the whole effect of this mighty statue depends, not on the positive efforts of Michel Angelo's chisel, but on the absence of light in a space of a few inches. He wrought the whole statue in harmony with that small part of it which he leaves to the spectator's imagination, and if he had erred at any point, the miracle would have been a failure; so that, working in marble, he has positively reached a degree of excellence above the capability of marble, sculpturing his highest touches upon air and duskiness.

Mr. Powers gave some amusing anecdotes of his early life, when he was a clerk in a store in Cincinnati. There was a museum opposite, the proprietor of which had a peculiar physiognomy that struck Powers, insomuch that he felt impelled to make continual caricatures of it. He used to draw them upon the door of the museum, and became so familiar with the face that he could draw them in the dark; so that, every morning, here was this absurd profile of himself greeting the museum man when he came to open his establishment. Often, too, it would reappear within an hour after it was rubbed out. The man was infinitely annoyed, and made all possible efforts to discover the unknown artist, but in vain; and finally concluded, I suppose, that the likeness broke out upon the door of its own accord, like the nettle-rash. Some years afterwards, the proprietor of the museum engaged Powers himself as an assistant; and one day Powers asked him if he remembered this mysterious profile. "Yes," said he, "did you know who drew them?" Powers took a piece of chalk, and touched off the very profile again, before the man's eyes. "Ah," said he, "if I had known it at the time, I would have broken every bone in your body!"

Before he began to work in marble, Powers had greater practice and success in making wax figures, and he produced a work of this kind called The Infernal Regions, which he seemed to imply had been very famous. He said he once wrought a face in wax which was life itself, having made the eyes on purpose for it, and put in every hair in the eyebrows individually, and finished the whole with similar minuteness; so that, within the distance of a foot or two, it was impossible to tell that the face did not live.

I have hardly ever before felt an impulse to write down a man's conversation as I do that of Mr. Powers. The chief reason is, probably, that it is so possible to do it, his ideas being square, solid, and tangible, and therefore readily grasped and retained. He is a very instructive man, and sweeps one's empty and dead notions out of the way with exceeding vigor ; but when you have his ultimate thought and perception, you feel inclined to think and see a little further for yourself. He sees too clearly what is within his range to be aware of any region of mystery beyond. Probably, however, this latter remark does him injustice. I like the man, and am always glad to encounter the mill-stream of his talk. . . . Yesterday he met me in the street (dressed in his linen blouse and slippers, with a little bit of a sculptor's cap on the side of his head), and gave utterance to a theory of colds, and a dissertation on the bad effects of draughts, whether of cold air or hot, and the dangers of transfusing blood from the veins of one living subject to those of another. On the last topic, he remarked that if a single particle of air found its way into the veins, along with the transfused blood, it caused convulsions and inevitable death ; otherwise the process might be of excellent effect.

Last evening we went to pass the evening
with Miss Blagden, who inhabits a villa at Bellosguardo, about a mile outside of the walls.
The situation is very lofty, and there are good
views from every window of the house, and an
especially fine one of Florence and the hills beyond from the balcony of the drawing-room.
By and by came Mr. Browning, Mr. Trollope,
Mr. Boott and his young daughter, and two or
three other gentlemen. . . .

Browning was very genial and full of life, as
usual, but his conversation has the effervescent
aroma which you cannot catch, even if you get
the very words that seem to be imbued with it.
He spoke most rapturously of a portrait of
Mrs. Browning, which an Italian artist is painting for the wife of an American gentleman, as
a present from her husband. The success was
already perfect, although there had been only
two sittings as yet, and both on the same day ;
and in this relation, Mr. Browning remarked
that P——, the American artist, had had no
less than seventy-three sittings of him for a portrait. In the result, every hair and speck of
him was represented ; yet, as I inferred from
what he did not say, this accumulation of minute truths did not, after all, amount to the
true whole.

I do not remember much else that Browning
said, except a playful abuse of a little King

Charles spaniel, named Frolic, Miss Blagden's lap-dog, whose venerable age (he is eleven years old) ought to have pleaded in his behalf. Browning's nonsense is of very genuine and excellent quality, the true babble and effervescence of a bright and powerful mind ; and he lets it play among his friends with the faith and simplicity of a child. He must be an amiable man. I should like him much, and should make him like me, if opportunities were favorable.

I conversed principally with Mr. Trollope, the son, I believe, of the Mrs. Trollope to whom America owes more for her shrewd criticisms than we are ever likely to repay. Mr. Trollope is a very sensible and cultivated man, and, I suspect, an author : at least, there is a literary man of repute of this name, though I have never read his works. He has resided in Italy eighteen years. It seems a pity to do this. It needs the native air to give life a reality ; a truth which I do not fail to take home regretfully to myself, though without feeling much inclination to go back to the realities of my own.

We had a pleasant cup of tea, and took a moonlight view of Florence from the balcony.

. . . .

June 28. — Yesterday afternoon Julian and I went to a horse-race, which took place in the Corso and contiguous line of streets, in further celebration of the Feast of St. John. A crowd of people was already collected, all along the line of the proposed race, as early as six o'clock ; and there were a great many carriages driving amid the throng, open barouches mostly, in which the beauty and gentility of Florence were freely displayed. It was a repetition of the scene in the Corso at Rome, at Carnival time, without the masks, the fun, and the *confetti*. The Grand Duke and Duchess and the Court likewise made their appearance in as many as seven or eight coaches-and-six, each with a coachman, three footmen, and a postilion in the royal livery, and attended by a troop of horsemen in scarlet coats and cocked hats. I did not particularly notice the Grand Duke himself ; but, in the carriage behind him, there sat only a lady, who favored the people along the street with a constant succession of bows, repeated at such short intervals, and so quickly, as to be little more than nods ; therefore not particularly graceful or majestic. Having the good fortune to be favored with one of these nods, I lifted my hat in response, and may therefore claim a bowing acquaintance with the Grand Duchess. She is a Bourbon of the Naples family, and was a pale, handsome woman, of princely aspect enough. The crowd evinced no enthusiasm, nor the slightest feeling of any kind, in acknowledgment of the presence of their rulers ; and, indeed, I think I never saw a crowd so well behaved ; that is, with so few salient points, so little ebullition, so absolutely tame, as the Florentine one. After all, and much contrary to my expectations, an American crowd has incomparably more life than any other; and, meeting on any casual occasion, it will talk, laugh, roar, and be diversified with a thousand characteristic incidents and gleams and shadows, that you see nothing of here. The people seems to have no part even in its own gatherings. It comes together merely as a mass of spectators, and must not so much as amuse itself by any activity of mind.

The race, which was the attraction that drew us all together, turned out a very pitiful affair. When we had waited till nearly dusk, the street being thronged quite across, insomuch that it seemed impossible that it should be cleared as a race-course, there came suddenly from every throat a quick, sharp exclamation, combining into a general shout. Immediately the crowd pressed back on each side of the street; a moment afterwards, there was a rapid pattering of hoofs over the earth with which the pavement was strewn, and I saw the head and back of a horse rushing past. A few seconds more, and another horse followed ; and at another little interval, a third. This was all that we had waited for ; all that I saw, or anybody else, except those who stood on the utmost verge of the course, at the risk of being trampled down and killed. Two men were killed in this way on Thursday, and certainly human life was never spent for a poorer object. The spectators at the windows, to be sure, having the horses in sight for a longer time, might get a little more enjoyment out of the affair. By the bye, the most picturesque aspect of the scene was the life given to it by the many faces, some of them fair ones, that looked out from window and balcony, all along the curving line of lofty palaces and edifices, between which the race - course lay; and from nearly every window, and over every balcony, was flung a silken texture, or cloth of brilliant hue, or piece of tapestry or carpet, or whatever adornment of the kind could be had, so as to dress up the street in gala attire. But the Feast of St. John, like the Carnival, is but a meagre semblance of festivity, kept alive factitiously, and dying a lingering death of centuries. It takes the exuberant mind and heart of a people to keep its holidays alive.

I do not know whether there be any populace in Florence, but I saw none that I recognized as such, on this occasion. All the people were respectably dressed and perfectly well behaved; and soldiers and priests were scattered abundantly among the throng. On my way home I saw the Teatro Goldoni, which is in our own street, lighted up for a representation

this Sunday evening. It shocked my New England prejudices a little.

This forenoon my wife and I went to the
Church of Santa Croce, the great monumental
deposit of Florentine worthies. The piazza
before it is a wide, gravelled square, where the
liberty of Florence, if it really ever had any
genuine liberty, came into existence some hundreds of years ago, by the people's taking its
own rights into its hands, and putting its own
immediate will in execution. The piazza has not
much appearance of antiquity, except that the
façade of one of the houses is quite covered with
ancient frescos, a good deal faded and obliterated, yet with traces enough of old glory to show
that the colors must have been well laid on.

The front of the church, the foundation of
which was laid six centuries ago, is still waiting
for its casing of marbles, and I suppose will wait
forever, though a carpenter's staging is now
erected before it, as if with the purpose of doing
something.

The interior is spacious, the length of the
church being between four and five hundred feet.
There is a nave, roofed with wooden cross-
beams, lighted by a clere-story and supported on
each side by seven great pointed arches, which
rest upon octagonal pillars. The octagon seems
to be a favorite shape in Florence. These pillars were clad in yellow and scarlet damask, in

honor of the feast of St. John.   The aisles, on
each side of the nave, are lighted with high and
somewhat narrow windows of painted glass, the
effect of which, however, is much diminished
by the flood of common daylight that comes in
through the windows of the clere-story.   It is
like admitting too much of the light of reason
and worldly intelligence into the mind, instead
of illuminating it wholly through a religious medium.   The many-hued saints and angels lose
their mysterious effulgence, when we get white
light enough, and find we see all the better
without their help.

The main pavement of the church is brickwork; but it is inlaid with many sepulchral slabs
of marble, on some of which knightly or priestly
figures are sculptured in bas-relief.   In both of
the side-aisles there are saintly shrines, alternating with mural monuments, some of which record names as illustrious as any in the world.
As you enter, the first monument on your right
is that of Michel Angelo, occupying the ancient
burial site of his family.   The general design is
a heavy sarcophagus of colored marble, with the
figures of Sculpture, Painting, and Architecture
as mourners, and Michel Angelo's bust above,
the whole assuming a pyramidal form.   You pass
a shrine, within its framework of marble pillars
and a pediment, and come next to Dante's monument, a modern work, with likewise its sarcoph-

agus, and some huge, cold images weeping and
sprawling over it, and an unimpressive statue of
Dante sitting above.

Another shrine intervenes, and next you see
the tomb of Alfieri, erected to his memory by
the Countess of Albany, who pays, out of a woman's love, the honor which his country owed
him. Her own monument is in one of the
chapels of the transept.

Passing the next shrine you see the tomb of
Macchiavelli, which, I think, was constructed
not many years after his death. The rest of the
monuments, on this side of the church, com-
memorate people of less than world-wide fame ;
and though the opposite side has likewise a monument alternating with each shrine, I remember
only the names of Raphael Morghen and of
Galileo. The tomb of the latter is over against
that of Michel Angelo, being the first large tomb
on the left-hand wall as you enter the church.
It has the usual heavy sarcophagus, surmounted
by a bust of Galileo, in the habit of his time, and
is, of course, duly provided with mourners in the
shape of Science or Astronomy, or some such
cold-hearted people. I wish every sculptor
might be at once imprisoned for life who shall
hereafter chisel an allegoric figure ; and as for
those who have sculptured them heretofore, let
them be kept in purgatory till the marble shall
have crumbled away. It is especially absurd to

assign to this frozen sisterhood of the allegoric
family the office of weeping for the dead, inasmuch as they have incomparably less feeling
than a lump of ice, which might contrive to shed
a tear if the sun shone on it.   But they seem to
let themselves out, like the hired mourners of
an English funeral, for the very reason that, having no interest in the dead person, nor any affections or emotions whatever, it costs them no
wear and tear of heart.

All round both transepts of the church there
is a series of chapels, into most of which we
went, and generally found an inscrutably dark
picture over the altar, and often a marble bust
or two, or perhaps a mediæval statue of a saint,
or a modern monumental bas-relief in marble,
as white as new-fallen snow.   A chapel of the
Bonapartes is here, containing memorials of two
female members of the family.   In several
chapels, moreover, there were some of those dis-
tressing frescos by Giotto, Cimabue, or their
compeers, which, whenever I see them, — poor,
faded relics, looking as if the Devil had been
rubbing and scrubbing them for centuries, in
spite against the saints, — my heart sinks and
my stomach sickens.   There is no other despondency like this ; it is a new shade of human misery, akin to the physical disease that comes from
dry-rot in a wall.   These frescos are to a church
what dreary, old remembrances are to a mind ;

the drearier because they were once bright:
Hope fading into Disappointment, Joy into
Grief, and festal splendor passing into funereal
duskiness, and saddening you all the more by
the grim identity that you find to exist between
gay things and sorrowful ones.   Only wait long
enough, and they turn out to be the very same.

All the time we were in the church some
great religious ceremony had been going forward ; the organ playing and the white-robed
priests bowing, gesticulating, and making Latin
prayers at the high altar, where at least a hundred wax tapers were burning in constellations.
Everybody knelt except ourselves, yet seemed
not to be troubled by the echoes of our passing
footsteps, nor to require that we should pray
along with them.   They consider us already
lost irrevocably, no doubt, and therefore right
enough in taking no heed of their devotions ;
not but what we take so much heed, however,
as to give the smallest possible disturbance.   By
and by we sat down in the nave of the church,
till the ceremony should be concluded ; and
then my wife left me to go in quest of yet
another chapel, where either Cimabue or Giotto,
or both, have left some of their now ghastly
decorations.   While she was gone I threw my
eyes about the church, and came to the conclusion that, in spite of its antiquity, its size,
its architecture, its painted windows, its tombs

of great men, and all the reverence and interest that broods over them, it is not an impressive edifice. Any little Norman church in England would impress me as much, and more. There is something, I do not know what, but it is in the region of the heart, rather than in the intellect, that Italian architecture, of whatever age or style, never seems to reach.

Leaving the Santa Croce, we went next in quest of the Riccardi Palace. On our way, in the rear of the Grand Ducal Piazza, we passed by the Bargello, formerly the palace of the Podestà of Florence, and now converted into a prison. It is an immense square edifice of dark stone, with a tall, lank tower rising high above it at one corner. Two stone lions, symbols of the city, lash their tails and glare at the passers-by ; and all over the front of the building windows are scattered irregularly, and grated with rusty iron bars ; also there are many square holes, which probably admit a little light and a breath or two of air into prisoners' cells. It is a very ugly edifice, but looks antique, and as if a vast deal of history might have been transacted within it, or have beaten, like fierce blasts, against its dark, massive walls, since the thirteenth century. When I first saw the city it struck me that there were few marks of antiquity in Florence ; but I am now inclined to think otherwise, although the bright Italian at-

mosphere, and the general squareness and monotony of the Italian architecture, have their
effect in apparently modernizing everything.
But everywhere we see the ponderous Tuscan
basements that never can decay, and which will
look, five hundred years hence, as they look
now ; and one often passes beneath an abbreviated remnant of what was once a lofty tower,
perhaps three hundred feet high, such as used
to be numerous in Florence when each noble
of the city had his own warfare to wage ; and
there are patches of sculpture that look old on
houses, the modern stucco of which causes them
to look almost new.   Here and there an un-
mistakable antiquity stands in its own impressive shadow ; the Church of Or San Michele,
for instance, once a market, but which grew to
be a church by some inherent fitness and inevitable consecration.   It has not the least the
aspect of a church, being high and square, like
a mediæval palace ; but deep and high niches
are let into its walls, within which stand great
statues of saints, masterpieces of Donatello, and
other sculptors of that age, before sculpture began to be congealed by the influence of Greek
art.

The Riccardi Palace is at the corner of the
Via Larga.   It was built by the first Cosmo de
Medici, the old banker, more than four cen-
turies ago, and was long the home of the ignobl

race of princes which he left behind him. It
looks fit to be still the home of a princely race,
being nowise dilapidated nor decayed externally,
nor likely to be so, its high Tuscan basement
being as solid as a ledge of rock, and its upper
portion not much less so, though smoothed
into another order of stately architecture. Entering its court from the Via Larga, we found
ourselves beneath a pillared arcade, passing
round the court like a cloister; and on the
walls of the palace, under this succession of
arches, were statues, bas-reliefs, and sarcophagi,
in which, first, dead Pagans had slept, and then
dead Christians, before the sculptured coffins
were brought hither to adorn the palace of
the Medici. In the most prominent place was a
Latin inscription of great length and breadth,
chiefly in praise of old Cosmo and his deeds
and wisdom. This mansion gives the visitor
a stately notion of the life of a commercial man
in the days when merchants were princes; not
that it seems to be so wonderfully extensive,
nor so very grand, for I suppose there are a
dozen Roman palaces that excel it in both these
particulars. Still, we cannot but be conscious
that it must have been, in some sense, a great
man who thought of founding a homestead like
this, and was capable of filling it with his per-
sonality, as the hand fills a glove. It has been
found spacious enough, since Cosmo's time,

for an emperor and a pope and a king, all of whom have been guests in this house. After being the family mansion of the Medici for nearly two centuries, it was sold to the Riccardis, but it was subsequently bought of them by the government and it is now occupied by public offices and societies.

After sufficiently examining the court and its antiquities, we ascended a noble staircase that passes, by broad flights and square turns, to the region above the basement. Here the palace is cut up and portioned off into little rooms and passages, and everywhere there were desks, inkstands, and men, with pens in their fingers or behind their ears. We were shown into a little antique chapel, quite covered with frescos in the Giotto style, but painted by a certain Gonzoli. They were in pretty good preservation, and, in fact, I am wrong in comparing them to Giotto's works, inasmuch as there must have been nearly two hundred years between the two artists. The chapel was furnished with curiously carved old chairs, and looked surprisingly venerable within its little precinct.

We were next guided into the grand gallery, a hall of respectable size, with a frescoed ceiling, on which is represented the blue sky, and various members of the Medici family ascending through it by the help of angelic personages,

who seem only to have waited for their society
to be perfectly happy. At least, this was the
meaning, so far as I could make it out. Along
one side of the gallery were oil pictures on
looking-glasses, rather good than otherwise;
but Rome, with her palaces and villas, takes
the splendor out of all this sort of thing elsewhere.

On our way home, and on our own side of
the Ponte Vecchio, we passed the Palazzo
Guicciardini, the ancient residence of the histo-
rian of Italy, who was a politic statesman of
his day, and probably as cruel and unprincipled
as any of those whose deeds he has recorded.
Opposite, across the narrow way, stands the
house of Macchiavelli, who was his friend, and,
I should judge, an honester man than he. The
house is distinguished by a marble tablet, let
into the wall, commemorative of Macchiavelli,
but has nothing antique or picturesque about
it, being in a contiguous line with other smooth-
faced and stuccoed edifices.

June 30. — Yesterday, at three o'clock P. M.,
I went to see the final horse-race of the Feast
of St. John, or rather to see the concourse of
people and grandees whom it brought together.
I took my stand in the vicinity of the spot whence
the Grand Duke and his courtiers view the race,
and from this point the scene was rather better

worth looking at than from the street corners whence I saw it before. The vista of the street, stretching far adown between two rows of lofty edifices, was really gay and gorgeous with the silks, damasks, and tapestries of all bright hues, that flaunted from windows and balconies, whence ladies looked forth and looked down, themselves making the liveliest part of the show. The whole capacity of the street swarmed with moving heads, leaving scarce room enough for the carriages, which, as on Sunday, passed up and down, until the signal for the race was given. Equipages, too, were constantly arriving at the door of the building which communicates with the open loggia, where the Grand Ducal party sit to see and to be seen. Two sentinels were standing at the door, and presented arms as each courtier or ambassador, or whatever dignity it might be, alighted. Most of them had on gold-embroidered court dresses ; some of them had military uniforms, and medals in abundance at the breast; and ladies also came, looking like heaps of lace and gauze in the carriages, but lightly shaking themselves into shape as they went up the steps. By and by a trumpet sounded, a drum beat, and again appeared a succession of half a dozen royal equipages, each with its six horses, its postilion, coachman, and three footmen, grand with cocked hats and embroidery ; and the gray-headed, bowing Grand

138

Duke and his nodding Grand Duchess as before.
The Noble Guard ranged themselves on horseback opposite the loggia; but there was no irksome and impertinent show of ceremony and
restraint upon the people.   The play-guard of
volunteer soldiers, who escort the President of
the United States in his Northern progresses,
keep back their fellow-citizens much more
sternly and immitigably than the Florentine
guard kept back the populace from its despotic
sovereign.

This morning Julian and I have been to the
Uffizi gallery.   It was his first visit there, and
he passed a sweeping condemnation upon everything he saw, except a fly, a snail-shell, a cater-
pillar, a lemon, a piece of bread, and a wineglass,
in some of the Dutch pictures.   The Venus di
Medici met with no sort of favor.   His feeling
of utter distaste reacted upon me, and I was
sensible of the same weary lack of appreciation
that used to chill me through, in my earlier
visits to picture galleries; the same doubt,
moreover, whether we do not bamboozle ourselves in the greater part of the admiration which
we learn to bestow.   I looked with some pleasure at one of Correggio's Madonnas in the
Tribune, — no divine and deep-thoughted mother of the Saviour, but a young woman playing
with her first child, as gay and thoughtless as
itself.   I looked at Michel Angelo's Madonna,

in which William Ware saw such prophetic depth of feeling; but I suspect it was one of the many instances in which the spectator sees more than the painter ever dreamed of.

Straying through the city, after leaving the gallery, we went into the Church of Or San Michele, and saw in its architecture the traces of its transformation from a market into a church. In its pristine state it consisted of a double row of three great open arches, with the wind blowing through them, and the sunshine falling aslantwise into them, while the bustle of the market, the sale of fish, flesh, or fruit went on within, or brimmed over into the streets that enclosed them on every side. But, four or five hundred years ago, the broad arches were built up with stone-work; windows were pierced through and filled with painted glass; a high altar, in a rich style of pointed Gothic, was raised; shrines and confessionals were set up; and here it is, a solemn and antique church, where a man may buy his salvation instead of his dinner. At any rate, the Catholic priests will insure it to him, and take the price. The sculpture, within the beautifully decorated niches, on the outside of the church, is very curious and interesting. The statues of those old saints seem to have that charm of earnestness which so attracts the admirers of the Pre-Raphaelite painters.

It appears that a picture of the Virgin used
to hang against one of the pillars of the market-
place while it was still a market, and in the year
1291 several miracles were wrought by it, insomuch that a chapel was consecrated for it.
So many worshippers came to the shrine that
the business of the market was impeded, and
ultimately the Virgin and St. Michael won the
whole space for themselves. The upper part
of the edifice was at that time a granary, and is
still used for other than religious purposes. This
church was one spot to which the inhabitants
betook themselves much for refuge and divine
assistance during the great plague described by
Boccaccio.

July 2. — We set out yesterday morning to
visit the Palazzo Buonarotti, Michel Angelo's
ancestral home. . . . It is in the Via Ghibel-
lina, an ordinary-looking, three-story house, with
broad-brimmed eaves, a stuccoed front, and two
or three windows painted in fresco, besides the
real ones.   Adown the street, there is a glimpse
of the hills outside of Florence. The sun shining heavily directly upon the front, we rang the
door-bell, and then drew back into the shadow
that fell from the opposite side of the street.
After we had waited some time a man looked
out from an upper window, and a woman from
a lower one, and informed us that we could not

be admitted now, nor for two or three months
to come, the house being under repairs.   It is a
pity, for I wished to see Michel Angelo's sword
and walking-stick and old slippers, and whatever other of his closest personalities are to be
shown. . . .

We passed into the Piazza of the Grand
Duke, and looked into the court of the Palazzo
Vecchio, with its beautifully embossed pillars ;
and, seeing just beyond the court a staircase of
broad and easy steps, we ascended it at a venture.   Upward and upward we went, flight after
flight of stairs, and through passages, till at last
we found an official who ushered us into a large
saloon.   It was the Hall of Audience.   Its
heavily embossed ceiling, rich with tarnished
gold, was a feature of antique magnificence, and
the only one that it retained, the floor being
paved with tiles and the furniture scanty or
none.   There were, however, three cabinets
standing against the walls, two of which contained very curious and exquisite carvings and
cuttings in ivory ; some of them in the Chinese
style of hollow, concentric balls; others, really
beautiful works of art : little crucifixes, statues,
saintly and knightly, and cups enriched with
delicate bas-reliefs.   The custode pointed to a
small figure of St. Sebastian, and also to a vase
around which the reliefs seemed to assume life.
Both these specimens, he said, were by Ben-

venuto Cellini, and there were many others that might well have been wrought by his famous hand.   The third cabinet contained a great number and variety of crucifixes, chalices, and whatever other vessels are needed in altar service, exquisitely carved out of amber.   They belong to the chapel of the palace, and into this holy closet we were now conducted.   It is large enough to accommodate comfortably perhaps thirty worshippers, and is quite covered with frescos by Ghirlandaio in good preservation, and with remnants enough of gilding and bright color to show how splendid the chapel must have been when the Medicean Grand Dukes used to pray here.   The altar is still ready for service, and I am not sure that some of the wax tapers were not burning; but Lorenzo the Magnificent was nowhere to be seen.

The custode now led us back through the Hall of Audience into a smaller room, hung with pictures, chiefly of the Medici and their connections, among whom was one Carolina, an intelligent and pretty child, and Bianca Capella.

There was nothing else to show us except a very noble and most spacious saloon, lighted by two large windows at each end, coming down level with the floor, and by a row of windows on one side just beneath the cornice.   A gilded framework divides the ceiling into squares, cir-

cles, and octagons, the compartments of which
are filled with pictures in oil; and the walls are
covered with immense frescos, representing various battles and triumphs of the Florentines.
Statues by Michel Angelo, John of Bologna,
and Bandinelli, as well historic as ideal, stand
round the hall, and it is really a fit theatre for
the historic scenes of a country to be acted in.
It was built, moreover, with the idea of its being the council hall of a free people; but our
own little Faneuil, which was meant, in all simplicity, to be merely a spot where the townspeople should meet to choose their selectmen,
has served the world better in that respect.   I
wish I had more room to speak of this vast,
dusky, historic hall.   [This volume of journal
closes here.]

July 4, 1858. — Yesterday forenoon we went
to see the Church of Santa Maria Novella.
We found the piazza, on one side of which the
church stands, encumbered with the amphithe-
atrical ranges of wooden seats that had been
erected to accommodate the spectators of the
chariot races at the recent Feast of St. John.
The front of the church is composed of black
and white marble, which, in the course of the
five centuries that it has been built, has turned
brown and yellow.   On the right hand, as you
approach, is a long colonnade of arches, extend-

ing on a line with the façade, and having a tomb
beneath every arch.   This colonnade forms one
of the enclosing walls of a cloister.   We found
none of the front entrances open, but on our
left, in a wall at right angles with the church,
there was an open gateway, approaching which,
we saw, within the four-sided colonnade, an enclosed green space of a cloister.   This is what
is called the Chiostro Verde, so named from the
prevailing color of the frescos with which the
walls beneath the arches are adorned.

This cloister is the reality of what I used to
imagine when I saw the half-ruinous colonnades
connected with English cathedrals, or endeav-
ored to trace out the lines along the broken
wall of some old abbey.   Not that this extant
cloister, still perfect and in daily use for its
original purposes, is nearly so beautiful as the
crumbling ruin which has ceased to be trodden
by monkish feet for more than three centuries.
The cloister of Santa Maria has not the seclusion that is desirable, being open, by its gateway, to the public square; and several of the
neighbors, women as well as men, were loitering within its precincts.   The convent, however, has another and larger cloister, which I
suppose is kept free from interlopers.   The
Chiostro Verde is a walk round the four sides
of a square, beneath an arched and groined roof.
One side of the walk looks upon an enclosed

green space with a fountain or a tomb (I forget which) in the centre ; the other side is ornamented all along with a succession of ancient frescos, representing subjects of Scripture history.   In the days when the designs were more distinct than now, it must have been a very effective way for a monk to read Bible history, to see its personages and events thus passing visibly beside him in his morning and evening walks.   Beneath the frescos on one side of the cloistered walk, and along the low stone parapet that separates it from the grass-plat on the other, are inscriptions to the memory of the dead who are buried underneath the pavement. The most of these were modern, and recorded the names of persons of no particular note. Other monumental slabs were inlaid with the pavement itself.   Two or three Dominican monks, belonging to the convent, passed in and out while we were there, in their white habits.

After going round three sides, we came to the fourth, formed by the wall of the church, and heard the voice of a priest behind a curtain that fell down before a door.   Lifting it aside, we went in, and found ourselves in the ancient chapter house, a large interior formed by two great pointed arches crossing one another in a groined roof.   The broad spaces of the walls were entirely covered with frescos that are rich

even now, and must have glowed with an inexpressible splendor when fresh from the artists' hands, five hundred years ago. There is
a long period, during which frescos illuminate
a church or a hall in a way that no other adornment can; when this epoch of brightness is
past, they become the dreariest ghosts of per-
ished magnificence. . . . This chapter house is
the only part of the church that is now used for
the purposes of public worship. There are
several confessionals, and two chapels or shrines,
each with its lighted tapers. A priest performed mass while we were there, and several
persons, as usual, stepped in to do a little devotion, either praying on their own account, or
uniting with the ceremony that was going forward. One man was followed by two little
dogs, and in the midst of his prayers, as one of
the dogs was inclined to stray about the church,
he kept snapping his fingers to call him back.
The cool, dusky refreshment of these holy
places, affording such a refuge from the hot
noon of the streets and piazzas, probably suggests devotional ideas to the people, and it may
be, when they are praying, they feel a breath
of Paradise fanning them. If we could only
see any good effects in their daily life, we might
deem it an excellent thing to be able to find incense and a prayer always ascending, to which
every individual may join his own. I really

wonder that the Catholics are not better men
and women.

When we had looked at the old frescos, . . .
we emerged into the cloister again, and thence
ventured into a passage which would have led
us to the Chiostro Grande, where strangers, and
especially ladies, have no right to go.   It was a
secluded corridor, very neatly kept, bordered
with sepulchral monuments, and at the end appeared a vista of cypress-trees, which, indeed,
were but an illusory perspective, being painted
in fresco.   While we loitered along . . . the
sacristan appeared and offered to show us the
church, and led us into the transept on the right
of the high altar, and ushered us into the sacristy, where we found two artists copying some
of Fra Angelico's pictures.   These were painted
on the three wooden leaves of a triptych, and,
as usual, were glorified with a great deal of
gilding, so that they seemed to float in the
brightness of a heavenly element.   Solomon
speaks of " apples of gold in pictures of silver."
The pictures of Fra Angelico, and other artists
of that age, are really pictures of gold ; and it
is wonderful to see how rich the effect, and how
much delicate beauty is attained (by Fra Angelico at least) along with it.   His miniature
heads appear to me much more successful than
his larger ones.   In a monkish point of view,
however, the chief value of the triptych of which

I am speaking does not lie in the pictures, for
they merely serve as the framework of some
relics, which are set all round the edges of the
three leaves. They consist of little bits and
fragments of bones, and of packages carefully
tied up in silk, the contents of which are signi-
fied in Gothic letters appended to each parcel.
The sacred vessels of the church are likewise
kept in the sacristy. . . .

Reëntering the transept, our guide showed us
the chapel of the Strozzi family, which is accessible by a flight of steps from the floor of the
church. The walls of this chapel are covered
with frescos by Orcagna, representing around
the altar The Last Judgment, and on one of
the walls heaven and the assembly of the blessed,
and on the other, of course, hell. I cannot
speak as to the truth of the representation; but,
at all events, it was purgatory to look at it. . . .

We next passed into the choir, which occupies the extreme end of the church behind
the great square mass of the high altar, and is
surrounded with a double row of ancient oaken
seats of venerable shape and carving. The
choir is illuminated by a threefold Gothic window, full of richly painted glass, worth all the
frescos that ever stained a wall or ceiling; but
these walls, nevertheless, are adorned with frescos by Ghirlandaio, and it is easy to see must
once have made a magnificent appearance. I

really was sensible of a sad and ghostly beauty
in many of the figures; but all the bloom, the
magic of the painter's touch, his topmost art,
have long ago been rubbed off, the white plaster
showing through the colors in spots, and even
in large spaces.   Any other sort of ruin acquires
a beauty proper to its decay, and often superior
to that of its pristine state; but the ruin of a
picture, especially of a fresco, is wholly unre-
deemed; and, moreover, it dies so slowly that
many generations are likely to be saddened by
it.

   We next saw the famous picture of the Virgin
by Cimabue, which was deemed a miracle in its
day, . . . and still brightens the sombre walls
with the lustre of its gold ground.   As to its
artistic merits, it seems to me that the babe
Jesus has a certain air of state and dignity; but
I could see no charm whatever in the broad-
faced Virgin, and it would relieve my mind and
rejoice my spirit if the picture were borne out
of the church in another triumphal procession
(like the one which brought it there), and reverently burnt.   This should be the final honor
paid to all human works that have served a good
office in their day, for when their day is over,
if still galvanized into false life, they do harm
instead of good. . . . The interior of Santa
Maria Novella is spacious and in the Gothic
style, though differing from English churches

of that order of architecture.   It is not now
kept open to the public, nor were any of the
shrines and chapels, nor even the high altar itself, adorned and lighted for worship.   The
pictures that decorated the shrines along the
side-aisles have been removed, leaving bare,
blank spaces of brickwork, very dreary and desolate to behold.   This is almost worse than a
black oil-painting or a faded fresco.   The church
was much injured by the French, and afterwards
by the Austrians, both powers having quartered
their troops within the holy precincts.   Its old
walls, however, are yet stalwart enough to out-
last another set of frescos, and to see the beginning and the end of a new school of painting
as long-lived as Cimabue's.   I should be sorry
to have the church go to decay, because it was
here that Boccaccio's dames and cavaliers encountered one another, and formed their plan
of retreating into the country during the
plague. . . .

At the door we bought a string of beads, with
a small crucifix appended, in memory of the
place.   The beads seem to be of a grayish, pear-
shaped seed, and the seller assured us that they
were the tears of St. Job.   They were cheap,
probably because Job shed so many tears in his
lifetime.

It being still early in the day, we went to the
Uffizi gallery, and after loitering a good while

among the pictures, were so fortunate as to find
the room of the bronzes open. The first object that attracted us was John of Bologna's
Mercury, poising himself on tiptoe, and looking not merely buoyant enough to float, but as
if he possessed more than the eagle's power of
lofty flight. It seems a wonder that he did not
absolutely fling himself into the air when the
artist gave him the last touch. No bolder work
was ever achieved; nothing so full of life has
been done since. I was much interested, too,
in the original little wax model, two feet high,
of Benvenuto Cellini's Perseus. The wax seems
to be laid over a wooden framework, and is but
roughly finished off. . . .

In an adjoining room are innumerable specimens of Roman and Etruscan bronzes, great
and small. A bronze Chimera did not strike
me as very ingeniously conceived, the goat's
head being merely an adjunct, growing out of
the back of the monster, without possessing
any original and substantive share in its nature.
The snake's head is at the end of the tail. The
object most really interesting was a Roman
eagle, the standard of the Twenty-fourth Legion,
about the size of a blackbird.

July 8. — On the 6th we went to the Church
of the Annunziata, which stands in the piazza of
the same name. On the corner of the Via dei

Servi is the palace which I suppose to be the one that Browning makes the scene of his poem, "The Statue and the Bust," and the statue of Duke Ferdinand sits stately on horseback, with his face turned towards the window, where the lady ought to appear. Neither she nor the bust, however, was visible, at least not to my eyes. The church occupies one side of the piazza, and in front of it, as likewise on the two adjoining sides of the square, there are pillared arcades, constructed by Brunelleschi or his scholars. After passing through these arches, and still before entering the church itself, you come to an ancient cloister, which is now quite enclosed in glass as a means of preserving some frescos of Andrea del Sarto and others, which are considered valuable.

Passing the threshold of the church, we were quite dazzled by the splendor that shone upon us from the ceiling of the nave, the great parallelograms of which, viewed from one end, look as if richly embossed all over with gold. The whole interior, indeed, has an effect of brightness and magnificence, the walls being covered mostly with light-colored marble, into which are inlaid compartments of rarer and richer marbles. The pillars and pilasters, too, are of variegated marbles, with Corinthian capitals, that shine just as brightly as if they were of solid gold, so faithfully have they been gilded and

burnished. The pavement is formed of squares
of black and white marble. There are no side-
aisles, but ranges of chapels, with communication
from one to another, stand round the whole
extent of the nave and choir; all of marble, all
decorated with pictures, statues, busts, and mural monuments; all worth, separately, a day's
inspection. The high altar is of great beauty
and richness, . . . and also the tomb of John
of Bologna in a chapel at the remotest extremity of the church. In this chapel there are some
bas-reliefs by him, and also a large crucifix with
a marble Christ upon it. I think there has been
no better sculptor since the days of Phidias. . . .

The church was founded by seven gentlemen
of Florence, who formed themselves into a religious order called " Servants of Mary." Many
miraculous cures were wrought here; and the
church, in consequence, was so thickly hung
with votive offerings of legs, arms, and other
things in wax, that they used to tumble upon
people's heads, so that finally they were all
cleared out as rubbish. The church is still, I
should imagine, looked upon as a place of peculiar sanctity; for while we were there it had an
unusual number of kneeling worshippers, and
persons were passing from shrine to shrine all
round the nave and choir, praying awhile at
each, and thus performing a pilgrimage at little
cost of time and labor. One old gentleman, I

observed, carried a cushion or pad, just big enough for one knee, on which he carefully adjusted his genuflections before each altar. An old woman in the choir prayed alternately to us and to the saints, with most success, I hope, in her petitions to the latter, though certainly her prayers to ourselves seemed the more fervent of the two.

When we had gone entirely round the church, we came at last to the chapel of the Annunziata, which stands on the floor of the nave, on the left hand as we enter. It is a very beautiful piece of architecture, — a sort of canopy of marble, supported upon pillars ; and its magnificence within, in marble and silver, and all manner of holy decoration, is quite indescribable. It was built four hundred years ago, by Pietro de' Medici, and has probably been growing richer ever since. The altar is entirely of silver, richly embossed. As many people were kneeling on the steps before it as could find room, and most of them when they finished their prayers, ascended the steps, kissed over and over again the margin of the silver altar, laid their foreheads upon it, and then deposited an offering in a box placed upon the altar's top. From the dulness of the chink in the only case when I heard it, I judged it to be a small copper coin.

In the inner part of this chapel is preserved a miraculous picture of the Santissima Annunzi-

ata, painted by angels, and held in such holy
repute that forty thousand dollars have lately
been expended in providing a new crown for
the sacred personage represented.   The picture
is now veiled behind a curtain ; and as it is a
fresco, and is not considered to do much credit
to the angelic artists, I was well contented not
to see it.

We found a side door of the church admitting us into the great cloister, which has a walk
of intersecting arches round its four sides, paved
with flat tombstones, and broad enough for six
people to walk abreast.   On the walls, in the
semicircles of each successive arch, are frescos
representing incidents in the lives of the seven
founders of the church, and all the lower part of
the wall is incrusted with marble inscriptions to
the memory of the dead, and mostly of persons
who have died not very long ago.   The space
enclosed by the cloistered walk, usually made
cheerful by green grass, has a pavement of tombstones laid in regular ranges.   In the centre
is a stone octagonal structure, which at first I
supposed to be the tomb of some deceased
mediæval personage ; but, on approaching, I
found it a well, with its bucket hanging within
the curb, and looking as if it were in constant
use.   The surface of the water lay deep beneath
the deepest dust of the dead people, and thence
threw up its picture of the sky ; but I think it

would not be a moderate thirst that would induce me to drink of that well.

On leaving the church we bought a little gilt crucifix. . . .

On Sunday evening I paid a short visit to Mr. Powers, and, as usual, was entertained and instructed with his conversation. It did not, indeed, turn upon artistical subjects; but the artistic is only one side of his character, and, I think, not the principal side. He might have achieved valuable success as an engineer and mechanician. He gave a dissertation on flying machines, evidently from his own experience, and came to the conclusion that it is impossible to fly by means of steam or any other motive power now known to man. No force hitherto attained would suffice to lift the engine which generated it. He appeared to anticipate that flying will be a future mode of locomotion, but not till the moral condition of mankind is so improved as to obviate the bad uses to which the power might be applied. Another topic discussed was a cure for complaints of the chest by the inhalation of nitric acid; and he produced his own apparatus for that purpose, being merely a tube inserted into a bottle containing a small quantity of the acid, just enough to produce the gas for inhalation. He told me, too, a remedy for burns accidentally discovered by himself; viz., to wear wash-leather, or something equivalent, over the burn, and keep it constantly wet. It prevents all pain, and cures by the exclusion of the air. He evidently has a great tendency to empirical remedies, and would have made a natural doctor of mighty potency, possessing the shrewd sense, inventive faculty, and self-reliance that such persons require. It is very singular that there should be an ideal vein in a man of this character.

This morning he called to see me, with intelligence of the failure of the new attempt to lay the electric cable between England and America ; and here, too, it appears the misfortune might have been avoided if a plan of his own for laying the cable had been adopted. He explained his process, and made it seem as practicable as to put up a bell-wire. I do not remember how or why (but appositely) he repeated some verses, from a pretty little ballad about fairies, that had struck his fancy, and he wound up his talk with some acute observations on the characters of General Jackson and other public men. He told an anecdote, illustrating the old general's small acquaintance with astronomical science, and his force of will in compelling a whole dinner party of better instructed people than himself to succumb to him in an argument about eclipses and the planetary system generally. Powers witnessed the scene himself. He thinks that General Jackson was

a man of the keenest and surest intuitions, in
respect to men and measures, but with no power
of reasoning out his own conclusions, or of
imparting them intellectually to other persons.
Men who have known Jackson intimately, and
in great affairs, would not agree as to this intellectual and argumentative deficiency, though
they would fully allow the intuitive faculty.   I
have heard General Pierce tell a striking instance of Jackson's power of presenting his own
view of a subject with irresistible force to the
mind of the auditor.   President Buchanan has
likewise expressed to me as high admiration of
Jackson as I ever heard one man award to another.   Surely he was a great man, and his
native strength, as well of intellect as character,
compelled every man to be his tool that came
within his reach ; and the more cunning the individual might be, it served only to make him
the sharper tool.

Speaking of Jackson, and remembering Raphael's picture of Pope Julius II., the best portrait in the whole world, and excellent in all its
repetitions, I wish it had been possible for Raphael to paint General Jackson !

Referring again to General Jackson's intuitions, and to Powers's idea that he was unable
to render a reason to himself or others for what
he chose to do, I should have thought that this
very probably might have been the case, were

there not such strong evidence to the contrary. The highest, or perhaps any high administrative ability, is intuitive, and precedes argument, and rises above it. It is a revelation of the very thing to be done, and its propriety and necessity are felt so strongly that very likely it cannot be talked about; if the doer can likewise talk, it is an additional and gratuitous faculty, as little to be expected as that a poet should be able to write an explanatory criticism on his own poem. The English overlook this in their scheme of government, which requires that the members of the national executive should be orators, and the readiest and most fluent orators that can be found. The very fact (on which they are selected) that they are men of words makes it improbable that they are likewise men of deeds. And it is only tradition and old custom, founded on an obsolete state of things, that assigns any value to parliamentary oratory. The world has done with it, except as an intellectual pastime. The speeches have no effect till they are converted into newspaper paragraphs ; and they had better be composed as such, in the first place, and oratory reserved for churches, courts of law, and public dinner tables.

July 10. — My wife and I went yesterday forenoon to see the Church of San Marco, with

which is connected a convent of Dominicans.
. . . The interior is not less than three or four
hundred years old, and is in the classic style,
with a flat ceiling, gilded, and a lofty arch, supported by pillars, between the nave and choir.
There are no side-aisles, but ranges of shrines
on both sides of the nave, each beneath its own
pair of pillars and pediments. The pavement
is of brick, with here and there a marble tomb-
stone inlaid. It is not a magnificent church;
but looks dingy with time and apparent neglect,
though rendered sufficiently interesting by statues of mediæval date by John of Bologna and
other old sculptors, and by monumental busts
and bas-reliefs : also, there is a wooden crucifix
by Giotto, with ancient gilding on it ; and a
painting of Christ, which was considered a wonderful work in its day. Each shrine, or most
of them, at any rate, had its dark old picture,
and there is a very old and hideous mosaic of
the Virgin and two saints, which I looked at
very slightly, with the purpose of immediately
forgetting it. Savonarola, the reforming monk,
was a brother of this convent, and was torn
from its shelter, to be subsequently hanged and
burnt in the Grand Ducal Piazza. A large
chapel in the left transept is of the Salviati family, dedicated to St. Anthony, and decorated
with several statues of saints, and with some old
frescos. When we had more than sufficiently

examined these, the custode proposed to show us some frescos of Fra Angelico, and conducted us into a large cloister, under the arches of which, and beneath a covering of glass, he pointed to a picture of St. Dominic kneeling at the Cross. There are two or three others by the angelic friar in different parts of the cloister, and a regular series, filling up all the arches, by various artists. Its four-sided, cloistered walk surrounds a square, open to the sky as usual, and paved with gray stones that have no inscriptions, but probably are laid over graves. Its walls, however, are incrusted, and the walk itself is paved with monumental inscriptions on marble, none of which, so far as I observed, were of ancient date. Either the fashion of thus commemorating the dead is not ancient in Florence, or the old tombstones have been removed to make room for new ones. I do not know where the monks themselves have their burial-place ; perhaps in an inner cloister which we did not see. All the inscriptions here, I believe, were in memory of persons not connected with the convent.

A door in the wall of the cloister admitted us into the chapter-house, its interior moderately spacious, with a roof formed by intersecting arches. Three sides of the walls were covered with blessed whitewash ; but on the fourth side, opposite to the entrance, was a great fresco

of the Crucifixion, by Fra Angelico, surrounded
with a border or pictured framework, in which
are represented the heads of saints, prophets,
and sibyls, as large as life. The cross of the
Saviour and those of the thieves were painted
against a dark red sky ; the figures upon them
were lean and attenuated, evidently the vague
conceptions of a man who had never seen a
naked figure. Beneath was a multitude of people, most of whom were saints who had lived
and been martyred long after the Crucifixion ;
and some of these had wounds from which gilded
rays shone forth, as if the inner glory and bless-
edness of the holy men blazed through them.
It is a very ugly picture, and its ugliness is not
that of strength and vigor, but of weakness and
incompetency. Fra Angelico should have confined himself to miniature heads, in which his
delicacy of touch and minute labor often produce an excellent effect. The custode informed
us that there were more frescos of this pious
artist in the interior of the convent, into which
I might be allowed admittance, but not my wife.
I declined seeing them, and heartily thanked
Heaven for my escape.

Returning through the church, we stopped to
look at a shrine on the right of the entrance,
where several wax candles were lighted, and the
steps of which were crowded with worshippers.
It was evidently a spot of special sanctity, and,

approaching the steps, we saw, behind a gilded framework of stars and protected by glass, a wooden image of the Saviour, naked, covered with spots of blood, crowned with thorns, and expressing all the human wretchedness that the carver's skill could represent. The whole shrine, within the glass, was hung with offerings, as well of silver and gold as of tinsel and trumpery, and the body of Christ glistened with gold chains and ornaments, and with watches of silver and gold, some of which appeared to be of very old manufacture, and others might be new. Amid all this glitter the face of pain and grief looked forth, not a whit comforted. While we stood there, a woman, who had been praying, arose from her knees and laid an offering of a single flower upon the shrine.

The corresponding arch, on the opposite side of the entrance, contained a wax-work within a large glass case, representing the Nativity. I do not remember how the Blessed Infant looked, but the Virgin was gorgeously dressed in silks, satins, and gauzes, with spangles and ornaments of all kinds, and I believe brooches of real diamonds on her bosom. Her attire, judging from its freshness and newness of glitter, might have been put on that very morning.

July 13. — We went for the second time, this morning, to the Academy of Fine Arts, and I

looked pretty thoroughly at the Pre-Raphaelite
pictures, few of which are really worth looking
at nowadays. Cimabue and Giotto might certainly be dismissed, henceforth and forever,
without any detriment to the cause of good art.
There is what seems to me a better picture than
either of these has produced, by Bonamico Buf-
falmacco, an artist of about their date or not
long after. The first real picture in the series
is The Adoration of the Magi, by Gentile da
Fabriano, a really splendid work in all senses,
with noble and beautiful figures in it, and a
crowd of personages, managed with great skill.
Three pictures by Perugino are the only other
ones I cared to look at. In one of these, the
face of the Virgin, who holds the dead Christ
on her knees, has a deeper expression of woe
than can ever have been painted since. After
Perugino the pictures cease to be interesting;
the art came forward with rapid strides, but the
painters and their productions do not take nearly
so much hold of the spectator as before. They
all paint better than Giotto and Cimabue, — in
some respects better than Perugino; but they
paint in vain, probably because they were not
nearly so much in earnest, and meant far less,
though possessing the dexterity to express far
more. Andrea del Sarto appears to have been
a good painter, yet I always turn away readily
from his pictures. I looked again, and for a

good while, at Carlo Dolce's portrait of the Eternal Father, for it is a miracle and masterpiece of absurdity, and almost equally a miracle of pictorial art. It is the All-powerless, a fairhaired, soft, consumptive deity, with a mouth that has fallen open through very weakness. He holds one hand on his stomach, as if the wickedness and wretchedness of mankind made him qualmish; and he is looking down out of heaven with an expression of pitiable appeal, or as if seeking somewhere for assistance in his heavy task of ruling the universe. You might fancy such a being falling on his knees before a strong-willed man, and beseeching him to take the reins of omnipotence out of his hands. No wonder that wrong gets the better of right, and that good and ill are confounded, if the Supreme Head were as here depicted; for I never saw, and nobody else ever saw, so perfect a representation of a person burdened with a task infinitely above his strength. If Carlo Dolce had been wicked enough to know what he was doing, the picture would have been most blasphemous, — a satire, in the very person of the Almighty, against all incompetent rulers, and against the rickety machine and crazy action of the universe. Heaven forgive me for such thoughts as this picture has suggested! It must be added that the great original defect in the character as here represented is an easy good-nature. I wonder what Michel Angelo would have said to this painting.

In the large, enclosed court connected with the Academy there are a number of statues, bas-reliefs, and casts, and, what was especially interesting, the vague and rude commencement of a statue of St. Matthew by Michel Angelo. The conceptions of this great sculptor were so godlike that he seems to have been discontented at not likewise possessing the godlike attribute of creating and embodying them with an instantaneous thought, and therefore we often find sculptures from his hand left at the critical point of their struggle to get out of the marble. The statue of St. Matthew looks like the antediluvian fossil of a human being of an epoch when humanity was mightier and more majestic than now, long ago imprisoned in stone, and half uncovered again.

July 16. — We went yesterday forenoon to see the Bargello. I do not know anything more picturesque in Florence than the great interior court of this ancient Palace of the Podestà, with the lofty height of the edifice looking down into the enclosed space, dark and stern, and the armorial bearings of a long succession of magistrates carved in stone upon the walls, a garland, as it were, of these Gothic devices extending quite round the court. The best feature of the whole is the broad stone staircase, with its heavy balustrade, ascending externally from the court to the iron-grated door in the second story. We passed the sentinels under the lofty archway that communicates with the street, and went up the stairs without being questioned or impeded. At the iron-grated door, however, we were met by two officials in uniform, who courteously informed us that there was nothing to be exhibited in the Bargello except an old chapel containing some frescos by Giotto, and that these could only be seen by making a previous appointment with the custode, he not being constantly on hand. I was not sorry to escape the frescos, though one of them is a portrait of Dante.

We next went to the Church of the Badia, which is built in the form of a Greek cross, with a flat roof embossed and once splendid with now tarnished gold. The pavement is of brick, and the walls of dark stone, similar to that of the interior of the Cathedral (*pietra serena*), and there being, according to Florentine custom, but little light, the effect was sombre, though the cool gloomy dusk was refreshing after the hot turmoil and dazzle of the adjacent street. Here we found three or four Gothic tombs, with figures of the deceased persons stretched in marble slumber upon them. There were likewise a picture or two, which it was impos-

Michel Angelo

sible to see; indeed, I have hardly ever met
with a picture in a church that was not utterly
wasted and thrown away in the deep shadows
of the chapel it was meant to adorn. If there
is the remotest chance of its being seen, the
sacristan hangs a curtain before it for the sake
of his fee for withdrawing it. In the chapel of
the Bianco family we saw (if it could be called
seeing) what is considered the finest oil-painting of Fra Filippo Lippi. It was evidently
hung with reference to a lofty window on the
other side of the church, whence sufficient light
might fall upon it to show a picture so vividly
painted as this is, and as most of Fra Filippo
Lippi's are. The window was curtained, however, and the chapel so dusky that I could make
out nothing.

Several persons came in to say their prayers
during the little time that we remained in the
church, and as we came out we passed a good
woman who sat knitting in the coolness of the
vestibule, which was lined with mural tombstones. Probably she spends the day thus,
keeping up the little industry of her fingers,
slipping into the church to pray whenever a
devotional impulse swells into her heart, and
asking an alms as often as she sees a person of
charitable aspect.

From the church we went to the Uffizi
gallery, and reinspected the greater part of it

pretty faithfully. We had the good fortune, too, again to get admittance into the cabinet of bronzes, where we admired anew the wonderful airiness of John of Bologna's Mercury, which, as I now observed, rests on nothing substantial, but on the breath of a zephyr beneath him. We also saw a bronze bust of one of the Medici by Benvenuto Cellini, and a thousand other things the curiosity of which is overlaid by their multitude. The Roman eagle, which I have recorded to be about the size of a blackbird, I now saw to be as large as a pigeon.

On our way towards the door of the gallery, at our departure, we saw the cabinet of gems open, and again feasted our eyes with its concentrated brilliances and magnificences. Among them were two crystal cups, with engraved devices, and covers of enamelled gold, wrought by Benvenuto Cellini, and wonderfully beautiful. But it is idle to mention one or two things, when all are so beautiful and curious; idle, too, because language is not burnished gold, with here and there a brighter word flashing like a diamond; and therefore no amount of talk will give the slightest idea of one of these elaborate handiworks.

July 27. — I seldom go out nowadays, having already seen Florence tolerably well, and the streets being very hot, and myself having been engaged in sketching out a romance,[1] which, whether it will ever come to anything, is a point yet to be decided. At any rate, it leaves me little heart for journalizing and describing new things; and six months of uninterrupted monotony would be more valuable to me just now, than the most brilliant succession of novelties.

Yesterday I spent a good deal of time in watching the setting out of a wedding party from our door; the bride being the daughter of an English lady, the Countess of ——. After all, there was nothing very characteristic. The bridegroom is a young man of English birth, son of the Countess of St. G——, who inhabits the third piano of this Casa del Bello. The very curious part of the spectacle was the swarm of beggars who haunted the street all day; the most wretched mob conceivable, chiefly women, with a few blind people, and some old men and boys. Among these the bridal party distributed their beneficence in the shape of some handfuls of copper, with here and there a half-paul intermixed; whereupon the whole wretched mob flung themselves in a heap upon the pavement, struggling, fighting, tumbling one over another, and then looking up to the windows with petitionary gestures for more and more, and still for more. Doubtless they had need enough, for they looked thin,

1 *The Marble Faun.* — S. H.

sickly, ill-fed, and the women ugly to the last degree. The wedding party had a breakfast above stairs, which lasted till four o'clock, and then the bridegroom took his bride in a barouche and pair, which was already crammed with his own luggage and hers. . . . He was a well-looking young man enough, in a uniform of French gray with silver epaulets; more agreeable in aspect than his bride, who, I think, will have the upper hand in their domestic life. I observed that, on getting into the barouche, he sat down on her dress, as he could not well help doing, and received a slight reprimand in consequence. After their departure the wedding guests took their leave; the most noteworthy person being the Pope's Nuncio (the young man being son of the Pope's Chamberlain, and one of the Grand Duke's Noble Guard), an ecclesiastical personage in purple stockings, attended by two priests, all of whom got into a coach, the driver and footmen of which wore gold-laced cocked hats and other splendors.

To-day I paid a short visit to the gallery of the Pitti Palace. I looked long at a Madonna of Raphael's, the one which is usually kept in the Grand Duke's private apartments, only brought into the public gallery for the purpose of being copied. It is the holiest of all Raphael's Madonnas, with a great reserve in the expression, a sense of being apart, and yet with the utmost tenderness and sweetness ; although she drops her eyelids before her like a veil, as it were, and has a primness of eternal virginity about the mouth. It is one of Raphael's earlier works, when he mixed more religious sentiment with his paint than afterwards. Perugino's pictures give the impression of greater sincerity and earnestness than Raphael's, though the genius of Raphael often gave him miraculous vision.

July 28. — Last evening we went to the Powers's, and sat with them on the terrace, at the top of the house, till nearly ten o'clock. It was a delightful, calm, summer evening, and we were elevated far above all the adjacent roofs, and had a prospect of the greater part of Florence and its towers, and the surrounding hills, while directly beneath us rose the trees of a garden, and they hardly sent their summits higher than we sat. At a little distance, with only a house or two between, was a theatre in full action, the Teatro Goldoni, which is an open amphitheatre, in the ancient fashion, without any roof. We could see the upper part of the proscenium, and, had we been a little nearer, might have seen the whole performance, as did several boys who crept along the tops of the surrounding houses. As it was, we heard the music and the applause, and now and then an

actor's stentorian tones, when we chose to listen.
Mrs. Powers and my wife, Una and Master
Bob, sat in a group together, and chatted in
one corner of our aerial drawing-room, while
Mr. Powers and myself leaned against the parapet, and talked of innumerable things. When
the clocks struck the hour, or the bells rung
from the steeples, as they are continually doing,
I spoke of the sweetness of the Florence bells,
the tones of some of them being as if the bell
were full of liquid melody, and shed it through
the air on being upturned. I had supposed, in
my lack of musical ear, that the bells of the
Campanile were the sweetest; but Mr. Powers
says that there is a defect in their tone, and that
the bell of the Palazzo Vecchio is the most melodious he ever heard. Then he spoke of his
having been a manufacturer of organs, or, at
least, of reeds for organs, at one period of his
life. I wonder what he has not been! He
told me of an invention of his in the musical
line, a jew's-harp with two tongues; and by and
by he produced it for my inspection. It was
carefully kept in a little wooden case, and was
very neatly and elaborately constructed, with
screws to tighten it, and a silver centre-piece between the two tongues. Evidently a great deal
of thought had been bestowed on this little
harp; but Mr. Powers told me that it was an
utter failure, because the tongues were apt to

interfere and jar with one another, although the strain of music was very sweet and melodious — as he proved, by playing on it a little — when everything went right. It was a youthful production, and he said that its failure had been a great disappointment to him at the time; whereupon I congratulated him that his failures had been in small matters and his successes in great ones.

We talked, furthermore, about instinct and reason, and whether the brute creation have souls, and, if they have none, how justice is to be done them for their sufferings here; and Mr. Powers came finally to the conclusion that brutes suffer only in appearance, and that God enjoys for them all that they seem to enjoy, and that man is the only intelligent and sentient being. We reasoned high about other states of being; and I suggested the possibility that there might be beings inhabiting this earth, contemporaneously with us, and close beside us, but of whose existence and whereabout we could have no perception, nor they of ours, because we are endowed with different sets of senses; for certainly it was in God's power to create beings who should communicate with nature by innumerable other senses than those few which we possess. Mr. Powers gave hospitable reception to this idea, and said that it had occurred to himself; and he has evidently thought much and

earnestly about such matters ; but is apt to let
his idea crystallize into a theory before he can
have sufficient data for it. He is a Sweden-
borgian in faith.

The moon had risen behind the trees while
we were talking, and Powers intimated his idea
that beings analogous to men — men in everything except the modification necessary to adapt
them to their physical circumstances — inhabited
the planets, and peopled them with beautiful
shapes. Each planet, however, must have its
own standard of the beautiful, I suppose ; and
probably his sculptor's eye would not see much
to admire in the proportions of an inhabitant
of Saturn.

The atmosphere of Florence, at least when
we ascend a little way into it, suggests planetary
speculations. Galileo found it so, and Mr.
Powers and I pervaded the whole universe ;
but finally crept down his garret-stairs, and
parted, with a friendly pressure of the hand.

VILLA MONTAUTO (MONTE BENI), *August* 2.
— We had grown weary of the heat of Florence
within the walls, . . . there being little opportunity for air and exercise except within the precincts of our little garden, which, also, we feared
might breed malaria, or something akin to it.
We have therefore taken this suburban villa for
the two next months, and, yesterday morning,

we all came out hither. Julian had preceded
us with B. P——.   The villa is on a hill called
Bellosguardo, about a mile beyond the Porta
Romana.   Less than half an hour's walk brought
us, who were on foot, to the iron gate of our
villa, which we found shut and locked. We
shouted to be let in, and, while waiting for
somebody to appear, there was a good opportunity to contemplate the external aspect of the
villa.   After we had waited a few minutes, Julian came racing down to the gate, laughing
heartily, and said that Bob and he had been in
the house, but had come out, shutting the door
behind them ; and as the door closed with a
spring-lock, they could not get in again.   Now
as the key of the outer gate as well as that of
the house itself was in the pocket of Julian's
coat, left inside, we were shut out of our own
castle, and compelled to carry on a siege against
it, without much likelihood of taking it, although
the garrison was willing to surrender.   But B.
P—— called in the assistance of the contadini
who cultivate the ground, and live in the farmhouse close by ; and one of them got into a
window by means of a ladder, so that the keys
were got, the gates opened, and we finally admitted.   Before examining any other part of
the house, we climbed to the top of the tower,
which, indeed, is not very high, in proportion
to its massive square. Very probably, its origi-

nal height was abbreviated, in compliance with
the law that lowered so many of the fortified
towers of noblemen within the walls of Florence. . . . The stairs were not of stone, built
in with the original mass of the tower, as in English castles, but of now decayed wood, which
shook beneath us, and grew more and more
crazy as we ascended. It will not be many
years before the height of the tower becomes
unattainable. . . . Near at hand, in the vicinity
of the city, we saw the convent of Monte Olivetto, and other structures that looked like convents, being built round an enclosed square ;
also numerous white villas, many of which had
towers, like that we were standing upon, square
and massive, some of them battlemented on the
summit, and others apparently modernized for
domestic purposes. Among them Una pointed
out Galileo's tower, whither she made an excursion the other day. It looked lower than our
own, but seemed to stand on a higher elevation.
We also saw the duke's villa, the Poggio, with a
long avenue of cypresses leading from it, as if a
funeral were going forth. And having wasted
thus much of description on the landscape, I will
finish with saying that it lacked only water to
be a very fine one. It is strange what a differ-
ence the gleam of water makes, and how a scene
awakens and comes to life wherever it is visible.
The landscape, moreover, gives the beholder

(at least, this beholder) a sense of oppressive sunshine and scanty shade, and does not incite a longing to wander through it on foot, as a really delightful landscape should. The vine, too, being cultivated in so trim a manner, does not suggest that idea of luxuriant fertility, which is the poetical notion of a vineyard. The olive orchards have a pale and unlovely hue. An English view would have been incomparably richer in its never-fading green; and in my own country the wooded hills would have been more delightful than these peaks and ridges of dreary and barren sunshine; and there would have been the bright eyes of half a dozen little lakes, looking heavenward within an extent like that of the Val d'Arno.

By and by mamma's carriage came along the dusty road, and passed through the iron gateway, which we had left open for her reception. We shouted down to her and Rose, and they waved their handkerchiefs upward to us; and, on my way down, I met Rose and the servant coming up through the ghostly rooms.

The rest of the day we spent mostly in exploring the premises. The house itself is of almost bewildering extent, insomuch that we might each of us have a suite of rooms individually. I have established myself on the ground floor, where I have a dressing-room, a large vaulted saloon, hung with yellow damask,

and a square writing-study, the walls and ceilings of the two latter apartments being ornamented with angels and cherubs aloft in fresco,
and with temples, statues, vases, broken columns, peacocks, parrots, vines, and sunflowers
below. I know not how many more saloons,
anterooms, and sleeping chambers there are on
this same basement story, besides an equal number over them, and a great subterranean establishment. I saw some immense jars there,
which I suppose were intended to hold oil ; and
iron kettles, for what purpose I cannot tell.
There is also a chapel in the house, but it is
locked up, and we cannot yet with certainty
find the door of it, nor, even in this great wilderness of a house, decide absolutely what space
the holy precincts occupy. Adjoining Una's
chamber, which is in the tower, there is a little
oratory, hung round with sacred prints of very
ancient date, and with crucifixes, holy-water
vases, and other consecrated things ; and here,
within a glass case, there is the representation
of an undraped little boy in wax, very prettily
modelled, and holding up a heart that looks
like a bit of red sealing-wax. If I had found
him anywhere else, I should have taken him
for Cupid ; but, being in an oratory, I presume him to have some religious signification.
In the servants' room a crucifix hung on one
side of the bed, and a little vase for holy water,

now overgrown with a cobweb, on the other; and, no doubt, all the other sleeping apartments would have been equally well provided, only that their occupants were to be heretics.

The lower floor of the house is tolerably furnished, and looks cheerful with its frescos, although the bare pavements in every room give an impression of discomfort. But carpets are universally taken up in Italy during summer time. It must have been an immense family that could have ever filled such a house with life. We go on voyages of discovery, and when in quest of any particular point, are likely enough to fetch up at some other. This morning I had difficulty in finding my way again to the top of the tower. One of the most peculiar rooms is constructed close to the tower, under the roof of the main building, but with no external walls on two sides! It is thus left open to the air, I presume for the sake of coolness. A parapet runs round the exposed sides for the sake of security. Some of the palaces in Florence have such open loggias in their upper stories, and I saw others on our journey hither, after arriving in Tuscany.

The grounds immediately around the house are laid out in gravel walks, and ornamented with shrubbery, and with what ought to be a grassy lawn; but the Italian sun is quite as little favorable to beauty of that kind as our own.

I have enjoyed the luxury, however, almost for the first time since I left my hilltop at the Wayside, of flinging myself at full length on the ground without any fear of catching cold. Moist England would punish a man soundly for taking such liberties with her greensward. A *podere*, or cultivated tract, comprising several acres, belongs to the villa, and seems to be fertile, like all the surrounding country. The possessions of different proprietors are not separated by fences, but only marked out by ditches; and it seems possible to walk miles and miles, along the intersecting paths, without obstruction. The rural laborers, so far as I have observed, go about in their shirt-sleeves, and look very much like tanned and sunburnt Yankees.

Last night it was really a work of time and toil to go about making our defensive preparations for the night; first closing the iron gate, then the ponderous and complicated fastenings of the house door, then the separate barricadoes of each iron-barred window on the lower floor, with a somewhat slighter arrangement above. There are bolts and shutters, however, for every window in the house, and I suppose it would not be amiss to put them all in use. Our garrison is so small that we must depend more upon the strength of our fortifications than upon our own active efforts in case of an attack. In England, in an insulated country house, we should need all these bolts and bars, and Italy is not thought to be the safer country of the two.

It deserves to be recorded that the Count Montauto, a nobleman, and seemingly a man of property, should deem it worth while to let his country seat, and reside during the hot months in his palace in the city, for the consideration of a comparatively small sum a month. He seems to contemplate returning hither for the autumn and winter, when the situation must be very windy and bleak, and the cold deathlike in these great halls ; and then, it is to be supposed, he will let his palace in town. The Count, through the agency of his son, bargained very stiffly for, and finally obtained, three dollars in addition to the sum which we at first offered him.   This indicates that even a little money is still a matter of great moment in Italy.   Signor del Bello, who, I believe, is also a nobleman, haggled with us about some cracked crockery at our late residence, and finally demanded and received fifty cents in compensation.   But this poor gentleman has been a spendthrift, and now acts as the agent of another.

August 3. — Yesterday afternoon William Story called on me, he being on a day or two's excursion from Siena, where he is spending the

summer with his family. He was very entertaining and conversative, as usual, and said, in
reply to my question whether he were not anxious to return to Cleopatra, that he had already
sketched out another subject for sculpture,
which would employ him during next winter.
He told me, what I was glad to hear, that his
sketches of Italian life, intended for the Atlantic Monthly, and supposed to be lost, have
been recovered. Speaking of the superstitious-
ness of the Italians, he said that they universally believe in the influence of the evil eye.
The evil influence is supposed not to be de-
pendent on the will of the possessor of the evil
eye; on the contrary, the persons to whom he
wishes well are the very ones to suffer by it. It
is oftener found in monks than in any other
class of people; and on meeting a monk, and
encountering his eye, an Italian usually makes
a defensive sign by putting both hands behind
him, with the forefingers and little fingers extended, although it is a controverted point
whether it be not more efficacious to extend the
hand with its outspread fingers towards the suspected person. It is considered an evil omen
to meet a monk on first going out for the day.
The evil eye may be classified with the phenomena of mesmerism. The Italians, especially the Neapolitans, very generally wear am-
ulets. Pio Nono, perhaps as being the chief of

all monks and other religious people, is supposed to have an evil eye of tenfold malignancy;
and its effect has been seen in the ruin of all
schemes for the public good so soon as they are
favored by him. When the pillar in the Piazza
di Spagna, commemorative of his dogma of the
Immaculate Conception, was to be erected, the
people of Rome refused to be present, or to
have anything to do with it, unless the pope
promised to abstain from interference. His
holiness did promise, but so far broke his word
as to be present one day while it was being
erected, and on that day a man was killed. A
little while ago there was a Lord Clifford, an
English Catholic nobleman, residing in Italy,
and, happening to come to Rome, he sent his
compliments to Pio Nono, and requested the
favor of an interview. The pope, as it happened, was indisposed, or for some reason could
not see his lordship, but very kindly sent him
his blessing. Those who knew of it shook their
heads, and intimated that it would go ill with
his lordship now that he had been blessed by
Pio Nono, and the very next day poor Lord
Clifford was dead! His holiness had better
construe the scriptural injunction literally, and
take to blessing his enemies.

I walked into town with Julian this morning,
and, meeting a monk in the Via Fornace, I
thought it no more than reasonable, as the good

father fixed his eyes on me, to provide against
the worst by putting both hands behind me,
with the forefingers and little fingers stuck out.

In speaking of the little oratory connected
with Una's chamber, I forgot to mention the
most remarkable object in it. It is a skull,
the size of life (or death). . . . This part of the
house must be very old, probably coeval with
the tower. The ceiling of Una's apartment is
vaulted with intersecting arches ; and adjoining
it is a very large saloon, likewise with a vaulted
and groined ceiling, and having a cushioned
divan running round the wall. The windows
of these rooms look out on the Val d'Arno.

The apartment above this saloon is of the
same size, and hung with engraved portraits,
printed on large sheets by the score and hundred together, and enclosed in wooden frames.
They comprise the whole series of Roman emperors, the succession of popes, the kings of
Europe, the doges of Venice, and the sultans of
Turkey. The engravings bear different dates
between 1685 and thirty years later, and were
executed at Rome.

August 4. — We ascended our tower yesterday afternoon to see the sunset. In my first
sketch of the Val d'Arno I said that the Arno
seemed to hold its course near the bases of the
hills. I now observe that the line of trees which

marks its current divides the valley into two pretty equal parts, and the river runs nearly east and west. . . . At last, when it was growing dark, we went down, groping our way over the shaky staircases, and peeping into each dark chamber as we passed. I gratified Julian exceedingly by hitting my nose against the wall. Reaching the bottom, I went into the great saloon, and stood at a window watching the lights twinkle forth, near and far, in the valley, and listening to the convent bells that sounded from Monte Olivetto, and more remotely still. The stars came out, and the constellation of the Dipper hung exactly over the Val d'Arno, pointing to the North Star above the hills on my right.

August 12. — We drove into town yesterday afternoon, with Miss Blagden, to call on Mr. Kirkup, an old Englishman who has resided a great many years in Florence. He is noted as an antiquarian, and has the reputation of being a necromancer, not undeservedly, as he is deeply interested in spirit rappings, and holds converse, through a medium, with dead poets and emperors. He lives in an old house, formerly a residence of the Knights Templars, hanging over the Arno, just as you come upon the Ponte Vecchio; and, going up a dark staircase and knocking at a door on one side of the landing-

place, we were received by Mr. Kirkup. He
had had notice of our visit, and was prepared
for it, being dressed in a blue frock-coat of
rather an old fashion, with a velvet collar, and
in a thin waistcoat and pantaloons fresh from
the drawer ; looking very sprucely, in short, and
unlike his customary guise, for Miss Blagden
hinted to us that the poor gentleman is generally so untidy that it is not quite pleasant to
take him by the hand. He is rather low of
stature, with a pale, shrivelled face, and hair
and beard perfectly white, and the hair of a
particularly soft and silken texture. He has a
high, thin nose, of the English aristocratic type ;
his eyes have a queer, rather wild look, and the
eyebrows are arched above them so that he
seems all the time to be seeing something that
strikes him with surprise. I judged him to be
a little crack-brained, chiefly on the strength of
this expression. His whole make is delicate,
his hands white and small, and his appearance
and manners those of a gentleman, with rather
more embroidery of courtesy than belongs to an
Englishman. He appeared to be very ner-
vous, tremulous, indeed, to his fingers' ends,
without being in any degree disturbed or em-
barrassed by our presence. Finally, he is very
deaf ; an infirmity that quite took away my
pleasure in the interview, because it is impossible to say anything worth while when one is

compelled to raise one's voice above its ordinary level.

He ushered us through two or three large rooms, dark, dusty, hung with antique-looking pictures, and lined with bookcases containing, I doubt not, a very curious library. Indeed, he directed my attention to one case, and said that he had collected those works, in former days, merely for the sake of laughing at them. They were books of magic and occult sciences. What he seemed really to value, however, were some manuscript copies of Dante, of which he showed us two : one, a folio on parchment, beautifully written in German text, the letters as clear and accurately cut as printed type ; the other a small volume, fit, as Mr. Kirkup said, to be carried in a capacious mediæval sleeve. This also was on vellum, and as elegantly executed as the larger one ; but the larger had beautiful illuminations, the vermilion and gold of which looked as brilliant now as they did five centuries ago. Both of these books were written early in the fourteenth century. Mr. Kirkup has also a plaster cast of Dante's face, which he believes to be the original one taken from his face after death ; and he has likewise his own accurate tracing from Giotto's fresco of Dante in the chapel of the Bargello. This fresco was discovered through Mr. Kirkup's means, and the tracing is particularly valuable, because the original has been almost destroyed by rough usage in drawing out a nail that had been driven into the eye. It represents the profile of a youthful but melancholy face, and has the general outline of Dante's features in other protraits.

Dante has held frequent communications with Mr. Kirkup through a medium, the poet being described by the medium as wearing the same dress seen in the youthful portrait, but as bearing more resemblance to the cast taken from his dead face than to the picture from his youthful one.

There was a very good picture of Savonarola in one of the rooms, and many other portraits, paintings, and drawings, some of them ancient, and others the work of Mr. Kirkup himself. He has the torn fragment of an exquisite drawing of a nude figure by Rubens, and a portfolio of other curious drawings. And besides books and works of art, he has no end of antique knickknackeries, none of which we had any time to look at; among others some instruments with which nuns used to torture themselves in their convents by way of penance. But the greatest curiosity of all, and no antiquity, was a pale, large-eyed little girl, about four years old, who followed the conjurer's footsteps wherever he went. She was the brightest and merriest little thing in the world, and frisked through those shadowy old chambers, among

the dead people's trumpery, as gayly as a butter-
fly flits among flowers and sunshine.

The child's mother was a beautiful girl named
Regina, whose portrait Mr. Kirkup showed us
on the wall. I never saw a more beautiful and
striking face claiming to be a real one. She was
a Florentine, of low birth, and she lived with
the old necromancer as his spiritual medium.
He showed us a journal, kept during her lifetime, and read from it his notes of an interview
with the Czar Alexander, when that potentate
communicated to Mr. Kirkup that he had been
poisoned. The necromancer set a great value
upon Regina, . . . and when she died he received her poor baby into his heart, and now
considers it absolutely his own. At any rate,
it is a happy belief for him, since he has nothing
else in the world to love, and loves the child
entirely, and enjoys all the bliss of fatherhood,
though he must have lived as much as seventy
years before he began to taste it.

The child inherits her mother's gift of communication with the spiritual world, so that the
conjurer can still talk with Regina through the
baby which she left, and not only with her, but
with Dante, and any other great spirit that may
choose to visit him. It is a very strange story,
and this child might be put at once into a romance, with all her history and environment:
the ancient Knight Templar palace, with the

Arno flowing under the iron-barred windows, and the Ponte Vecchio, covered with its jewellers' shops, close at hand ; the dark, lofty chambers with faded frescos on the ceilings, black pictures hanging on the walls, old books on the shelves, and hundreds of musty antiquities, emitting an odor of past centuries ; the shrivelled, white-bearded old man, thinking all the time of ghosts, and looking into the child's eyes to seek them ; and the child herself springing so freshly out of the soil, so pretty, so intelligent, so playful, with never a playmate save the conjurer and a kitten. It is a Persian kitten, and lay asleep in a window ; but when I touched it, it started up at once in as gamesome a mood as the child herself.

The child looks pale, and no wonder, seldom or never stirring out of that old palace, or away from the river atmosphere. Miss Blagden advised Mr. Kirkup to go with her to the seaside or into the country, and he did not deny that it might do her good, but seemed to be hampered by an old man's sluggishness and dislike of change. I think he will not live a great while, for he seems very frail. When he dies, the little girl will inherit what property he may leave. A lady, Catharine Fleming, an Englishwoman, and a friend of Mr. Kirkup, has engaged to take her in charge. She followed us merrily to the door, and so did the Persian kitten, and

Mr. Kirkup shook hands with us, over and over again, with vivacious courtesy, his manner having been characterized by a great deal of briskness throughout the interview. He expressed himself delighted to have met me (whose books he had read), and said that the day would be a memorable one to him, — which I did not in the least believe.

Mr. Kirkup is an intimate friend of Trelawney, author of Adventures of a Younger Son, and, long ago, the latter promised him that, if he ever came into possession of the family estate, he would divide it with him. Trelawney did really succeed to the estate, and lost no time in forwarding to his friend the legal documents, entitling him to half of the property. But Mr. Kirkup declined the gift, as he himself was not destitute, and Trelawney had a brother. There were two pictures of Trelawney in the saloons, one a slight sketch on the wall, the other a half-length portrait in a Turkish dress; both handsome, but indicating no very amiable character. It is not easy to forgive Trelawney for uncovering dead Byron's limbs, and telling that terrible story about them, — equally disgraceful to himself, be it truth or a lie.

It seems that Regina had a lover, and a sister who was very disreputable. . . . It rather adds than otherwise to the romance of the affair, — the idea that this pretty little elf has no right whatever to the asylum which she has found. Her name is Imogen.

The small manuscript copy of Dante which he showed me was written by a Florentine gentleman of the fourteenth century, one of whose ancestors the poet had met and talked with in Paradise.

August 19. — Here is a good Italian incident, which I find in Valery. Andrea del Castagno was a painter in Florence in the fifteenth century; and he had a friend, likewise a painter, Domenico of Venice. The latter had the secret of painting in oils, and yielded to Castagno's entreaties to impart it to him. Desirous of being the sole possessor of this great secret, Castagno waited only the night to assassinate Domenico, who so little suspected his treachery that he besought those who found him bleeding and dying to take him to his friend Castagno, that he might die in his arms. The murderer lived to be seventy-four years old, and his crime was never suspected till he himself revealed it on his death-bed. Domenico did actually die in Castagno's arms. The death scene would have been a good one for the latter to paint in oils.

September 1. — Few things journalizable have happened during the last month, because Flor-

ence and the neighborhood have lost their novelty ; and furthermore, I usually spend the
whole day at home, having been engaged in
planning and sketching out a romance. I have
now done with this for the present, and mean
to employ the rest of the time we stay here
chiefly in revisiting the galleries, and seeing
what remains to be seen in Florence.

Last Saturday, August 28, we went to take
tea at Miss Blagden's, who has a weekly reception on that evening. We found Mr. Powers
there, and by and by Mr. Boott and Mr. Trollope came in. Miss —— has lately been exer-
cising her faculties as a spiritual writing-med-
ium ; and, the conversation turning on that
subject, Mr. Powers related some things that
he had witnessed through the agency of Mr.
Home, who had held a session or two at his
house. He described the apparition of two
mysterious hands from beneath a table round
which the party were seated. These hands pur-
ported to belong to the aunt of the Countess
Cotterel, who was present, and were a pair of
thin, delicate, aged, ladylike hands and arms,
appearing at the edge of the table, and terminating at the elbow in a sort of white mist. One
of the hands took up a fan and began to use
it. The countess then said, " Fan yourself as
you used to do, dear aunt ; " and forthwith the
hands waved the fan back and forth in a pecul-

iar manner, which the countess recognized as
the manner of her dead aunt.   The spirit was
then requested to fan each member of the party ;
and accordingly, each separate individual round
the table was fanned in turn, and felt the breeze
sensibly upon his face.   Finally, the hands
sank beneath the table, I believe Mr. Powers
said ; but I am not quite sure that they did not
melt into the air.   During this apparition, Mr.
Home sat at the table, but not in such a position or within such distance that he could have
put out or managed the spectral hands ; and
of this Mr. Powers satisfied himself by taking
precisely the same position after the party had
retired.   Mr. Powers did not feel the hands at
this time, but he afterwards felt the touch of
infant hands, which were at the time invisible.
He told of many of the wonders, which seem
to have as much right to be set down as facts
as anything else that depends on human testi-
mony.   For example, Mr. K——, one of the
party, gave a sudden start and exclamation.   He
had felt on his knee a certain token, which
could have been given him only by a friend,
long ago in his grave.   Mr. Powers inquired
what was the last thing that had been given as
a present to a deceased child, and suddenly
both he and his wife felt a prick, as of some
sharp instrument, on their knees.   The present had been a penknife.   I have forgotten

other incidents quite as striking as these; but,
with the exception of the spirit hands, they
seemed to be akin to those that had been produced by mesmerism, returning the inquirer's
thoughts and veiled recollections to himself,
as answers to his queries. The hands are certainly an inexplicable phenomenon. Of course,
they are not portions of a dead body, nor any
other kind of substance: they are impressions
on the two senses, sight and touch, but how
produced I cannot tell. Even admitting their
appearance, — and certainly I do admit it as
freely and fully as if I had seen them myself, —
there is no need of supposing them to come
from the world of departed spirits.

Powers seems to put entire faith in the verity
of spiritual communications, while acknowledging the difficulty of identifying spirits as being
what they pretend to be. He is a Swedenbor-
gian, and so far prepared to put faith in many
of these phenomena. As for Home, Powers
gives a decided opinion that he is a knave, but
thinks him so organized, nevertheless, as to be
a particularly good medium for spiritual communications. Spirits, I suppose, like earthly people,
are obliged to use such instruments as will answer their purposes; but rather than receive a
message from a dead friend through the organ-
ism of a rogue or charlatan, methinks I would
choose to wait till we meet. But what most

astonishes me is the indifference with which I listen to these marvels. They throw old ghost stories quite into the shade ; they bring the whole world of spirits down amongst us, visibly and audibly ; they are absolutely proved to be sober facts by evidence that would satisfy us of any other alleged realities ; and yet I cannot force my mind to interest myself in them. They are facts to my understanding, which, it might have been anticipated, would have been the last to acknowledge them ; but they seem not to be facts to my intuitions and deeper percep- tions. My inner soul does not in the least admit them ; there is a mistake somewhere. So idle and empty do I feel these stories to be, that I hesitated long whether or no to give up a few pages of this not very important journal to the record of them.

We have had written communications through Miss —— with several spirits ; my wife's father, mother, two brothers, and a sister, who died long ago, in infancy ; a certain Mary Hall, who announces herself as the guardian spirit of Miss —— ; and, queerest of all, a Mary Run- nel, who seems to be a wandering spirit, having relations with nobody, but thrusts her finger into everybody's affairs. My wife's mother is the principal communicant; she expresses strong affection, and rejoices at the opportunity of con- versing with her daughter. She often says very pretty things; for instance, in a dissertation upon heavenly music; but there is a lack of substance in her talk, a want of gripe, a delusive show, a sentimental surface, with no bottom beneath it. The same sort of thing has struck me in all the poetry and prose that I have read from spiritual sources. I should judge that these effusions emanated from earthly minds, but had undergone some process that had deprived them of solidity and warmth. In the communications between my wife and her mother, I cannot help thinking that (Miss —— being unconsciously in a mesmeric state) all the responses are conveyed to her fingers from my wife's mind. . . .

We have tried the spirits by various test questions, on every one of which they have failed egregiously. Here, however, the aforesaid Mary Runnel comes into play. The other spirits have told us that the veracity of this spirit is not to be depended upon; and so, whenever it is possible, poor Mary Runnel is thrust forward to bear the odium of every mistake or falsehood. They have avowed themselves responsible for all statements signed by themselves, and have thereby brought themselves into more than one inextricable dilemma; but it is very funny, where a response or a matter of fact has not been thus certified, how invariably Mary Runnel is made to assume the discredit

of it, on its turning out to be false. It is the
most ingenious arrangement that could possibly
have been contrived; and somehow or other
the pranks of this lying spirit give a reality to
the conversations which the more respectable
ghosts quite fail in imparting.

The whole matter seems to me a sort of
dreaming awake. It resembles a dream, in that
the whole material is, from the first, in the
dreamer's mind, though concealed at various
depths below the surface; the dead appear alive,
as they always do in dreams; unexpected com-
binations occur, as continually in dreams; the
mind speaks through the various persons of the
drama, and sometimes astonishes itself with its
own wit, wisdom, and eloquence, as often in
dreams; but, in both cases, the intellectual
manifestations are really of a very flimsy texture.
Mary Runnel is the only personage who does
not come evidently from dreamland; and she,
I think, represents that lurking scepticism, that
sense of unreality, of which we are often conscious, amid the most vivid phantasmagoria of
a dream. I should be glad to believe in the
genuineness of these spirits, if I could; but the
above is the conclusion to which my soberest
thoughts tend. There remains, of course, a
great deal for which I cannot account, and I
cannot sufficiently wonder at the pigheadedness
both of metaphysicians and physiologists, in not

accepting the phenomena, so far as to make them the subject of investigation.

In writing the communications, Miss —— holds the pencil rather loosely between her fingers ; it moves rapidly, and with equal facility whether she fixes her eyes on the paper or not. The handwriting has far more freedom than her own. At the conclusion of a sentence the pencil lays itself down. She sometimes has a perception of each word before it is written ; at other times she is quite unconscious what is to come next. Her integrity is absolutely indubitable, and she herself totally disbelieves in the spiritual authenticity of what is communicated through her medium.

September 3. — We walked into Florence yesterday, betimes after breakfast, it being comfortably cool, and a gray, English sky ; though, indeed, the clouds had a tendency to mass themselves more than they do on an overcast English day. We found it warmer in Florence, but not inconveniently so, even in the sunniest streets and squares.

We went to the Uffizi gallery, the whole of which, with its contents, is now familiar to us, except the room containing drawings ; and our to-day's visit was especially to them. The door giving admittance to them is the very last in the gallery ; and the rooms, three in number, are, I should judge, over the Loggia de Lanzi, looking on the Grand Ducal Piazza. The drawings hang on the walls, framed and glazed; and number, perhaps, from one to two hundred in each room; but this is only a small portion of the collection, which amounts, it is said, to twenty thousand, and is reposited in portfolios. The sketches on the walls are changed from time to time, so as to exhibit all the most interesting ones in turn. Their whole charm is artistic, imaginative, and intellectual, and in no degree of the upholstery kind; their outward presentment being, in general, a design hastily shadowed out, by means of colored crayons, on tinted paper, or perhaps scratched rudely in pen and ink; or drawn in pencil or charcoal, and half rubbed out; very rough things, indeed, in many instances, and the more interesting on that account, because it seems as if the artist had bestirred himself to catch the first glimpse of an image that did but reveal itself and vanish. The sheets, or sometimes scraps of paper, on which they are drawn, are discolored with age, creased, soiled; but yet you are magnetized by the hand of Raphael, Michel Angelo, Leonardo, or whoever may have jotted down those rough-looking master-touches. They certainly possess a charm that is lost in the finished picture; and I was more sensible of forecasting thought, skill, and prophetic design in these sketches than in the most consummate works that have been elaborated from them.   There is something more divine in these; for I suppose the first idea of a picture is real inspiration, and all the subsequent elaboration of the master serves but to cover up the celestial germ with something that belongs to himself.   At any rate, the first sketch is the more suggestive, and sets the spectator's imagination at work; whereas the picture, if a good one, leaves him nothing to do; if bad, it confuses, stupefies, disenchants, and disheartens him.   First thoughts have an aroma and fragrance in them, that they do not lose in three hundred years; for so old, and a good deal more, are some of these sketches.

None interested me more than some drawings, on separate pieces of paper, by Perugino, for his picture of the mother and friends of Jesus round his dead body, now at the Pitti Palace.   The attendant figures are distinctly made out, as if the Virgin, and John, and Mary Magdalen had each favored the painter with a sitting; but the body of Jesus lies in the midst, dimly hinted with a few pencil marks.

There were several designs by Michel Angelo, none of which made much impression on me; the most striking was a very ugly demon, afterwards painted in the Sistine Chapel.   Raphael shows several sketches of Madonnas, — one of which has flowered into the Grand Duke's especial Madonna at the Pitti Palace, but with a different face. His sketches were mostly very rough in execution ; but there were two or three designs for frescos, I think, in the Vatican, very carefully executed ; perhaps because these works were mainly to be done by other hands than his own. It seems to me that the Pre-Raphaelite artists made more careful drawings than the later ones ; and it rather surprised me to see how much science they possessed.

We looked at few other things in the gallery ; and, indeed, it was not one of the days when works of art find me impressible. We stopped a little while in the Tribune, but the Venus di Medici seemed to me to-day little more than any other piece of yellowish white marble. How strange that a goddess should stand before us absolutely unrecognized, even when we know, by previous revelations, that she is nothing short of divine ! It is also strange that, unless when one feels the ideal charm of a statue, it becomes one of the most tedious and irksome things in the world. Either it must be a celestial thing or an old lump of stone, dusty and time-soiled, and tiring out your patience with eternally looking just the same. Once in a while you penetrate through the crust of the old sameness, and see the statue forever new and immortally young.

Leaving the gallery we walked towards the
Duomo, and on our way stopped to look at the
beautiful Gothic niches hollowed into the exterior walls of the Church of San Michele
They are now in the process of being cleaned,
and each niche is elaborately inlaid with precious
marbles and some of them magnificently gilded ;
and they are all surmounted with marble canopies as light and graceful as frost-work. Within
stand statues, St. George, and many other saints,
by Donatello and others, and all taking a hold
upon one's sympathies, even if they be not beautiful.   Classic statues escape you with their slip-
pery beauty, as if they were made of ice.   Rough
and ugly things can be clutched.   This is nonsense, and yet it means something. . . . The
streets were thronged and vociferative with more
life and outcry than usual.   It must have been
market day in Florence, for the commerce of
the streets was in great vigor, narrow tables
being set out in them and in the squares, burdened with all kinds of small merchandise, such
as cheap jewelry, glistening as brightly as what
we had just seen in the gem-room of the Uffizi ;
crockery ware ; toys, books, Italian and French ;
silks ; slippers ; old iron ; all advertised by the
dealers with terribly loud and high voices, that
reverberated harshly from side to side of the
narrow streets.   Italian street-cries go through

the head, not that they are so very sharp, but exceedingly hard, like a blunt iron bar.

We stood at the base of the Campanile, and looked at the bas-reliefs which wreathe it round; and, above them, a row of statues; and from bottom to top a marvellous minuteness of inlaid marbles, filling up the vast and beautiful design of this heaven-aspiring tower. Looking upward to its lofty summit, — where angels might alight, lapsing downward from heaven, and gaze curiously at the bustle of men below, — I could not but feel that there is a moral charm in this faithful minuteness of Gothic architecture, filling up its outline with a million of beauties that perhaps may never be studied out by a single spectator. It is the very process of nature, and no doubt produces an effect that we know not of. Classic architecture is nothing but an outline, and affords no little points, no interstices where human feelings may cling and overgrow it like ivy. The charm, as I said, seems to be moral rather than intellectual; for in the gemroom of the Uffizi you may see fifty designs, elaborated on a small scale, that have just as much merit as the design of the Campanile. If it were only five inches long, it might be a case for some article of toilet; being two hundred feet high, its prettiness develops into grandeur as well as beauty, and it becomes really one of the wonders of the world. The design of the

Pantheon, on the contrary, would retain its sublimity on whatever scale it might be represented.

Returning homewards, we crossed the Ponte Vecchio, and went to the Museum of Natural History, where we gained admittance into the rooms dedicated to Galileo. They consist of a vestibule, a saloon, and a semicircular tribune, covered with a frescoed dome, beneath which stands a colossal statue of Galileo, long-bearded, and clad in a student's gown, or some voluminous garb of that kind. Around the tribune, beside and behind the statue, are six niches, — in one of which is preserved a forefinger of Galileo, fixed on a little gilt pedestal, and pointing upward, under a glass cover. It is very much shrivelled and mummylike, of the color of parchment, and is little more than a finger-bone, with the dry skin of flesh flaking away from it; on the whole, not a very delightful relic; but Galileo used to point heavenward with this finger, and I hope has gone whither he pointed.

Another niche contains two telescopes, wherewith he made some of his discoveries; they are perhaps a yard long, and of very small calibre. Other astronomical instruments are displayed in the glass cases that line the rooms; but I did not understand their use any better than the monks, who wished to burn Galileo for his heterodoxy about the planetary system. . . .

After dinner I climbed to the tower. . . . Florence lay in the sunshine, level, compact, and small of compass. Above the tiled roofs rose the tower of Palazzo Vecchio, the loftiest and the most picturesque, though built, I suppose, with no idea of making it so. But it attains, in a singular degree, the end of causing the imagination to fly upward and alight on its airy battlements. Near it I beheld the square mass of Or San Michele, and farther to the left the bulky Duomo, and the Campanile close beside it, like a slender bride or daughter; the dome of San Lorenzo too. The Arno is nowhere visible. Beyond, and on all sides of the city, the hills pile themselves lazily upward in ridges, here and there developing into a peak; towards their bases white villas were strewn numerously, but the upper region was lonely and bare.

As we passed under the arch of the Porta Romana this morning, on our way into the city, we saw a queer object. It was what we at first took for a living man, in a garb of light reddish or yellowish red color, of antique or priestly fashion, and with a cowl falling behind. His face was of the same hue, and seemed to have been powdered, as the faces of maskers sometimes are. He sat in a cart, which he seemed to be driving into the city with a load of earthen jars and pipkins, the color of which was precisely like his own.   On closer inspection, this priestly figure proved to be likewise an image of earthenware, but his lifelikeness had a very strange and rather ghastly effect.   Adam, perhaps, was made of just such red earth, and had the complexion of this figure.

September 7. — I walked into town yesterday morning, by way of the Porta San Frediano. The gate of a city might be a good locality for a chapter in a novel, or for a little sketch by itself, whether by painter or writer.   The great arch of the gateway, piercing through the depth and height of the massive masonry beneath the battlemented summit ;   the shadow brooding below in the immense thickness of the wall, and beyond it the vista of the street, sunny and swarming with life ;   outside of the gate, a throng of carts, laden with fruits, vegetables, small flat barrels of wine, waiting to be examined by the custom-house officers ;   carriages, too, and foot-passengers entering, and others swarming outward.   Under the shadowy arch are the offices of the police and customs, and probably the guard-room of the soldiers, all hollowed out in the mass of the gateway.   Civil officers loll on chairs in the shade, perhaps with an awning over their heads.   Where the sun falls aslantwise under the arch a sentinel, with musket and bayonet, paces to and fro in the entrance, and other soldiers lounge close by.   The life of the city seems to be compressed and made more intense by this barrier; and on passing within it you do not breathe quite so freely, yet are sensible of an enjoyment in the close elbowing throng, the clamor of high voices from side to side of the street, and the million of pretty sights, actions, traffics, and personalities, all so squeezed together as to become a great whole.

The street by which I entered led me to the Carraja Bridge; crossing which, I kept straight onward till I came to the Church of Santa Maria Novella.   Doubtless, it looks just the same as when Boccaccio's party stood in a cluster on its broad steps arranging their excursion to the villa.   Thence I went to the Church of St. Lorenzo, which I entered by the side door, and found the organ sounding and a religious ceremony going forward.   It is a church of sombre aspect, with its gray walls and pillars, but was decked out for some festivity with hangings of scarlet damask and gold.   I sat awhile to rest myself, and then pursued my way to the Duomo.   I entered, and looked at Sir John Hawkwood's painted effigy, and at several busts and statues, and at the windows of the chapel surrounding the dome, through which the sunshine glowed, white in the outer air, but a hundred-hued splendor within.   I tried to bring up the scene of Lorenzo de' Medici's attempted assassination, but with no great success ; and after listening a little while to the chanting of the priests and acolytes, I went to the Bank. It is in a palace of which Raphael was the architect, in the Piazza Gran Duca.

I next went, as a matter of course, to the Uffizi gallery, and, in the first place, to the Tribune, where the Venus de' Medici deigned to reveal herself rather more satisfactorily than at my last visit. . . . I looked into all the rooms, bronzes, drawings, and gem-room ; a volume might easily be written upon either subject. The contents of the gem-room especially require to be looked at separately in order to convince one's self of their minute magnificences ; for, among so many, the eye slips from one to another with only a vague outward sense that here are whole shelves full of little miracles, both of nature's material and man's workmanship. Greater [larger] things can be reasonably well appreciated with a less scrupulous though broader attention ; but in order to estimate the brilliancy of the diamond eyes of a little agate bust, for instance, you have to screw your mind down to them and nothing else. You must sharpen your faculties of observation to a point, and touch the object exactly on the right spot, or you do not appreciate it at all. It is a troublesome process when there are a thousand such objects to be seen.

I stood at an open window in the transverse corridor, and looked down upon the Arno, and across at the range of edifices that impend over it on the opposite side. The river, I should judge, may be a hundred or a hundred and fifty yards wide in its course between the Ponte alle Grazie and the Ponte Vecchio ; that is, the width between strand and strand is at least so much. The river, however, leaves a broad margin of mud and gravel on its right bank, on which water-weeds grow pretty abundantly, and creep even into the stream. On my first arrival in Florence I thought the goose-pond green of the water rather agreeable than otherwise ; but its hue is now that of unadulterated mud, as yellow as the Tiber itself, yet not impressing me as being enriched with city sewerage like that other famous river. From the Ponte alle Grazie downward, halfway towards the Ponte Vecchio, there is an island of gravel, and the channel on each side is so shallow as to allow the passage of men and horses, wading not overleg. I have seen fishermen wading the main channel from side to side, their feet sinking into the dark mud, and thus discoloring the yellow water with a black track visible, step by step, through its shallowness. But still the Arno is a mountain stream, and liable to be tetchy and turbulent like all its kindred, and no doubt it often finds its borders of hewn stone not too far apart for its convenience.

Along the right shore, beneath the Uffizi and the adjacent buildings, there is a broad paved way, with a parapet; on the opposite shore the edifices are built directly upon the river's edge, and impend over the water, supported upon arches and machicolations, as I think that peculiar arrangement of buttressing arcades is called. The houses are picturesquely various in height, from two or three stories to seven; picturesque in hue likewise, — pea-green, yellow, white, and of aged discoloration, — but all with green blinds; picturesque also in the courts and galleries that look upon the river, and in the wide arches that open beneath, intended perhaps to afford a haven for the household boat. Nets were suspended before one or two of the houses, as if the inhabitants were in the habit of fishing out of window. As a general effect, the houses, though often palatial in size and height, have a shabby, neglected aspect, and are jumbled too closely together. Behind their range the city swells upward in a hillside, which rises to a great height above, forming, I believe, a part of the Boboli Gardens.

I returned homewards over the Ponte Vecchio, which is a continuous street of ancient houses, except over the central arch, so that a stranger might easily cross the river without knowing it. In these small, old houses there is a community of goldsmiths, who set out their glass cases, and hang their windows with rings, bracelets, necklaces, strings of pearl, ornaments of malachite and coral, and especially with Florentine mosaics ; watches, too, and snuff-boxes of old fashion or new ; offerings for shrines also, such as silver hearts pierced with swords ; an infinity of pretty things, the manufacture of which is continually going on in the little back room of each little shop. This gewgaw business has been established on the Ponte Vecchio for centuries, although, long since, it was an art of far higher pretensions than now. Benvenuto Cellini had his workshop here, probably in one of these self-same little nooks. It would have been a ticklish affair to be Benvenuto's fellow workman within such narrow limits.

Going out of the Porta Romana, I walked for some distance along the city wall, and then, turning to the left, toiled up the hill of Bellosguardo, through narrow zigzag lanes between high walls of stone or plastered brick, where the sun had the fairest chance to frizzle me. There were scattered villas and houses, here and there concentrating into a little bit of a street, paved with flag-stones from side to side, as in the city, and shadowed quite across its narrowness by the height of the houses. Mostly, however, the way was inhospitably sunny, and shut out by the high wall from every glimpse of a view, except in one spot, where Florence spread itself before my eyes, with every tower, dome, and spire which it contains. A little way farther on my own gray tower rose before me, the most welcome object that I had seen in the course of the day.

September 10. — I went into town again yesterday, by way of the Porta San Frediano, and observed that this gate (like the other gates of Florence as far as I have observed) is a tall, square structure of stone or brick, or both, rising high above the adjacent wall, and having a range of open loggie in the upper story. The arch externally is about half the height of the structure. Inside, towards the town, it rises nearly to the roof. On each side of the arch there is much room for offices, apartments, storehouses, or whatever else. On the outside of the gate, along the base, are those iron rings and sockets for torches, which are said to be the distinguishing symbol of illustrious houses. As contrasted with the vista of the narrow, swarming street through the arch from without, the view from the inside might be presented with a glimpse of the free blue sky.

I strolled a little about Florence, and went into two or three churches ; into that of the Annunziata for one. I have already described

this church, with its general magnificence, and
it was more magnificent than ever to-day, being
hung with scarlet silk and gold embroidery.
A great many people were at their devotions,
thronging principally around the Virgin's shrine.
I was struck now with the many bas-reliefs and
busts in the costume of their respective ages,
and seemingly with great accuracy of portraiture,
in the passage leading from the front of the
church into the cloisters. The marble was not
at all abashed nor degraded by being made to
assume the guise of the mediæval furred robe,
or the close-fitting tunic with elaborate ruff, or
the breastplate and gorget, or the flowing wig,
or whatever the actual costume might be ; and
one is sensible of a rectitude and reality in the
affair, and respects the dead people for not putting themselves into an eternal masquerade.
The dress of the present day will look equally
respectable in one or two hundred years.

The fair is still going on, and one of its
principal centres is before this church, in the
Piazza of the Annunziata. Cloth is the chief
commodity offered for sale, and none of the
finest ; coarse, unbleached linen and cotton
prints for country-people's wear, together with
yarn, stockings, and here and there an assort-
ment of bright-colored ribbons. Playthings,
of a very rude fashion, were also displayed ;
likewise books in Italian and French ; and a

great deal of iron-work. Both here and in Rome
they have this odd custom of offering rusty iron
implements for sale, spread out on the pavements. There was a good deal of tinware, too,
glittering in the sunshine, especially around the
pedestal of the bronze statue of Duke Ferdinand, who curbs his horse and looks down upon
the bustling piazza in a very stately way. . . .
The people attending the fair had mostly a rustic appearance ; sunburnt faces, thin frames ;
no beauty, no bloom, no joyousness of young
or old ; an anxious aspect, as if life were no easy
or holiday matter with them ; but I should take
them to be of a kindly nature, and reasonably
honest.   Except the broad-brimmed Tuscan
hats of the women, there was no peculiarity of
costume. At a careless glance I could very
well have mistaken most of the men for Yankees ; as for the women, there is very little resemblance between them and ours, — the old
being absolutely hideous, and the young ones
very seldom pretty.   It was a very dull crowd.
They do not generate any warmth among themselves by contiguity ; they have no pervading
sentiment, such as is continually breaking out
in rough merriment from an American crowd ;
they have nothing to do with one another ;
they are not a crowd, considered as one mass,
but a collection of individuals. A despotic
government has perhaps destroyed their prin-

ciple of cohesion, and crumbled them to atoms.
Italian crowds are noted for their civility; possibly they deserve credit for native courtesy
and gentleness; possibly, on the other hand,
the crowd has not spirit and self-consciousness
enough to be rampant. I wonder whether they
will ever hold another parliament in the Piazza
of Santa Croce !

I paid a visit to the gallery of the Pitti Palace. There is too large an intermixture of
Andrea del Sarto's pictures in this gallery;
everywhere you see them, cold, proper, and un-
criticisable, looking so much like first-rate excellence, that you inevitably quarrel with your
own taste for not admiring them. . . .

It was one of the days when my mind mis-
gives me whether the pictorial art be not a hum-
bug, and when the minute accuracy of a fly in a
Dutch picture of fruit and flowers seems to me
something more reliable than the master-touches
of Raphael. The gallery was considerably
thronged, and many of the visitors appeared
to be from the country, and of a class intermediate between gentility and labor. Is there
such a rural class in Italy ? I saw a respectable-
looking man feeling awkward and uncomfortable
in a new and glossy pair of pantaloons not yet
bent and creased to his natural movement.

Nothing pleased me better to-day than some
amber cups, in one of the cabinets of curiosities.

They are richly wrought, and the material is as if the artist had compressed a great deal of sunshine together, and, when sufficiently solidified, had moulded these cups out of it, and let them harden. This simile was suggested by —— .

Leaving the palace, I entered the Boboli Gardens, and wandered up and down a good deal of its uneven surface, through broad, well-kept edges of box, sprouting loftily, trimmed smoothly, and strewn between with cleanly gravel; skirting along plantations of aged trees, throwing a deep shadow within their precincts; passing many statues, not of the finest art, yet approaching so near it as to serve just as good a purpose for garden ornament; coming now and then to the borders of a fish-pool, or a pond, where stately swans circumnavigated an island of flowers, — all very fine and very wearisome. I have never enjoyed this garden; perhaps because it suggests dress-coats, and such elegant formalities.

September 11. — We have heard a good deal of spirit matters of late, especially of wonderful incidents that attended Mr. Home's visit to Florence, two or three years ago. Mrs. Powers told a very marvellous thing; how that when Mr. Home was holding a séance in her house, and several persons present, a great scratching was heard in a neighboring closet. She addressed the spirit, and requested it not to disturb the company then, as they were busy with other affairs, promising to converse with it on a future occasion. On a subsequent night, accordingly, the scratching was renewed, with the utmost violence; and in reply to Mrs. Powers's questions, the spirit assured her that it was not *one*, but legion, being the ghosts of twenty-seven monks, who were miserable and without hope! The house now occupied by Powers was formerly a convent, and I suppose these were the spirits of all the wicked monks that had ever inhabited it; at least, I hope that there were not such a number of damnable sinners extant at any one time. These ghostly fathers must have been very improper persons in their lifetime, judging by the indecorousness of their behavior even after death, and in such dreadful circumstances; for they pulled Mrs. Powers's skirts so hard as to break the gathers. . . . It was not ascertained that they desired to have anything done for their eternal welfare, or that their situation was capable of amendment anyhow; but, being exhorted to refrain from further disturbance, they took their departure, after making the sign of the cross on the breast of each person present. This was very singular in such reprobates, who, by their own confession, had forfeited all claim to be benefited by that holy symbol: it curiously suggests that the forms of religion may still be kept up in purgatory and hell itself. The sign was made in a way that conveyed the sense of something devilish and spiteful; the perpendicular line of the cross being drawn gently enough, but the transverse one sharply and violently, so as to leave a painful impression. Perhaps the monks meant this to express their contempt and hatred for heretics; and how queer, that this antipathy should survive their own damnation! But I cannot help hoping that the case of these poor devils may not be so desperate as they think. They cannot be wholly lost, because their desire for communication with mortals shows that they need sympathy, therefore are not altogether hardened, therefore, with loving treatment, may be restored.

A great many other wonders took place within the knowledge and experience of Mrs. Powers. She saw, not one pair of hands only, but many. The head of one of her dead children, a little boy, was laid in her lap, not in ghastly fashion, as a head out of the coffin and the grave, but just as the living child might have laid it on his mother's knees. It was invisible, by the bye, and she recognized it by the features and the character of the hair, through the sense of touch. Little hands grasped hers. In short, these soberly attested incredibilities are so numerous that

I forget nine tenths of them, and judge the others too cheap to be written down. Christ spoke the truth, surely, in saying that men would not believe, " though one rose from the dead." In my own case, the fact makes absolutely no impression. I regret such confirmation of truth as this.

Within a mile of our villa stands the Villa Columbaria, a large house, built round a square court. Like Mr. Powers's residence, it was formerly a convent. It is inhabited by Major Gregorie, an old soldier of Waterloo and various other fights, and his family consists of Mrs. ——, the widow of one of the major's friends, and her two daughters. We have become acquainted with the family, and Mrs. ——, the married daughter, has lent us a written statement of her experiences with a ghost, who has haunted the Villa Columbaria for many years back. He had made Mrs. —— aware of his presence in her room by a sensation of extreme cold, as if a wintry breeze were blowing over her ; also by a rustling of the bed-curtains ; and, at such times, she had a certain consciousness, as she says, that she was not ALONE. Through Mr. Home's agency the ghost was enabled to explain himself, and declared that he was a monk, named Giannana, who died a very long time ago in Mrs. ——'s present bedchamber. He was a murderer, and had been in a restless and miserable state ever since his death, wandering up and down the house, but especially haunting his own death-chamber and a staircase that communicated with the chapel of the villa. All the interviews with this lost spirit were attended with a sensation of severe cold, which was felt by every one present. He made his communications by means of table-rapping, and by the movements of chairs and other articles, which often assumed an angry character. The poor old fellow does not seem to have known exactly what he wanted with Mrs. ———, but promised to refrain from disturbing her any more, on condition that she would pray that he might find some repose. He had previously declined having any masses said for his soul. Rest, rest, rest, appears to be the continual craving of unhappy spirits; they do not venture to ask for positive bliss: perhaps, in their utter weariness, would rather forego the trouble of active enjoyment, but pray only for rest. The cold atmosphere around this monk suggests new ideas as to the climate of Hades. If all the aforementioned twenty-seven monks had a similar one, the combined temperature must have been that of a polar winter.

Mrs. ——— saw, at one time, the fingers of her monk, long, yellow, and skinny; these fingers grasped the hands of individuals of the party, with a cold, clammy, and horrible touch.

After the departure of this ghost other séances were held in her bedchamber, at which good and holy spirits manifested themselves, and behaved in a very comfortable and encouraging way. It was their benevolent purpose, apparently, to purify her apartments from all traces of the evil spirit, and to reconcile her to what had been so long the haunt of this miserable monk, by filling it with happy and sacred associations, in which, as Mrs. —— intimates, they entirely succeeded.

These stories remind me of an incident that took place at the Old Manse, in the first summer of our marriage. . . .

September 17.—We walked yesterday to Florence, and visited the Church of St. Lorenzo, where we saw, for the second time, the famous Medici statues of Michel Angelo. I found myself not in a very appreciative state, and, being a stone myself, the statue of Lorenzo was at first little more to me than another stone; but it was beginning to assume life, and would have impressed me as it did before if I had gazed long enough. There was a better light upon the face, under the helmet, than at my former visit, although still the features were enough overshadowed to produce that mystery on which, according to Mr. Powers, the effect of the statue depends. I observe that the costume of the figure, instead of being mediæval as I believe I have stated, is Roman; but, be it what it may, the grand and simple character of the figure imbues the robes with its individual propriety. I still think it the greatest miracle ever wrought in marble.

We crossed the church and entered a cloister on the opposite side, in quest of the Laurentian Library. Ascending a staircase we found an old man blowing the bellows of the organ, which was in full blast in the church; nevertheless he found time to direct us to the library door. We entered a lofty vestibule, of ancient aspect and stately architecture, and thence were admitted into the library itself; a long and wide gallery or hall, lighted by a row of windows on which were painted the arms of the Medici. The ceiling was inlaid with dark wood, in an elaborate pattern, which was exactly repeated in terra-cotta on the pavement beneath our feet. Long desks, much like the old-fashioned ones in schools, were ranged on each side of the mid-aisle, in a series from end to end, with seats for the convenience of students; and on these desks were rare manuscripts, carefully preserved under glass; and books, fastened to the desks by iron chains, as the custom of studious antiquity used to be. Along the centre of the hall, between the two ranges of desks, were tables and chairs, at which two or three scholarly persons were seated, diligently consulting volumes in manuscript or old type. It was a very quiet place, imbued with a cloistered sanctity, and remote from all street cries and rumble of the city, — odorous of old literature, — a spot where the commonest ideas ought not to be expressed in less than Latin.

The librarian — or custode he ought rather to be termed, for he was a man not above the fee of a paul — now presented himself, and showed us some of the literary curiosities ; a vellum manuscript of the Bible, with a splendid illumination by Ghirlandaio, covering two folio pages, and just as brilliant in its color as if finished yesterday.   Other illuminated manuscripts — or at least separate pages of them, for the volumes were kept under glass, and not to be turned over — were shown us, very magnificent, but not to be compared with this of Ghirlandaio. Looking at such treasures I could almost say that we have left behind us more splendor than we have kept alive to our own age.   We publish beautiful editions of books, to be sure, and thousands of people enjoy them ; but in ancient times the expense that we spread thinly over a thousand volumes was all compressed into one, and it became a great jewel of a book, a heavy folio, worth its weight in gold.   Then, what a spiritual charm it gives to a book to feel that every letter has been individually wrought, and the pictures glow for that individual page alone! Certainly the ancient reader had a luxury which the modern one lacks. I was surprised, moreover, to see the clearness and accuracy of the chirography. Print does not surpass it in these respects.

The custode showed us an ancient manuscript of the Decameron; likewise, a volume containing the portraits of Petrarch and of Laura, each covering the whole of a vellum page, and very finely done. They are authentic portraits, no doubt, and Laura is depicted as a fair-haired beauty, with a very satisfactory amount of loveliness. We saw some choice old editions of books in a small separate room; but as these were all ranged in shut bookcases, and, as each volume, moreover, was in a separate cover or modern binding, this exhibition did us very little good. By the bye, there is a conceit struggling blindly in my mind about Petrarch and Laura, suggested by those two lifelike portraits, which have been sleeping cheek to cheek through all these centuries. But I cannot lay hold of it.

September 21. — Yesterday morning the Val d' Arno was entirely filled with a thick fog, which extended even up to our windows, and concealed objects within a very short distance. It began to dissipate itself betimes, however, and was the forerunner of an unusually bright and warm day.

We set out after breakfast and walked into town, where we looked at mosaic brooches. These are very pretty little bits of manufacture; but there seems to have been no infusion of fresh fancy work, and the specimens present little variety.   It is the characteristic commodity of the place; the central mart and manufacturing locality being on the Ponte Vecchio, from end to end of which they are displayed in cases; but there are other mosaic shops scattered about the town.   The principal devices are roses, — pink, yellow, or white, — jasmines, lilies of the valley, forget-me-nots, orange blossoms, and others, single or in sprigs, or twined into wreaths; parrots, too, and other birds of gay plumage, — often exquisitely done, and sometimes with precious materials, such as lapis lazuli, malachite, and still rarer gems.   Bracelets, with several different, yet relative designs, are often very beautiful.   We find, at different shops, a great inequality of prices for mosaics that seemed to be of much the same quality.

We went to the Uffizi gallery, and found it much thronged with the middle and lower classes of Italians; and the English, too, seemed more numerous than I have lately seen them. Perhaps the tourists have just arrived here, starting at the close of the London season.   We were amused with a pair of Englishmen who

went through the gallery; one of them criticis-
ing the pictures and statues audibly, for the benefit of his companion. The critic I should take
to be a country squire, and wholly untravelled;
a tall, well-built, rather rough, but gentlemanly
man enough; his friend, a small personage,
exquisitely neat in dress, and of artificial deportment, every attitude and· gesture appearing to
have been practised before a glass. Being but
a small pattern of a man, physically and intellectually, he had thought it worth while to finish
himself off with the elaborateness of a Florentine mosaic; and the result was something like
a dancing-master, though without the exuberant
embroidery of such persons. Indeed, he was a
very quiet little man, and, though so thoroughly
made up, there was something particularly green,
fresh, and simple in him. Both these Englishmen were elderly, and the smaller one had perfectly white hair, glossy and silken. It did not
make him in the least venerable, however, but
took his own character of neatness and prettiness. He carried his well-brushed and glossy
hat in his hand in such a way as not to ruffle its
surface; and I wish I could put into one word
or one sentence the prettiness, the minikin-fini-
cal effect of this little man; his self-consciousness
so lifelong, that, in some sort, he forgot himself
even in the midst of it; his propriety, his clean-
liness and unruffledness; his prettiness and

nicety of manifestation, like a bird hopping daintily about.

His companion, as I said, was of a completely different type ; a tall, gray-haired man, with the rough English face, a little tinted with port wine ; careless, natural manner, betokening a man of position in his own neighborhood ; a loud voice, not vulgar, nor outraging the rules of society, but betraying a character incapable of much refinement.   He talked continually in his pro-gress through the gallery, and audibly enough for us to catch almost everything he said, at many yards' distance.   His remarks and criti-cisms, addressed to his small friend, were so en-tertaining, that we strolled behind him for the sake of being benefited by them ; and I think he soon became aware of this, and addressed him-self to us as well as to his more immediate friend. Nobody but an Englishman, it seems to me, has just this kind of vanity, — a feeling mixed up with scorn and good nature ; self-complacency on his own merits, and as an Englishman ; pride at being in foreign parts ; contempt for every-body around him ; a rough kindliness towards people in general.   I liked the man, and should be glad to know him better.   As for his criti-cism, I am sorry to remember only one.   It was upon the picture of the Nativity, by Correggio, in the Tribune, where the mother is kneeling before the Child, and adoring it in an awful rapture, because she sees the eternal God in its baby face and figure.   The Englishman was highly delighted with this picture, and began to gesticulate, as if dandling a baby, and to make a chirruping sound.   It was to him merely a representation of a mother fondling her infant.   He then said, " If I could have my choice of the pictures and statues in the Tribune, I would take this picture, and that one yonder " (it was a good enough Enthronement of the Virgin, by Andrea del Sarto) "and the Dancing Faun, and let the rest go."   A delightful man ; I love that wholesome coarseness of mind and heart, which no education nor opportunity can polish out of the genuine Englishman, — a coarseness without vulgarity.   When a Yankee is coarse he is pretty sure to be vulgar too.

The two critics seemed to be considering whether it were practicable to go from the Uffizi to the Pitti gallery ; but " it confuses one," remarked the little man, "to see more than one gallery in a day."   (I should think so, — the Pitti Palace tumbling into his small receptacle on the top of the Uffizi.)   " It *does* so," responded the big man, with heavy emphasis.

September 23. — The vintage has been going on in our *podere* for about a week, and I saw a part of the process of making wine, under one of our back windows.   It was on a very small

231

scale, the grapes being thrown into a barrel, and crushed with a sort of pestle; and as each estate seems to make its own wine, there are probably no very extensive and elaborate appliances in general use for the manufacture. The cider-making of New England is far more picturesque; the great heap of golden or rosy apples under the trees, and the cider mill worked by a circumgyratory horse, and all agush with sweet juice. Indeed, nothing connected with the grape culture and the vintage here has been picturesque, except the large inverted pyramids in which the clusters hang; those great bunches, white or purple, really satisfy my idea both as to aspect and taste. We can buy a large basketful for less than a paul; and they are the only things that one can never devour too much of — and there is no enough short of a little too much — without subsequent repentance. It is a shame to turn such delicious juice into such sour wine as they make in Tuscany. I tasted a sip or two of a flask which the contadini sent us for trial, — the rich result of the process I had witnessed in the barrel. It took me altogether by surprise; for I remembered the nectareousness of the new cider, which I used to sip through a straw in my boyhood, and I never doubted that this would be as dulcet, but finer and more ethereal; as much more delectable, in short, as these grapes are better than puckery

cider apples. Positively, I never tasted anything so detestable, such a sour and bitter juice,
still lukewarm with fermentation; it was a wail
of woe, squeezed out of the wine-press of trib-
ulation, and the more a man drinks of such, the
sorrier he will be.

Besides grapes, we have had figs, and I have
now learned to be very fond of them. When
they first began to appear, two months ago, they
had scarcely any sweetness, and tasted very like
a decaying squash : this was an early variety,
with purple skins. There are many kinds of
figs, the best being green-skinned, growing yel-
lower as they ripen ; and the riper they are, the
more the sweetness within them intensifies, till
they resemble dried figs in everything, except
that they retain the fresh fruit flavor; rich, lus-
cious, yet not palling. We have had pears,
too, some of them very tolerable ; and peaches,
which look magnificently, as regards size and
downy blush, but have seldom much more taste
than a cucumber. A succession of fruits has
followed us, ever since our arrival in Florence :
first, and for a long time, abundance of cherries ; then apricots, which lasted many weeks,
till we were weary of them ; then plums, pears,
and finally figs, peaches, and grapes. Except
the figs and grapes, a New England summer
and autumn would give us better fruit than any
we have found in Italy.

Italy beats us, I think, in mosquitoes; they are horribly pungent little satanic particles. They possess strange intelligence, and exquisite acuteness of sight and smell, — prodigious audacity and courage to match it, insomuch that they venture on the most hazardous attacks, and get safe off. One of them flew into my mouth, the other night, and stung me far down in my throat; but luckily I coughed him up in halves. They are bigger than American mosquitoes; and if you crush them, after one of their feasts, it makes a terrific blood spot. It is a sort of suicide — at least, a shedding of one's own blood — to kill them; but it gratifies the old Adam to do it. It shocks me to feel how revengeful I am; but it is impossible not to impute a certain malice and intellectual venom to these diabolical insects. I wonder whether our health, at this season of the year, requires that we should be kept in a state of irritation, and so the mosquitoes are Nature's prophylactic remedy for some disease; or whether we are made for the mosquitoes, not they for us. It is possible, just possible, that the infinitesimal doses of poison which they infuse into us are a homœopathic safeguard against pestilence; but medicine never was administered in a more disagreeable way.

The moist atmosphere about the Arno, I suppose, produces these insects, and fills the

234

broad, ten-mile valley with them; and as we are just on the brim of the basin, they overflow into our windows.

September 25. — Una and I walked to town yesterday morning, and went to the Uffizi gallery. It is not a pleasant thought that we are so soon to give up this gallery, with little prospect (none or hardly any, on my part) of ever seeing it again. It interests me and all of us far more than the gallery of the Pitti Palace, wherefore I know not, for the latter is the richer of the two in admirable pictures. Perhaps it is the picturesque variety of the Uffizi — the combination of painting, sculpture, gems, and bronzes — that makes the charm. The Tribune, too, is the richest room in all the world; a heart that draws all hearts to it. The Dutch pictures, moreover, give a homely, human interest to the Uffizi; and I really think that the frequency of Andrea del Sarto's productions at the Pitti Palace — looking so very like masterpieces, yet lacking the soul of art and nature — have much to do with the weariness that comes from better acquaintance with the latter gallery. The splendor of the gilded and frescoed saloons is perhaps another bore; but, after all, my memory will often tread there as long as I live. What shall we do in America?

Speaking of Dutch pictures, I was much

struck yesterday, as frequently before, with a small picture by Teniers the elder. It seems to be a pawnbroker in the midst of his pledges; old earthen jugs, flasks, a brass kettle, old books, and a huge pile of worn-out and broken rubbish, which he is examining. These things are represented with vast fidelity, yet with bold and free touches, unlike the minute, microscopic work of other Dutch masters; and a wonderful picturesqueness is wrought out of these humble materials, and even the figure and head of the pawnbroker have a strange grandeur.

We spent no very long time at the Uffizi, and afterwards crossed the Ponte alle Grazie, and went to the convent of San Miniato, which stands on a hill outside of the Porta San Gallo. A paved pathway, along which stand crosses marking stations at which pilgrims are to kneel and pray, goes steeply to the hilltop, where, in the first place, is a smaller church and convent than those of San Miniato. The latter are seen at a short distance to the right, the convent being a large, square battlemented mass, adjoining which is the church, showing a front of aged white marble, streaked with black, and having an old stone tower behind. I have seen no other convent or monastery that so well corresponds with my idea of what such structures were. The sacred precincts are enclosed by a high wall, gray, ancient, and luxuriously ivy-grown, and lofty and strong enough for the rampart of a fortress. We went through the gateway and entered the church, which we found in much disarray, and masons at work upon the pavement. The tribune is elevated considerably above the nave, and accessible by marble staircases; there are great arches and a chapel, with curious monuments in the Gothic style, and ancient carvings and mosaic works, and, in short, a dim, dusty, and venerable interior, well worth studying in detail. . . . The view of Florence from the church door is very fine, and seems to include every tower, dome, or whatever object emerges out of the general mass.

September 28. — I went to the Pitti Palace yesterday, and the Uffizi to-day, paying them probably my last visit, yet cherishing an unreasonable doubt whether I may not see them again. At all events, I have seen them enough for the present, even what is best of them; and, at the same time, with a sad reluctance to bid them farewell forever, I experience an utter weariness of Raphael's old canvas, and of the time-yellowed marble of the Venus di Medici. When the material embodiment presents itself outermost, and we perceive them only by the grosser sense, missing their ethereal spirit, there is nothing so heavily burdensome as masterpieces of painting and sculpture. I threw my farewell glance at the Venus di Medici to-day with strange insensibility.

The nights are wonderfully beautiful now. When the moon was at the full, a few nights ago, its light was an absolute glory, such as I seem only to have dreamed of heretofore, and that only in my younger days.   At its rising I have fancied that the orb of the moon has a kind of purple brightness, and that this tinge is communicated to its radiance until it has climbed high aloft and sheds a flood of white over hill and valley. Now that the moon is on the wane, there is a gentler lustre, but still bright ; and it makes the Val d'Arno with its surrounding hills, and its soft mist in the distance, as beautiful a scene as exists anywhere out of heaven. And the morning is quite as beautiful in its own way. This mist, of which I have so often spoken, sets it beyond the limits of actual sense and makes it ideal ; it is as if you were dreaming about the valley, — as if the valley itself were dreaming, and met you halfway in your own dream. If the mist were to be withdrawn I believe the whole beauty of the valley would go with it.

Until pretty late in the morning we have the comet streaming through the sky, and dragging its interminable tail among the stars.   It keeps brightening from night to night, and I should think must blaze fiercely enough to cast a

The Pitti Gardens, Florence

shadow by and by. I know not whether it be
in the vicinity of Galileo's tower, and in the influence of his spirit, but I have hardly ever
watched the stars with such interest as now.

September 29. — Last evening I met Mr.
Powers at Miss Blagden's and he talked about
his treatment by our government in reference
to an appropriation of twenty-five thousand
dollars made by Congress for a statue by him.
Its payment and the purchase of the statue were
left at the option of the President, and he conceived himself wronged because the affair was
never concluded. . . . As for the President, he
knows nothing of art, and probably acted in the
matter by the advice of the director of public
works. No doubt a sculptor gets commissions as
everybody gets public employment and emolu-
ment of whatever kind from our government,
not by merit of fitness, but by political influence
skilfully applied. As Powers himself observed,
the ruins of our Capitol are not likely to afford
sculptures equal to those which Lord Elgin took
from the Parthenon, if this be the system under
which they are produced. . . . I wish our great
Republic had the spirit to do as much, according to its vast means, as Florence did for sculpture and architecture when it was a republic ;
but we have the meanest government and the
shabbiest, and — if truly represented by it —

we are the meanest and shabbiest people known in history. And yet the less we attempt to do for art the better, if our future attempts are to have no better result than such brazen troopers as the equestrian statue of General Jackson, or even such naked respectabilities as Greenough's Washington. There is something false and affected in our highest taste for art; and I suppose, furthermore, we are the only people who seek to decorate their public institutions, not by the highest taste among them, but by the average at best.

There was also at Miss Blagden's, among other company, Mr. ——, an artist in Florence, and a sensible man. I talked with him about Home, the medium, whom he had many opportunities of observing when the latter was in these parts. Mr. —— says that Home is unquestionably a knave, but that he himself is as much perplexed at his own preternatural performances as any other person; he is startled and affrighted at the phenomena which he produces. Nevertheless, when his spiritual powers fall short, he does his best to eke them out with imposture. This moral infirmity is a part of his nature, and I suggested that perhaps if he were of a firmer and healthier moral make, if his character were sufficiently sound and dense to be capable of steadfast principle, he would not have possessed the impressibility that fits him for the

so-called spiritual influences.   Mr. —— says
that Louis Napoleon is literally one of the
most skilful jugglers in the world, and that
probably the interest he has taken in Mr.
Home was caused partly by a wish to acquire
his art.

This morning Mr. Powers invited me to go
with him to the Grand Duke's new foundry, to
see the bronze statue of Webster, which has
just been cast from his model.   It is the second
cast of the statue, the first having been shipped
some months ago on board of a vessel which
was lost; and, as Powers observed, the statue
now lies at the bottom of the Atlantic Ocean
somewhere in the vicinity of the telegraphic
cable.

We were received with much courtesy and
emphasis by the director of the foundry, and
conducted into a large room walled with bare,
new brick, where the statue was standing in
front of the extinct furnace : a majestic Webster
indeed, eight feet high, and looking even more
colossal than that.   The likeness seemed to me
perfect, and, like a sensible man, Powers has
dressed him in his natural costume, such as I
have seen Webster have on while making a
speech in the open air at a mass meeting in
Concord, — dress-coat buttoned pretty closely
across the breast, pantaloons and boots, —
everything finished even to a seam and a stitch.

Not an inch of the statue but is Webster; even his coat-tails are imbued with the man, and this true artist has succeeded in showing him through the broadcloth as nature showed him. He has felt that a man's actual clothes are as much a part of him as his flesh, and I respect him for disdaining to shirk the difficulty by throwing the meanness of a cloak over it, and for recognizing the folly of masquerading our Yankee statesman in a Roman toga, and the indecorousness of presenting him as a brassy nudity. It would have been quite as unjustifiable to strip him to his skeleton as to his flesh. Webster is represented as holding in his right hand the written roll of the Constitution, with which he points to a bundle of fasces, which he keeps from falling by the grasp of his left, thus symbolizing him as the preserver of the Union. There is an expression of quiet, solid, massive strength in the whole figure; a deep pervading energy, in which any exaggeration of gesture would lessen and lower the effect. He looks really like a pillar of the state. The face is very grand, very Webster; stern and awful, because he is in the act of meeting a great crisis, and yet with the warmth of a great heart glowing through it. Happy is Webster to have been so truly and adequately sculptured; happy the sculptor in such a subject, which no idealization of a demigod could have supplied him with.   Perhaps the statue at the bottom of the sea will be cast up in some future age, when the present race of man is forgotten, and if so, that far posterity will look up to us as a grander race than we find ourselves to be.   Neither was Webster altogether the man he looked.   His physique helped him out, even when he fell somewhat short of its promise ; and if his eyes had not been in such deep caverns their fire would not have looked so bright.

Powers made me observe how the surface of the statue was wrought to a sort of roughness instead of being smoothed, as is the practice of other artists.   He said that this had cost him great pains, and certainly it has an excellent effect.   The statue is to go to Boston, and I hope will be placed in the open air, for it is too mighty to be kept under any roof that now exists in America. . . .

After seeing this, the director showed us some very curious and exquisite specimens of castings, such as baskets of flowers, in which the most delicate and fragile blossoms, the curl of a petal, the finest veins in a leaf, the lightest flower spray that ever quivered in a breeze, were perfectly preserved; and the basket contained an abundant heap of such sprays.   There were likewise a pair of hands, taken actually from life, clasped together as they were, and they looked like parts of a man who had been changed suddenly from flesh to brass.   They were worn and rough and unhandsome hands, and so very real, with all their veins and the pores of the skin, that it was shocking to look at them.   A bronze leaf, cast also from the life, was as curious and more beautiful.

Taking leave of Powers, I went hither and thither about Florence, seeing for the last time things that I have seen many times before : the market, for instance, blocking up a line of narrow streets with fruit stalls, and obstreperous dealers crying their peaches, their green lemons, their figs, their delicious grapes, their mushrooms, their pomegranates, their radishes, their lettuces. They use one vegetable here which I have not known so used elsewhere : that is, very young pumpkins or squashes, of the size of apples, and to be cooked by boiling.   They are not to my taste, but the people here like unripe things, — unripe fruit, unripe chickens, unripe lamb. This market is the noisiest and swarmiest centre of noisy and swarming Florence, and I always like to pass through it on that account.

I went also to Santa Croce, and it seemed to me to present a longer vista and broader space than almost any other church, perhaps because the pillars between the nave and aisles are not so massive as to obstruct the view.   I looked into the Duomo, too, and was pretty well content to leave it.   Then I came homeward, and lost my way, and wandered far off through the white sunshine, and the scanty shade of the vineyard walls, and the olive-trees that here and there branched over them. At last I saw our own gray battlements at a distance on one side, quite out of the direction in which I was travelling, so was compelled to the grievous mortification of retracing a great many of my weary footsteps. It was a very hot day. This evening I have been on the tower top, star-gazing, and looking at the comet, which waves along the sky like an immense feather of flame. Over Florence there was an illuminated atmosphere, caused by the lights of the city gleaming upward into the mists which sleep and dream above that portion of the valley, as well as the rest of it. I saw dimly, or fancied I saw, the hill of Fiesole on the other side of Florence, and remembered how ghostly lights were seen passing thence to the Duomo on the night when Lorenzo the Magnificent died. From time to time the sweet bells of Florence rang out, and I was loath to come down into the lower world, knowing that I shall never again look heavenward from an old tower top in such a soft calm evening as this. Yet I am not loath to go away; impatient rather; for, taking no root, I soon weary of any soil in which I may be temporarily deposited. The same impatience I sometimes feel or conceive of as regards this earthly life. . . .

I forgot to mention that Powers showed me, in his studio, the model of the statue of America, which he wished the government to buy. It has great merit, and embodies the ideal of youth, freedom, progress, and whatever we consider as distinctive of our country's character and destiny. It is a female figure, vigorous, beautiful, planting its foot lightly on a broken chain, and pointing upward. The face has a high look of intelligence and lofty feeling; the form, nude to the middle, has all the charms of womanhood, and is thus warmed and redeemed out of the cold allegoric sisterhood who have generally no merit in chastity, being really without sex. I somewhat question whether it is quite the thing, however, to make a genuine woman out of an allegory: we ask, Who is to wed this lovely virgin? and we are not satisfied to banish her into the realm of chilly thought. But I liked the statue, and all the better for what I criticise, and was sorry to see the huge package in which the finished marble lies bundled up, ready to be sent to our country, — which does not call for it.

Mr. Powers and his two daughters called to take leave of us, and at parting I expressed a hope of seeing him in America. He said that it would make him very unhappy to believe that

he should never return thither; but it seems to
me that he has no such definite purpose of return as would be certain to bring itself to pass.
It makes a very unsatisfactory life, thus to spend
the greater part of it in exile.   In such a case we
are always deferring the reality of life till a future
moment, and, by and by, we have deferred it
till there are no future moments; or, if we do
go back, we find that life has shifted whatever
of reality it had to the country where we deemed
ourselves only living temporarily; and so between two stools we come to the ground, and
make ourselves a part of one or the other country only by laying our bones in its soil.   It is
particularly a pity in Powers's case, because he
is so very American in character, and the only
convenience for him of his Italian residence is,
that here he can supply himself with marble,
and with workmen to chisel it according to his
designs.

SIENA, *October* 2. — Yesterday morning, at six
o'clock, we left our ancient tower, and threw a
parting glance — and a rather sad one — over
the misty Val d' Arno. This summer will look
like a happy one in our children's retrospect,
and also, no doubt, in the years that remain to
ourselves; and, in truth, I have found it a peaceful and not uncheerful one.

It was not a pleasant morning, and Monte

Morello, looking down on Florence, had on its cap, betokening foul weather, according to the proverb. Crossing the suspension bridge, we reached the Leopoldo railway without entering the city. By some mistake, — or perhaps because nobody ever travels by first-class carriages in Tuscany, — we found we had received second-class tickets, and were put into a long, crowded carriage, full of priests, military men, commercial travellers, and other respectable people, facing one another lengthwise along the carriage, and many of them smoking cigars. They were all perfectly civil, and I think I must own that the manners of this second-class would compare favorably with those of an American first-class one.

At Empoli, about an hour after we started, we had to change carriages, the main train proceeding to Leghorn. . . . My observations along the road were very scanty : a hilly country, with several old towns seated on the most elevated hilltops, as is common throughout Tuscany, or sometimes a fortress with a town on the plain at its base ; or, once or twice, the towers and battlements of a mediæval castle, commanding the pass below it. Near Florence the country was fertile in the vine and olive, and looked as unpicturesque as that sort of fertility usually makes it ; not but what I have come to think better of the tint of the olive leaf

than when I first saw it.   In the latter part of
our journey I remember a wild stream, of a
greenish hue, but transparent, rushing along
over a rough bed, and before reaching Siena we
rumbled into a long tunnel, and emerged from
it near the city. . . .

We drove up hill and down (for the surface
of Siena seems to be nothing but an irregularity)
through narrow old streets, and were set down
at the Aquila Neva, a grim-looking albergo near
the centre of the town.   Mrs. S—— had already taken rooms for us there, and to these
we were now ushered up the highway of a dingy
stone staircase, and into a small, brick-paved
parlor.   The house seemed endlessly old, and
all the glimpses that we caught of Siena out of
window seemed more ancient still.   Almost
within arm's reach, across a narrow street, a tall
palace of gray, time-worn stone clambered sky-
ward, with arched windows, and square windows,
and large windows and small, scattered up and
down its side.   It is the Palazzo Tolomei, and
looks immensely venerable.   From the windows of our bedrooms we looked into a broader
street, though still not very wide, and into a
small piazza, the most conspicuous object in
which was a column, bearing on its top a bronze
wolf suckling Romulus and Remus.   This symbol is repeated in other parts of the city, and
seems to indicate that the Sienese people pride

themselves in a Roman origin. In another direction, over the tops of the houses, we saw a very high tower, with battlements projecting around its summit, so that it was a fortress in the air ; and this I have since found to be the Palazzo Publico. It was pleasant, looking downward into the little old piazza and narrow streets, to see the swarm of life on the pavement, the life of to-day, just as new as if it had never been lived before ; the citizens, the priests, the soldiers, the mules and asses with their panniers, the diligence lumbering along, with a postilion in a faded crimson coat bobbing up and down on the off horse. Such a bustling scene, vociferous, too, with various street cries, is wonderfully set off by the gray antiquity of the town, and makes the town look older than if it were a solitude.

Soon Mr. and Mrs. Story came, and accompanied us to look for lodgings. They also drove us about the city in their carriage, and showed us the outside of the Palazzo Publico, and of the Cathedral, and other remarkable edifices. The aspect of Siena is far more picturesque than that of any other town in Italy, so far as I know Italian towns ; and yet, now that I have written it, I remember Perugia, and feel that the observation is a mistake. But at any rate Siena is remarkably picturesque, standing on such a site, on the verge and within the

crater of an extinct volcano, and therefore being as uneven as the sea in a tempest; the
streets so narrow, ascending between tall, ancient palaces, while the side streets rush headlong down, only to be threaded by sure-footed
mules, such as climb Alpine heights; old stone
balconies on the palace fronts; old arched doorways, and windows set in frames of Gothic
architecture; arcades, resembling canopies of
stone, with quaintly sculptured statues in the
richly wrought Gothic niches of each pillar, —
everything massive and lofty, yet minutely interesting when you look at it stone by stone.
The Florentines, and the Romans too, have
obliterated, as far as they could, all the interest
of their mediæval structures by covering them
with stucco, so that they have quite lost their
character, and affect the spectator with no rever-
ential idea of age. Here the city is all over-
written with black-letter, and the glad Italian
sun makes the effect so much the stronger.

We took a lodging, and afterwards Julian
and I rambled about, and went into the Cathedral for a moment, and strayed also into the
Piazza del Campo, the great public square of
Siena. I am not in the mood for further description of public places now, so shall say a
word or two about the old palace in which we
have established ourselves. We have the second piano, and dwell amid faded grandeur,

having for our saloon what seems to have been a ballroom. It is ornamented with a great fresco in the centre of the vaulted ceiling, and others covering the sides of the apartment, and surrounded with arabesque frameworks, where Cupids gambol and chase one another. The subjects of the frescos I cannot make out, not that they are faded like Giotto's, for they are as fresh as roses, and are done in an exceedingly workmanlike style; but they are allegories of Fame and Plenty and other matters, such as I could never understand. Our whole accommodation is in similar style, — spacious, magnificent, and mouldy.

In the evening Miss S—— and I drove to the railway, and on the arrival of the train from Florence we watched with much eagerness the unlading of the luggage van. At last the whole of our ten trunks and tin bandbox were produced, and finally my leather bag, in which was my journal and a manuscript book containing my sketch of a romance. It gladdened my very heart to see it, and I shall think the better of Tuscan promptitude and accuracy for so quickly bringing it back to me. (It was left behind, under one of the rail carriage seats.) We find all the public officials, whether of railway, police, or custom house, extremely courteous and pleasant to encounter ; they seem willing to take trouble and reluctant to give it, and

it is really a gratification to find that such civil
people will sometimes oblige you by taking a
paul or two aside.

October 3. — I took several strolls about the
city yesterday, and find it scarcely extensive
enough to get lost in; and if we go far from
the centre we soon come to silent streets, with
only here and there an individual ; and the inhabitants stare from their doors and windows at
the stranger, and turn round to look at him
after he has passed. The interest of the old
town would soon be exhausted for the traveller,
but I can conceive that a thoughtful and shy
man might settle down here with the view of
making the place a home, and spend many
years in a sombre kind of happiness. I should
prefer it to Florence as a residence, but it would
be terrible without an independent life in one's
own mind.

Una and I walked out in the afternoon, and
went into the Piazza del Campo, the principal
place of the city, and a very noble and peculiar
one. It is much in the form of an amphitheatre, and the surface of the ground seems to be
slightly scooped out, so that it resembles the
shallow basin of a shell. It is thus a much
better site for an assemblage of the populace
than if it were a perfect level. A semicircle or
truncated ellipse of stately and ancient edifices

surround the piazza, with arches opening beneath them through which streets converge hitherward. One side of the piazza is a straight line, and is occupied by the Palazzo Publico, which is a most noble and impressive Gothic structure. It has not the mass of the Palazzo Vecchio at Florence, but is more striking. It has a long battlemented front, the central part of which rises eminent above the rest, in a great square bulk, which is likewise crowned with battlements. This is much more picturesque than the one great block of stone into which the Palazzo Vecchio is consolidated. At one extremity of this long front of the Palazzo Publico rises a tower, shooting up its shaft high, high into the air, and bulging out there into a battlemented fortress, within which the tower, slenderer than before, climbs to a still higher region. I do not know whether the summit of the tower is higher or so high as that of the Palazzo Vecchio ; but the length of the shaft, free of the edifice, is much greater, and so produces the more elevating effect. The whole front of the Palazzo Publico is exceedingly venerable, with arched windows, Gothic carvings, and all the old-time ornaments that betoken it to have stood a great while, and the gray strength that will hold it up at least as much longer. At one end of the façade, beneath the shadow of the tower, is a grand and beautiful

porch, supported on square pillars, within each
of which is a niche containing a statue of mediæval sculpture.

The great Piazza del Campo is the market-
place of Siena. In the morning it was thronged
with booths and stalls, especially of fruit and
vegetable dealers; but as in Florence, they
melted away in the sunshine, gradually withdrawing themselves into the shadow thrown
from the Palazzo Publico.

On the side opposite the palace is an antique
fountain of marble, ornamented with two statues and a series of bas-reliefs; and it was so
much admired in its day that its sculptor received the name " Del Fonte." I am loath to
leave the piazza and palace without finding some
word or two to suggest their antique majesty,
in the sunshine and the shadow; and how fit
it seemed, notwithstanding their venerableness,
that there should be a busy crowd filling up the
great, hollow amphitheatre, and crying their
fruit and little merchandises, so that all the
curved line of stately old edifices helped to re-
verberate the noise. The life of to-day, within
the shell of a time past, is wonderfully fascinat-
ing.

Another point to which a stranger's footsteps
are drawn by a kind of magnetism, so that he
will be apt to find himself there as often as he
strolls out of his hotel, is the Cathedral. It

255

stands in the highest part of the city, and almost every street runs into some other street which meanders hitherward. On our way thither, Una and I came to a beautiful front of black and white marble, in somewhat the same style as the Cathedral ; in fact, it was the baptistery, and should have made a part of it, according to the original design, which contemplated a structure of vastly greater extent than this actual one. We entered the baptistery, and found the interior small, but very rich in its clustered columns and intersecting arches, and its frescos, pictures, statues, and ornaments. Moreover, a father and mother had brought their baby to be baptized, and the poor little thing, in its gay swaddling-clothes, looked just like what I have seen in old pictures, and a good deal like an Indian pappoose. It gave one little slender squeak when the priest put the water on its forehead, and then was quiet again.

We now went round to the façade of the Cathedral. . . . It is of black and white marble, with, I believe, an intermixture of red and other colors ; but time has toned them down, so that white, black, and red do not contrast so strongly with one another as they may have done five hundred years ago. The architecture is generally of the pointed Gothic style, but there are likewise carved arches over the doors and windows, and a variety which does not produce the effect of confusion, — a magnificent eccentricity, an exuberant imagination flowering out in stone. On high, in the great peak of the front, and throwing its colored radiance into the nave within, there is a round window of immense circumference, the painted figures in which we can see dimly from the outside. But what I wish to express, and never can, is the multitudinous richness of the ornamentation of the front; the arches within arches, sculptured inch by inch, of the deep doorways; the statues of saints, some making a hermitage of a niche, others standing forth; the scores of busts, that look like faces of ancient people gazing down out of the Cathedral; the projecting shapes of stone lions, — the thousand forms of Gothic fancy, which seemed to soften the marble and express whatever it liked, and allow it to harden again to last forever. But my description seems like knocking off the noses of some of the busts, the fingers and toes of the statues, the projecting points of the architecture, jumbling them all up together, and flinging them down upon the page. This gives no idea of the truth, nor, least of all, can it shadow forth that solemn whole, mightily combined out of all these minute particulars, and sanctifying the entire space of ground over which this cathedral front flings its shadow, or on which it reflects the sun. A majesty and a minuteness, neither interfering with the other, each assisting the other; this is what I love in Gothic architecture. We went in and walked about; but I mean to go again before sketching the interior in my poor water colors.

October 4. — On looking again at the Palazzo Publico, I see that the pillared portal, which I have spoken of, does not cover an entrance to the palace, but is a chapel, with an altar, and frescos above it.   Bouquets of fresh flowers are on the altar, and a lamp burns, in all the daylight, before the crucifix.   The chapel is quite unenclosed, except by an open-work balustrade of marble, on which the carving looks very ancient.   Nothing could be more convenient for the devotions of the crowd in the piazza, and no doubt the daily prayers offered at the shrine might be numbered by the thousand, — brief, but I hope earnest, — like those glimpses I used to catch at the blue sky, revealing so much in an instant, while I was toiling at Brook Farm.   Another picturesque thing about the Palazzo Publico is a great stone balcony, quaintly wrought, about midway in the front and high aloft, with two arched windows opening into it.

After another glimpse at the Cathedral, too, I realize how utterly I have failed in conveying the idea of its elaborate ornament, its twisted and clustered pillars, and numberless devices of sculpture; nor did I mention the venerable statues that stand all round the summit of the edifice, relieved against the sky,—the highest of all being one of the Saviour, on the top-most peak of the front; nor the tall tower that ascends from one side of the building, and is built of layers of black and white marble piled one upon another in regular succession; nor the dome that swells upward close beside this tower.

Had the Cathedral been constructed on the plan and dimensions at first contemplated, it would have been incomparably majestic; the finished portion, grand as it is, being only what was intended for a transept. One of the walls of what was to have been the nave is still stand-ing, and looks like a ruin, though, I believe, it has been turned to account as the wall of a palace, the space of the never-completed nave being now a court or street.

The whole family of us were kindly taken out yesterday, to dine and spend the day at the Villa Belvidere with our friends Mr. and Mrs. Story. The vicinity of Siena is much more agreeable than that of Florence, being cooler, breezier, with more foliage and shrubbery both near at hand and in the distance; and the pros-pect, Mr. Story told us, embraces a diameter of about a hundred miles between hills north and south. The Villa Belvidere was built and owned by an Englishman now deceased, who has left it to his butler, and its lawns and shrubbery have something English in their character, and there was almost a dampness in the grass, which really pleased me in this parched Italy. Within the house the walls are hung with fine old-fashioned engravings from the pictures of Gainsborough, West, and other English painters. The Englishman, though he had chosen to live and die in Italy, had evidently brought his native tastes and peculiarities along with him. Mr. Story thinks of buying this villa: I do not know but I might be tempted to buy it myself if Siena were a practicable residence for the entire year; but the winter here, with the bleak mountain winds of a hundred miles round about blustering against it, must be terribly disagreeable.

We spent a very pleasant day, turning over books or talking on the lawn, whence we could behold scenes picturesque afar, and rich vineyard glimpses near at hand. Mr. Story is the most variously accomplished and brilliant person, the fullest of social life and fire, whom I have ever met; and without seeming to make an effort, he kept us amused and entertained the whole day long; not wearisomely entertained neither, as we should have been if he had not let his fountain play naturally. Still, though he bubbled and brimmed over with fun, he left the impression on me that . . . there is a pain and care, bred, it may be, out of the very richness of his gifts and abundance of his outward prosperity.   Rich, in the prime of life, . . . and children budding and blossoming around him as fairly as his heart could wish, with sparkling talents, — so many, that if he choose to neglect or fling away one, or two, or three, he would still have enough left to shine with, — who should be happy if not he? . . .

Towards sunset we all walked out into the *podere*, pausing a little while to look down into a well that stands on the verge of the lawn. Within the spacious circle of its stone curb was an abundant growth of maidenhair, forming a perfect wreath of thickly clustering leaves quite round, and trailing its tendrils downward to the water, which gleamed beneath.   It was a very pretty sight.   Mr. Story bent over the well and uttered deep, musical tones, which were reverberated from the hollow depths with wonderful effect, as if a spirit dwelt within there, and (unlike the spirits that speak through mediums) sent him back responses even profounder and more melodious than the tones that awakened them.   Such a responsive well as this might have been taken for an oracle in old days.

We went along paths that led from one vineyard to another, and which might have led us for miles across the country. The grapes had been partly gathered, but still there were many purple or white clusters hanging heavily on the vines. We passed cottage doors, and saw groups of contadini and contadine in their festal attire, and they saluted us graciously ; but it was observable that one of the men generally lingered on our track to see that no grapes were stolen, for there were a great many young people and children in our train, not only our own, but some from a neighboring villa. These Italian peasants are a kindly race, but, I doubt, not very hospitable of grape or fig.

There was a beautiful sunset, and by the time we reached the house again the comet was already visible amid the unextinguished glow of daylight. A Mr. and Mrs. B——, Scotch people from the next villa, had come to see the Storys, and we sat till tea-time reading, talking, William Story drawing caricatures for his children's amusement and ours, and all of us sometimes getting up to look at the comet, which blazed brighter and brighter till it went down into the mists of the horizon. Among the caricatures was one of a Presidential candidate, evidently a man of very malleable principles, and likely to succeed.

Late in the evening (too late for little Rosebud), we drove homeward. The streets of old Siena looked very grim at night, and it seemed like gazing into caverns to glimpse down some of the side streets as we passed, with a light burning dimly at the end of them. It was after ten when we reached home, and climbed up our gloomy staircase, lighted by the glimmer of some wax *moccoli* which I had in my pocket.

October 5. — I have been two or three times into the Cathedral; . . . the whole interior is of marble, in alternate lines of black and white, each layer being about eight inches in width and extending horizontally. It looks very curiously, and might remind the spectator of a stuff with horizontal stripes. Nevertheless, the effect is exceedingly rich, these alternate lines stretching away along the walls and round the clustered pillars, seen aloft, and through the arches ; everywhere, this inlay of black and white. Every sort of ornament that could be thought of seems to have been crammed into the Cathedral in one place or another : gilding, frescos, pictures ; a roof of blue, spangled with golden stars ; a magnificent wheel window of old painted glass over the entrance, and another at the opposite end of the Cathedral ; statues, some of marble, others of gilded bronze ; pulpits of carved marble ; a gilded organ ; a cornice of marble busts of the popes, extending round the entire church ; a pavement, covered all over with a strange kind of mosaic-work in various

263

marbles, wrought into marble pictures of sacred
subjects ; immense clustered pillars supporting
the round arches that divide the nave from
the side aisles ; a clere-story of windows within
pointed arches, — it seemed as if the spectator
were reading an antique volume written in black-
letter of a small character, but conveying a high
and solemn meaning. I can find no way of
expressing its effect on me, so quaint and venerable as I feel this cathedral to be in its im-
mensity of striped waistcoat, now dingy with five
centuries of wear. I ought not to say anything
that might detract from the grandeur and sanctity of the blessed edifice, for these attributes
are really uninjured by any of the Gothic oddi-
ties which I have hinted at.

We went this morning to the Institute of the
Fine Arts, which is interesting as containing a
series of the works of the Sienese painters from
a date earlier than that of Cimabue. There is a
dispute, I believe, between Florence and Siena
as to which city may claim the credit of having
originated the modern art of painting. The Florentines put forward Cimabue as the first artist,
but as the Sienese produce a picture, by Guido
da Siena, dated before the birth of Cimabue, the
victory is decidedly with them. As to pictorial
merit, to my taste there is none in either of these
old painters, nor in any of their successors for a
long time afterwards. At the Institute there are

several rooms hung with early productions of
the Sienese school, painted before the invention
of oil colors, on wood shaped into Gothic altar-
pieces. The backgrounds still retain a be-
dimmed splendor of gilding. There is a plentiful use of red, and I can conceive that the
pictures must have shed an illumination through
the churches where they were displayed. There
is often, too, a minute care bestowed on the
faces in the pictures, and sometimes a very
strong expression, stronger than modern artists
get, and it is very strange how they attained this
merit while they were so inconceivably rude
in other respects. It is remarkable that all the
early faces of the Madonna are especially stupid,
and all of the same type, a sort of face such as
one might carve on a pumpkin, representing a
heavy, sulky, phlegmatic woman, with a long
and low arch of the nose. This same dull face
continues to be assigned to the Madonna, even
when the countenances of the surrounding saints
and angels are characterized with power and
beauty, so that I think there must have been
some portrait of this sacred personage reckoned
authentic, which the early painters followed and
religiously repeated.

At last we came to a picture by Sodoma, the
most illustrious representative of the Sienese
school. It was a fresco; Christ bound to the
pillar, after having been scourged. I do believe

that painting has never done anything better, so far as expression is concerned, than this figure. In all these generations since it was painted it must have softened thousands of hearts, drawn down rivers of tears, been more effectual than a million of sermons.   Really, it is a thing to stand and weep at. No other painter has done anything that can deserve to be compared to this.

There are some other pictures by Sodoma, among them a Judith, very noble and admirable, and full of a profound sorrow for the deed which she has felt it her mission to do.

AQUILA NERA, *October* 7. — Our lodgings in Siena had been taken only for five days, as they were already engaged after that period; so yesterday we returned to our old quarters at the Black Eagle.

In the forenoon Julian and I went out of one of the gates (the road from it leads to Florence) and had a pleasant country walk. Our way wound downward, round the hill on which Siena stands, and gave us views of the Duomo and its campanile, seemingly pretty near, after we had walked long enough to be quite remote from them. Sitting awhile on the parapet of a bridge, I saw a laborer chopping the branches off a poplar-tree which he had felled; and, when it was trimmed, he took up the large trunk on

one of his shoulders and carried it off, seemingly
with ease.   He did not look like a particularly
robust man; but I have never seen such an
herculean feat attempted by an Englishman or
American.   It has frequently struck me that the
Italians are able to put forth a great deal of
strength in such insulated efforts as this ; but
I have been told that they are less capable of
continued endurance and hardship than our own
race.   I do not know why it should be so, except that I presume their food is less strong
than ours.   There was no other remarkable incident in our walk, which lay chiefly through
gorges of the hills, winding beneath high cliffs
of the brown Siena earth, with many pretty
scenes of rural landscape ; vineyards everywhere,
and olive-trees; a mill on its little stream, over
which there was an old stone bridge, with a
graceful arch ; farmhouses ; a villa or two ; subterranean passages, passing from the roadside
through the high banks into the vineyards. At
last we turned aside into a road which led us
pretty directly to another gate of the city, and
climbed steeply upward among tanneries, where
the young men went about with their well-shaped
legs bare, their trousers being tucked up till they
were strictly breeches and nothing else.   The
campanile stood high above us ; and by and by,
and very soon, indeed, the steep ascent of the
street brought us into the neighborhood of the

Piazza del Campo, and of our own hotel. . . .
From about twelve o'clock till one, I sat at my
chamber window watching the specimens of
human life as displayed in the Piazza Tolomei.
[Here follow several pages of moving objects.]
. . . Of course, a multitude of other people
passed by, but the curiousness of the catalogue
is the prevalence of the martial and religious ele-
ments. The general costume of the inhabitants
is frocks or sacks, loosely made, and rather
shabby; often, shirt-sleeves; or the coat hung
over one shoulder. They wear felt hats and
straw. People of respectability seem to prefer
cylinder hats, either black or drab, and broadcloth frock-coats in the French fashion; but, like
the rest, they look a little shabby. Almost all
the women wear shawls. Ladies in swelling petticoats, and with fans, some of which are highly
gilded, appear. The people generally are not
tall, but have a sufficient breadth of shoulder;
in complexion, similar to Americans; bearded,
universally. The vehicle used for driving is a
little gig without a top; but these are seldom
seen, and still less frequently a cab or other
carriages. The gait of the people has not the
energy of business or decided purpose. Everybody appears to lounge, and to have time for
a moment's chat, and a disposition to rest, reason or none.

   After dinner I walked out of another gate of

the city, and wandered among some pleasant country lanes, bordered with hedges, and wearing an English aspect; at least, I could fancy so. The vicinity of Siena is delightful to walk about in; there being a verdant outlook, a wide prospect of purple mountains, though no such level valley as the Val d' Arno; and the city stands so high that its towers and domes are seen more picturesquely from many points than those of Florence can be. Neither is the pedestrian so cruelly shut into narrow lanes, between high stone walls, over which he cannot get a glimpse of landscape. As I walked by the hedges yesterday, I could have fancied that the olive trunks were those of apple-trees, and that I were in one or other of the two lands that I love better than Italy. But the great white villas and the farmhouses were unlike anything I have seen elsewhere, or that I should wish to see again, though proper enough to Italy.

October 9. — Thursday forenoon, 8th, we went to see the Palazzo Publico. There are some fine old halls and chapels, adorned with ancient frescos and pictures, of which I remember a picture of the Virgin by Sodoma, very beautiful, and other fine pictures by the same master. The architecture of these old rooms is grand, the roofs being supported by ponderous arches, which are covered with frescos, still

magnificent, though faded, darkened, and defaced. We likewise saw an antique casket of
wood, enriched with gilding, which had once
contained an arm of John the Baptist, — so the
custode told us. One of the halls was hung
with the portraits of eight popes and nearly
forty cardinals, who were natives of Siena. I
have done hardly any other sight-seeing except
a daily visit to the Cathedral, which I admire
and love the more the oftener I go thither. Its
striped peculiarity ceases entirely to interfere
with the grandeur and venerable beauty of its
impression; and I am never weary of gazing
through the vista of its arches, and noting continually something that I had not seen before
in its exuberant adornment. The pavement
alone is inexhaustible, being covered all over
with figures of life-size or larger, which look like
immense engravings of Gothic or Scriptural
scenes. There is Absalom hanging by his hair,
and Joab slaying him with a spear. There is
Samson belaboring the Philistines with the jaw-
bone of an ass. There are armed knights in the
tumult of battle, all wrought with wonderful
expression. The figures are in white marble,
inlaid with darker stone, and the shading is
effected by means of engraved lines in the marble, filled in with black. It would be possible,
perhaps, to print impressions from some of these
vast plates, for the process of cutting the lines

was an exact anticipation of the modern art of engraving. However, the same thing was done — and I suppose at about the same period — on monumental brasses, and I have seen impressions or rubbings from those for sale in the old English churches.

Yesterday morning, in the Cathedral, I watched a woman at confession, being curious to see how long it would take her to tell her sins, the growth of a week perhaps. I know not how long she had been confessing when I first observed her, but nearly an hour passed before the priest came suddenly from the confessional, looking weary and moist with perspiration, and took his way out of the Cathedral. The woman was left on her knees. This morning I watched another woman, and she too was very long about it, and I could see the face of the priest behind the curtain of the confessional, scarcely inclining his ear to the perforated tin through which the penitent communicated her outpourings. It must be very tedious to listen, day after day, to the minute and commonplace iniquities of the multitude of penitents, and it cannot be often that these are redeemed by the treasure-trove of a great sin. When her confession was over the woman came and sat down on the same bench with me, where her broad-brimmed straw hat was lying. She seemed to be a country woman, with a simple, matronly face, which was solemnized and softened with the comfort that she had obtained by disburdening herself of the soil of worldly frailties and receiving absolution. An old woman, who haunts the Cathedral, whispered to her, and she went and knelt down where a procession of priests were to pass, and then the old lady begged a crazia of me, and got a half-paul. It almost invariably happens, in church or cathedral, that beggars address their prayers to the heretic visitor, and probably with more unction than to the Virgin or saints. However, I have nothing to say against the sincerity of this people's devotion. They give all the proof of it that a mere spectator can estimate.

Last evening we all went out to see the comet, which then reached its climax of lustre. It was like a lofty plume of fire, and grew very brilliant as the night darkened.

October 10. — This morning too we went to the Cathedral, and sat long listening to the music of the organ and voices, and witnessing rites and ceremonies which are far older than even the ancient edifice where they were exhibited. A good many people were present, sitting, kneeling, or walking about, — a freedom that contrasts very agreeably with the grim formalities of English churches and our own meeting-houses. Many persons were in their best

attire ; but others came in, with unabashed simplicity, in their old garments of labor, sunburnt
women from their toil among the vines and
olives. One old peasant I noticed with his
withered shanks in breeches and blue yarn
stockings. The people of whatever class are
wonderfully tolerant of heretics, never manifest-
ing any displeasure or annoyance, though they
must see that we are drawn thither by curiosity alone, and merely pry while they pray. I
heartily wish the priests were better men, and
that human nature, divinely influenced, could
be depended upon for a constant supply and
succession of good and pure ministers, their religion has so many admirable points. And then
it is a sad pity that this noble and beautiful
cathedral should be a mere fossil shell, out of
which the life has died long ago. But for
many a year yet to come the tapers will burn
before the high altar, the Host will be elevated, the incense diffuse its fragrance, the
confessionals be open to receive the penitents.
I saw a father entering with two little bits of
boys, just big enough to toddle along, holding
his hand on either side. The father dipped his
fingers into the marble font of holy water, —
which, on its pedestals, was two or three times
as high as those small Christians, — and wetted
a hand of each, and taught them how to cross
themselves. When they come to be men it

will be impossible to convince those children that there is no efficacy in holy water, without plucking up all religious faith and sentiment by the roots. Generally, I suspect, when people throw off the faith they were born in, the best soil of their hearts is apt to cling to its roots.

Raised several feet above the pavement, against every clustered pillar along the nave of the Cathedral, is placed a statue of Gothic sculpture. In various places are sitting statues of popes of Sienese nativity, all of whom, I believe, have a hand raised in the act of blessing. Shrines and chapels, set in grand, heavy frames of pillared architecture, stand all along the aisles and transepts, and these seem in many instances to have been built and enriched by noble families, whose arms are sculptured on the pedestals of the pillars, sometimes with a cardinal's hat above to denote the rank of one of its members. How much pride, love, and reverence in the lapse of ages must have clung to the sharp points of all this sculpture and architecture ! The Cathedral is a religion in itself, — something worth dying for to those who have an hereditary interest in it. In the pavement, yesterday, I noticed the gravestone of a person who fell six centuries ago in the battle of Monte Aperto, and was buried here by public decree as a meed of valor.

This afternoon I took a walk out of one of

the city gates, and found the country about Siena as beautiful in this direction as in all others. I came to a little stream flowing over into a pebbly bed, and collecting itself into pools, with a scanty rivulet between. Its glen was deep, and was crossed by a bridge of several lofty and narrow arches like those of a Roman aqueduct. It is a modern structure, however. Farther on, as I wound round along the base of a hill which fell down upon the road by precipitous cliffs of brown earth, I saw a gray, ruined wall on the summit, surrounded with cypress-trees. This tree is very frequent about Siena, and the scenery is made soft and beautiful by a variety of other trees and shrubbery, without which these hills and gorges would have scarcely a charm. The road was thronged with country people, mostly women and children, who had been spending the feast-day in Siena ; and parties of boys were chasing one another through the fields, pretty much as boys do in New England of a Sunday, but the Sienese lads had not the sense of Sabbath-breaking like our boys. Sunday with these people is like any other feast-day, and consecrated to cheerful enjoyment. So much religious observance, as regards outward forms, is diffused through the whole week that they have no need to intensify the Sabbath except by making it gladden the other days.

Returning through the same gate by which I

had come out, I ascended into the city by a long and steep street, which was paved with bricks set edgewise. This pavement is common in many of the streets, which, being too steep for horses and carriages, are meant only to sustain the lighter tread of mules and asses. The more level streets are paved with broad, smooth flag-stones, like those of Florence, — a fashion which I heartily regret to change for the little peniten-tial blocks of Rome. The walls of Siena in their present state, and so far as I have seen them, are chiefly brick ; but there are inter-mingled fragments of ancient stone-work, and I wonder why the latter does not prevail more largely. The Romans, however, — and Siena had Roman characteristics, — always liked to build of brick, a taste that has made their ruins (now that the marble slabs are torn off) much less grand than they ought to have been. I am grateful to the old Sienese for having used stone so largely in their domestic architecture, and thereby rendered their city so grimly pic-turesque, with its black palaces frowning upon one another from arched windows, across narrow streets, to the height of six stories, like opposite ranks of tall men looking sternly into one an-other's eyes.

October 11. — Again I went to the Cathe-dral this morning, and spent an hour listening to

the music and looking through the orderly intricacies of the arches, where many vistas open
away among the columns of the choir. There
are five clustered columns on each side of the
nave ; then under the dome there are two more
arches, not in a straight line, but forming the
segment of a circle ; and beyond the circle of
the dome there are four more arches, extending
to the extremity of the chancel. I should have
said, instead of " clustered columns," as above,
that there are five arches along the nave supported by columns. This cathedral has certainly bewitched me, to write about it so much,
effecting nothing with my pains. I should
judge the width of each arch to be about twenty
feet, and the thickness of each clustered pillar
is eight or ten more, and the length of the entire building may be between two and three
hundred feet ; not very large, certainly, but it
makes an impression of grandeur independent
of size. . . .

I never shall succeed even in reminding myself of the venerable magnificence of this min-
ster, with its arches, its columns, its cornice of
popes' heads, its great wheel-windows, its mani-
fold ornament, all combining in one vast effect,
though many men have labored individually,
and through a long course of time, to produce
this multifarious handiwork and headwork.

I now took a walk out of the city. A road

turned immediately to the left as I emerged from the city, and soon proved to be a rustic lane leading past several villas and farmhouses. It was a very pleasant walk, with vineyards and olive orchards on each side, and now and then glimpses of the towers and sombre heaped-up palaces of Siena, and now a rural seclusion again ; for the hills rise and the valleys fall like the swell and subsidence of the sea after a gale, so that Siena may be quite hidden within a quarter of a mile of its wall, or may be visible, I doubt not, twenty miles away. It is a fine old town, with every promise of health and vigor in its atmosphere ; and really, if I could take root anywhere, I know not but it could as well be here as in another place. It would only be a kind of despair, however, that would ever make me dream of finding a home in Italy ; a sense that I had lost my country through absence or incongruity, and that earth is not an abiding-place. I wonder that we Americans love our country at all, it having no limits and no oneness ; and when you try to make it a matter of the heart, everything falls away except one's native State ; neither can you seize hold of that unless you tear it out of the Union, bleeding and quivering. Yet, unquestionably, we do stand by our national flag as stoutly as any people in the world, and I myself have felt the heart throb at sight of it as sensibly as other men. I think the singularity of our form of government contributes to give us a kind of patriotism, by separating us from other nations more entirely. If other nations had similar institutions, — if England, especially, were a democracy, — we should as readily make ourselves at home in another country as now in a new State.

October 12. — And again we went to the Cathedral this forenoon, and the whole family, except myself, sketched portions of it. Even Rosebud stood gravely sketching some of the inlaid figures of the pavement. As for me, I can but try to preserve some memorial of this beautiful edifice in ill-fitting words that never hit the mark. This morning visit was not my final one, for I went again after dinner and walked quite round the whole interior. I think I have not yet mentioned the rich carvings of the old oaken seats round the choir, and the curious mosaic of lighter and darker woods, by which figures and landscapes are skilfully represented on the backs of some of the stalls. The process seems to be the same as the inlaying and engraving of the pavement, the material in one case being marble, in the other wood. The only other thing that I particularly noticed was, that in the fonts of holy water at the front entrance, marble fish are sculptured in the depths of the basin, and eels and shellfish crawl-ing round the brim. Have I spoken of the sumptuous carving of the capitals of the col-umns? At any rate I have left a thousand beauties without a word. Here I drop the sub-ject. As I took my parting glance, the Cathe-dral had a gleam of golden sunshine in its far depths, and it seemed to widen and deepen itself, as if to convince me of my error in saying, yes-terday, that it is not very large. I wonder how I could say it.

After taking leave of the Cathedral, I found my way out of another of the city gates, and soon turned aside into a green lane. . . . Soon the lane passed through a hamlet consisting of a few farmhouses, the shabbiest and dreariest that can be conceived, ancient, and ugly, and di-lapidated, with iron-grated windows below, and heavy wooden shutters on the windows above, — high, ruinous walls shutting in the courts, and ponderous gates, one of which was off its hinges. The farmyards were perfect pictures of disarray and slovenly administration of home affairs. Only one of these houses had a door opening on the road, and that was the meanest in the hamlet. A flight of narrow stone stairs ascended from the threshold to the second story. All these houses were specimens of a rude an-tiquity, built of brick and stone, with the marks of arched doors and windows where a subsequent generation had shut up the lights, or the accesses which the original builders had opened. Humble as these dwellings are, — though large and high compared with rural residences in other countries, — they may very probably date back to the times when Siena was a warlike republic, and when every house in its neighborhood had need to be a fortress. I suppose, however, prowling banditti were the only enemies against whom a defence would be attempted. What lives must now be lived there, — in beastly ignorance, mental sluggishness, hard toil for little profit, filth, and a horrible discomfort of fleas; for if the palaces of Italy are overrun with these pests, what must the country hovels be! . . .

We are now all ready for a start to-morrow.

RADICOFANI, *October* 13. — We arranged to begin our journey at six. . . . It was a chill, lowering morning, and the rain blew a little in our faces before we had gone far, but did not continue long. The country soon lost the pleasant aspect which it wears immediately about Siena, and grew very barren and dreary. Then it changed again for the better, the road leading us through a fertility of vines and olives, after which the dreary and barren hills came back again, and formed our prospect throughout most of the day. We stopped for our *déjeuner à la fourchette* at a little old town called San Querico, which we entered through a ruined gateway, the town being entirely surrounded by its ancient wall. This wall is far more picturesque than that of Siena, being lofty and built of stone, with a machicolation of arches running quite round its top, like a cornice. It has little more than a single street, perhaps a quarter of a mile long, narrow, paved with flag-stones in the Florentine fashion, and lined with two rows of tall, rusty, stone houses, without a gap between them from end to end. The cafés were numerous in relation to the size of the town, and here were two taverns, — our own, the Eagle, being doubtless the best, and having three arched entrances in its front. Of these, the middle one led to the guests' apartments, the one on the right to the barn, and that on the left to the stable, so that, as is usual in Italian inns, the whole establishment was under one roof. We were shown into a brick-paved room on the first floor, adorned with a funny fresco of Aurora on the ceiling, and with some colored prints, both religious and profane. . . .

As we drove into the town we noticed a Gothic church with two doors of peculiar architecture, and while our *déjeuner* was being prepared we went to see it. The interior had little that was remarkable, for it had been repaired early in the last century, and spoilt of course ;

but an old triptych is still hanging in a chapel beside the high altar. It is painted on wood, and dates back beyond the invention of oil painting, and represents the Virgin and some saints and angels. Neither is the exterior of the church particularly interesting, with the exception of the carving and ornaments of two of the doors. Both of them have round arches, deep and curiously wrought, and the pillars of one of the two are formed of a peculiar knot or twine in stone-work, such as I cannot well describe, but it is both ingenious and simple. These pillars rest on two nondescript animals, which look as much like walruses as anything else. The pillars of the other door consist of two figures supporting the capitals, and themselves standing on two handsomely carved lions. The work is curious, and evidently very ancient, and the material a red freestone.

After lunch, Julian and I took a walk out of the gate of the town opposite to that of our entrance. There were no soldiers on guard, as at city gates of more importance ; nor do I think that there is really any gate to shut, but the massive stone gateway still stands entire over the empty arch. Looking back after we had passed through, I observed that the lofty upper story is converted into a dovecot, and that pumpkins were put to ripen in some open chambers at one side. We passed near the base of

283

a tall, square tower, which is said to be of Roman origin. The little town is in the midst of a barren region, but its immediate neighborhood is fertile, and an olive orchard, venerable of aspect, lay on the other side of the pleasant lane with its English hedges, and olive-trees grew likewise along the base of the city wall. The arched machicolations, which I have before mentioned, were here and there interrupted by a house which was built upon the old wall or incorporated into it; and from the windows of one of them I saw ears of Indian corn hung out to ripen in the sun, and somebody was winnowing grain at a little door that opened through the wall. It was very pleasant to see the ancient warlike rampart thus overcome with rustic peace. The ruined gateway is partly overgrown with ivy.

Returning to our inn, along the street, we saw —— sketching one of the doors of the Gothic church, in the midst of a crowd of the good people of San Querico, who made no scruple to look over her shoulder, pressing so closely as hardly to allow her elbow-room. I must own that I was too cowardly to come forward and take my share of this public notice, so I turned away to the inn and there awaited her coming. Indeed, she has seldom attempted to sketch without finding herself the nucleus of a throng.

VITERBO, THE BLACK EAGLE, *October* 14. —
Perhaps I had something more to say of San
Querico, but I shall merely add that there is a
stately old palace of the Piccolomini close to
the church above described. It is built in the
style of the Roman palaces, and looked almost
large enough to be one of them. Nevertheless,
the basement story, or part of it, seems to be
used as a barn and stable, for I saw a yoke of
oxen in the entrance. I cannot but mention a
most wretched team of vettura-horses which
stopped at the door of our albergo : poor, lean,
downcast creatures, with deep furrows between
their ribs ; nothing but skin and bone, in short,
and not even so much skin as they should have
had, for it was partially worn off from their
backs. The harness was fastened with ropes,
the traces and reins were ropes ; the carriage was
old and shabby, and out of this miserable equi-
page there alighted an ancient gentleman and
lady, whom our waiter affirmed to be the Pre-
fect of Florence and his wife.

We left San Querico at two o'clock, and followed an ascending road till we got into the
region above the clouds ; the landscape was
very wide, but very dreary and barren, and grew
more and more so till we began to climb the
mountain of Radicofani, the peak of which had
been blackening itself on the horizon almost the
whole day. When we had come into a pretty

high region we were assailed by a real mountain tempest of wind, rain, and hail, which pelted down upon us in good earnest, and cooled the air a little below comfort.   As we toiled up the mountain, its upper region presented a very striking aspect, looking as if a precipice had been smoothed and squared for the purpose of rendering the old castle on its summit more inaccessible than it was by nature.   This is the castle of the robber-knight, Ghino di Tacco, whom Boccaccio introduces into the Decameron. A freebooter of those days must have set a higher value on such a rock as this than if it had been one mass of diamond, for no art of mediæval warfare could endanger him in such a fortress.   Drawing yet nearer, we found the hillside immediately above us strewn with thousands upon thousands of great fragments of stone.   It looked as if some great ruin had taken place there, only it was too vast a ruin to have been the dismemberment and dissolution of anything made by man.

We could now see the castle on the height pretty distinctly.   It seemed to impend over the precipice ; and close to the base of the latter we saw the street of a town on as strange and inconvenient a foundation as ever one was built upon.   I suppose the inhabitants of the village were dependants of the old knight of the castle ; this brotherhood of robbers, as they

married and had families, settled there under
the shelter of the eagle's nest. But the singularity is, how a community of people have contrived to live and perpetuate themselves so far
out of the reach of the world's help, and seemingly with no means of assisting in the world's
labor. I cannot imagine how they employ
themselves except in begging, and even that
branch of industry appears to be left to the old
women and the children. No house was ever
built in this immediate neighborhood for any
such natural purpose as induces people to build
them on other sites. Even our hotel, at which
we now arrived, could not be said to be a natural growth of the soil; it had originally been a
whim of one of the Grand Dukes of Tuscany,
— a hunting-palace, — intended for habitation
only during a few weeks of the year. Of all
dreary hotels I ever alighted at, methinks this
is the most so; but on first arriving I merely
followed the waiter to look at our rooms, across
stone-paved basement halls dismal as Etruscan
tombs; up dim staircases, and along shivering
corridors, all of stone, stone, stone, nothing but
cold stone. After glancing at these pleasant
accommodations, my wife and I, with Julian,
set out to ascend the hill and visit the town of
Radicofani.

It is not more than a quarter of a mile above
our hotel, and is accessible by a good piece of

road, though very steep. As we approached the town we were assailed by some little beggars; but this is the case all through Italy, in city or solitude, and I think the mendicants of Radicofani are fewer than its proportion. We had not got far towards the village when, looking back over the scene of many miles that lay stretched beneath us, we saw a heavy shower apparently travelling straight towards us over hill and dale. It seemed inevitable that it should soon be upon us, so I persuaded my wife to return to the hotel; but Julian and I kept onward, being determined to see Radicofani with or without a drenching. We soon entered the street; the blackest, ugliest, rudest old street, I do believe, that ever human life incrusted itself with. The first portion of it is the over-brimming of the town in generations subsequent to that in which it was surrounded by a wall; but after going a little way we came to a high, square tower planted right across the way, with an arched gateway in its basement story, so that it looked like a great short-legged giant striding over the street of Radicofani. Within the gateway is the proper and original town, though indeed the portion outside of the gate is as densely populated, as ugly, and as ancient, as that within.

The street was very narrow, and paved with flag-stones not quite so smooth as those of

Florence; the houses are tall enough to be stately, if they were not so inconceivably dingy and shabby; but, with their half-dozen stories, they make only the impression of hovel piled upon hovel, — squalor immortalized in unde-caying stone. It was now getting far into the twilight, and I could not distinguish the partic-ularities of the little town, except that there were shops, a café or two, and as many churches, all dusky with age, crowded closely together, inconvenient, stifled, too, in spite of the breadth and freedom of the mountain atmo-sphere outside the scanty precincts of the street. It was a death-in-life little place, a fossilized place, and yet the street was thronged, and had all the bustle of a city; even more noise than a city's street, because everybody in Radicofani knows everybody, and probably gossips with everybody, being everybody's blood relation, as they cannot fail to have become after they and their forefathers have been shut up together within the narrow walls for many hundred years. They looked round briskly at Julian and me, but were courteous, as Italians always are, and made way for us to pass through the throng as we kept on still ascending the steep street.   It took us but a few minutes to reach the still steeper and winding pathway which climbs to-wards the old castle.

After ascending above the village, the path,

though still paved, becomes very rough, as if the hoofs of Ghino di Tacco's robber cavalry had displaced the stones and they had never been readjusted. On every side, too, except where the path just finds space enough, there is an enormous rubbish of huge stones, which seems to have fallen from the precipice above, or else to have rained down out of the sky. We kept on, and by and by reached what seemed to have been a lower outwork of the castle on the top ; there was the massive old arch of a gateway, and a great deal of ruin of man's work, beside the large stones that here, as elsewhere, were scattered so abundantly. Within the wall and gateway just mentioned, however, there was a kind of farmhouse, adapted, I suppose, out of the old ruin, and I noticed some ears of Indian corn hanging out of a window. There were also a few stacks of hay, but no signs of human or animal life ; and it is utterly inexplicable to me where these products of the soil could have come from, for certainly they never grew amid that barrenness.

We had not yet reached Ghino's castle, and, being now beneath it, we had to bend our heads far backward to see it rising up against the clear sky while we were now in twilight. The path upward looked terribly steep and rough, and if we had climbed it we should probably have broken our necks in descending again into the lower obscurity. We therefore stopped here, much against Julian's will, and went back as we came, still wondering at the strange situation of Radicofani; for its aspect is as if it had stepped off the top of the cliff and lodged at its base, though still in danger of sliding farther down the hillside. Emerging from the compact, grimy life of its street, we saw that the shower had swept by, or probably had expended itself in a region beneath us, for we were above the scope of many of the showery clouds that haunt a hill country. There was a very bright star visible, I remember, and we saw the new moon, now a third towards the full, for the first time this evening. The air was cold and bracing.

But I am excessively sleepy, so will not describe our great dreary hotel, where a blast howled in an interminable corridor all night. It did not seem to have anything to do with the wind out of doors, but to be a blast that had been casually shut in when the doors were closed behind the last Grand Duke who came hither and departed, and ever since it has been kept prisoner, and makes a melancholy wail along the corridor. The dreamy stupidity of the conceit proves how sleepy I am.

SETTE VENE, *October* 15. — We left Radicofani long before sunrise, and I saw that cere-

mony take place from the coupé of the vettura
for the first time in a long while.   A sunset is
the better sight of the two.   I have always
suspected it, and have been strengthened in the
idea whenever I have had an opportunity of
comparison.   Our departure from Radicofani
was most dreary, except that we were very glad
to get away ; but the cold discomfort of dress-
ing in a chill bedroom by candlelight, and our
uncertain wandering through the immense hotel with a dim taper in search of the breakfast-
room, and our poor breakfast of eggs, Italian
bread, and coffee, — all these things made me
wish that people were created with roots like
trees, so that they could not befool themselves
with wandering about.   However, we had not
long been on our way before the morning air
blew away all our troubles, and we rumbled
cheerfully onward, ready to encounter even the
papal custom-house officers at Ponte Centino.
Our road thither was a pretty steep descent. I
remember the barren landscape of hills, with
here and there a lonely farmhouse, which there
seemed to be no occasion for, where nothing
grew.

At Ponte Centino my passport was examined,
and I was invited into an office where sat the
papal custom-house officer, a thin, subtle-look-
ing, keen-eyed, sallow personage, of aspect very
suitable to be the agent of a government of

priests. I communicated to him my wish to
pass the custom house without giving the officers the trouble of examining my luggage. He
inquired whether I had any dutiable articles,
and wrote for my signature a declaration in the
negative ; and then he lifted a sand-box, beneath which was a little heap of silver coins.
On this delicate hint I asked what was the
usual fee, and was told that fifteen pauls was
the proper sum. I presume it was entirely an
illegal charge, and that he had no right to pass
any luggage without examination ; but the thing
is winked at by the authorities, and no money
is better spent for the traveller's convenience
than these fifteen pauls. There was a papal
military officer in the room, and he, I believe,
cheated me in the change of a napoleon, as
his share of the spoil. At the door a soldier
met me with my passport, and looked as if he
expected a fee for handing it to me, but in this
he was disappointed. After I had resumed my
seat in the coupé, the porter of the custom
house — a poor, sickly looking creature, half
dead with the malaria of the place — appeared,
and demanded a fee for doing nothing to my
luggage. He got three pauls, and looked but
half contented. This whole set of men seem
to be as corrupt as official people can possibly
be ; and yet I hardly know whether to stigma-
tize them as corrupt, because it is not their

individual delinquency, but the operation of a regular system. Their superiors know what men they are, and calculate upon their getting a living by just these means. And, indeed, the custom-house and passport regulations, as they exist in Italy, would be intolerable if there were not this facility of evading them at little cost. Such laws are good for nothing but to be broken.

We now began to ascend again, and the country grew fertile and picturesque. We passed many mules and donkeys, laden with a sort of deep firkin on each side of the saddle, and these were heaped up with grapes, both purple and white. We bought some, and got what we should have thought an abundance at small price, only we used to get twice as many at Montauto for the same money. However, a Roman paul bought us three or four pounds even here. We still ascended, and came soon to the gateway of the town of Acquapendente, which stands on a height that seems to descend by natural terraces to the valley below. . . .

French soldiers, in their bluish-gray coats and scarlet trousers, were on duty at the gate, and one of them took my passport and the vetturino's, and we then drove into the town to wait till they should be viséd. We saw but one street, narrow, with tall, rusty, aged houses, built of stone, evil smelling; in short, a kind of place

that would be intolerably dismal in cloudy England, and cannot be called cheerful even under
the sun of Italy. . . . Priests passed and burly
friars, one of whom was carrying a wine-barrel
on his head. Little carts, laden with firkins of
grapes, and donkeys with the same genial burden, brushed past our vettura, finding scarce
room enough in the narrow street. All the idlers
of Acquapendente — and they were many — assembled to gaze at us, but not discourteously.
Indeed, I never saw an idle curiosity exercised
in such a pleasant way as by the country people
of Italy. It almost deserves to be called a kindly
interest and sympathy, instead of a hard and
cold curiosity, like that of our own people, and
it is displayed with such simplicity that it is
evident no offence is intended.

By and by the vetturino brought his passport
and my own, with the official visé and we kept
on our way, still ascending, passing through
vineyards and olives, and meeting grape-laden
donkeys, till we came to the town of San Lorenzo Nuovo, a place built by Pius VI. as the
refuge for the people of a lower town which had
been made uninhabitable by malaria. The new
town, which I suppose is hundreds of years old,
with all its novelty shows strikingly the differ-
ence between places that grow up and shape out
their streets of their own accord, as it were, and
one that is built on a settled plan of malice afore-

thought. This little rural village has gates of classic architecture, a spacious piazza, and a great breadth of straight and rectangular streets, with houses of uniform style, airy and wholesome looking to a degree seldom seen on the Continent. Nevertheless, I must say that the town looked hatefully dull and ridiculously prim, and of the two, I had rather spend my life in Radicofani. We drove through it, from gate to gate, without stopping, and soon came to the brow of a hill, whence we beheld, right beneath us, the beautiful lake of Bolsena ; not exactly at our feet, however, for a portion of level ground lay between, haunted by the pestilence which has depopulated all these shores, and made the lake and its neighborhood a solitude. It looked very beautiful, nevertheless, with a sheen of a silver and a gray like that of steel as the wind blew and the sun shone over it ; and, judging by my own feelings, I should really have thought that the breeze from its surface was bracing and healthy.

Descending the hill, we passed the ruins of the old town of San Lorenzo, of which the prim village on the hilltop may be considered the daughter. There is certainly no resemblance between parent and child, the former being situated on a sort of precipitous bluff, where there could have been no room for piazzas and spacious streets, nor accessibility except by mules,

donkeys, goats, and people of Alpine habits.
There was an ivy-covered tower on the top of
the bluff, and some arched cavern mouths that
looked as if they opened into the great darkness. These were the entrances to Etruscan
tombs, for the town on top had been originally
Etruscan, and the inhabitants had buried themselves in the heart of the precipitous bluffs
after spending their lives on its summit.

Reaching the plain, we drove several miles
along the shore of the lake, and found the soil
fertile and generally well cultivated, especially
with the vine, though there were tracts apparently too marshy to be put to any agricultural
purpose. We met now and then a flock of
sheep, watched by sallow-looking and spiritless
men and boys, who, we took it for granted,
would soon perish of malaria, though, I presume, they never spend their nights in the immediate vicinity of the lake. I should like to
inquire whether animals suffer from the bad
qualities of the air. The lake is not nearly so
beautiful on a nearer view as it is from the hill
above, there being no rocky margin, nor bright,
sandy beach, but everywhere this interval of
level ground, and often swampy marsh, betwixt the water and the hill. At a considerable
distance from the shore we saw two islands,
one of which is memorable as having been the
scene of an empress's murder, but I cannot

stop to fill my journal with historical reminiscences.

We kept onward to the town of Bolsena, which stands nearly a mile from the lake, and on a site higher than the level margin, yet not so much so, I should apprehend, as to free it from danger of malaria. We stopped at an albergo outside of the wall of the town, and before dinner had time to see a good deal of the neighborhood. The first aspect of the town was very striking, with a vista into its street through the open gateway, and high above it an old, gray, square-built castle, with three towers visible at the angles, one of them battlemented, one taller than the rest, and one partially ruined. Outside of the town gate there were some fragments of Etruscan ruin, capitals of pillars and altars with inscriptions ; these we glanced at, and then made our entrance through the gate.

There it was again, — the same narrow, dirty, time-darkened street of piled-up houses which we have so often seen ; the same swarm of ill-to-do people, grape-laden donkeys, little stands or shops of roasted chestnuts, peaches, tomatoes, white and purple figs ; the same evidence of a fertile land, and grimy poverty in the midst of abundance which nature tries to heap into their hands. It seems strange that they can never grasp it.

We had gone but a little way along this street

when we saw a narrow lane that turned aside from it and went steeply upward. Its name was on the corner, — the Via di Castello, — and as the castle promised to be more interesting than anything else, we immediately began to ascend. The street — a strange name for such an avenue — clambered upward in the oddest fashion, passing under arches, scrambling up steps, so that it was more like a long irregular pair of stairs than anything that Christians call a street ; and so large a part of it was under arches that we scarcely seemed to be out of doors. At last Una, who was in advance, emerged into the upper air, and cried out that we had ascended to an upper town, and a larger one than that beneath.

It really seemed like coming up out of the earth into the midst of the town, when we found ourselves so unexpectedly in upper Bolsena. We were in a little nook, surrounded by old edifices, and called the Piazza del Orologio, on account of a clock that was apparent somewhere. The castle was close by, and from its platform there was a splendid view of the lake and all the near hill country. The castle itself is still in good condition, and apparently as strong as ever it was as respects the exterior walls ; but within there seemed to be neither floor nor chamber, nothing but the empty shell of the dateless old fortress. The stones at the base and lower part of the building were so massive that I should think the Etrurians must have laid them ; and then perhaps the Romans built a little higher, and the mediæval people raised the battlements and towers. But we did not look long at the castle, our attention being drawn to the singular aspect of the town itself which — to speak first of its most prominent characteristic — is the very filthiest place, I do believe, that was ever inhabited by man. Defilement was everywhere ; in the piazza, in nooks and corners, strewing the miserable lanes from side to side, the refuse of every day, and of accumulated ages. I wonder whether the ancient Romans were as dirty a people as we everywhere find those who have succeeded them ; for there seems to have been something in the places that have been inhabited by Romans, or made famous in their history, and in the monuments of every kind that they have raised, that puts people in mind of their very earthiness, and incites them to defile therewith whatever temple, column, ruined palace, or triumphal arch may fall in their way. I think it must be an hereditary trait, probably weakened and robbed of a little of its horror by the influence of milder ages ; and I am much afraid that Cæsar trod narrower and fouler ways in his path to power than those of modern Rome, or even of this disgusting town of Bolsena. I cannot imagine anything worse than these, however. Rotten vegetables thrown everywhere about, musty straw, standing puddles, running rivulets of dissolved nastiness, — these matters were a relief amid viler objects. The town was full of great black hogs wallowing before every door, and they grunted at us with a kind of courtesy and affability as if the town were theirs, and it was their part to be hospitable to strangers. Many donkeys likewise accosted us with braying; children, growing more uncleanly every day they lived, pestered us with begging; men stared askance at us as they lounged in corners, and women endangered us with slops which they were flinging from doorways into the street. No decent words can describe, no admissible image can give an idea of this noisome place. And yet, I remember, the donkeys came up the height loaded with fruit, and with little flat-sided barrels of wine; the people had a good atmosphere — except as they polluted it themselves — on their high site, and there seemed to be no reason why they should not live a beautiful and jolly life.

I did not mean to write such an ugly description as the above, but it is well, once for all, to have attempted conveying an idea of what disgusts the traveller, more or less, in all these Italian towns. Setting aside this grand characteristic, the upper town of Bolsena is a most curious and interesting place. It was originally

NOTES OF TRAVEL [October

an Etruscan city, the ancient Volsinii, and when taken and destroyed by the Romans was said to contain two thousand statues. Afterwards the Romans built a town upon the site, including, I suppose, the space occupied by the lower city, which looks as if it had brimmed over like Radicofani, and fallen from the precipitous height occupied by the upper. The latter is a strange confusion of black and ugly houses, piled massively out of the ruins of former ages, built rudely and without plan, as a pauper would build his hovel, and yet with here and there an arched gateway, a cornice, a pillar, that might have adorned a palace. . . . The streets are the narrowest I have seen anywhere, — of no more width, indeed, than may suffice for the passage of a donkey with his panniers. They wind in and out in strange confusion, and hardly look like streets at all, but, nevertheless, have names printed on the corners, just as if they were stately avenues. After looking about us awhile and drawing half-breaths so as to take in the less quantity of gaseous pollution, we went back to the castle, and descended by a path winding downward from it into the plain outside of the town gate.

It was now dinner-time, . . . and we had, in the first place, some fish from the pestiferous lake ; not, I am sorry to say, the famous stewed eels which, Dante says, killed Pope Martin, but

302

some trout. . . . By the bye, the meal was not dinner, but our midday *colazione*. After despatching it, we again wandered forth and strolled round the outside of the lower town, which, with the upper one, made as picturesque a combination as could be desired. The old wall that surrounds the lower town has been appropriated, long since, as the back wall of a range of houses; windows have been pierced through it; upper chambers and loggie have been built upon it; so that it looks something like a long row of rural dwellings with one continuous front or back, constructed in a strange style of massive strength, contrasting with the vines that here and there are trained over it, and with the wreaths of yellow corn that hang from the windows. But portions of the old battlements are interspersed with the line of homely chambers and tiled house-tops. Within the wall the town is very compact, and above its roofs rises a rock, the sheer, precipitous bluff on which stands the upper town, whose foundations impend over the highest roof in the lower. At one end is the old castle, with its towers rising above the square battlemented mass of the main fortress, and if we had not seen the dirt and squalor that dwells within this venerable outside, we should have carried away a picture of gray, grim dignity, presented by a long past age to the present one, to put its mean ways and

modes to shame. —— sat diligently sketching,
and children came about her, exceedingly unfra-
grant, but very courteous and gentle, looking over
her shoulders, and expressing delight as they
saw each familiar edifice take its place in the
sketch. They are a lovable people, these Italians, as I find from almost all with whom we
come in contact; they have great and little
faults, and no great virtues that I know of;
but still are sweet, amiable, pleasant to encounter, save when they beg, or when you have to
bargain with them.

We left Bolsena and drove to Viterbo, passing the gate of the picturesque town of Montefiascone, over the wall of which I saw spires and
towers, and the dome of a cathedral. I was
sorry not to taste, in its own town, the celebrated *est*, which was the death-draught of the
jolly prelate. At Viterbo, however, I called
for some wine of Montefiascone, and had a
little straw-covered flask, which the waiter assured us was the genuine est-wine. It was of
golden color, and very delicate, somewhat resembling still champagne, but finer, and re-
quiring a calmer pause to appreciate its subtle
delight. Its good qualities, however, are so
evanescent, that the finer flavor became almost
imperceptible before we finished the flask.

Viterbo is a large, disagreeable town, built at
the foot of a mountain, the peak of which is

seen through the vista of some of the narrow
streets. . . .

There are more fountains in Viterbo than I
have seen in any other city of its size, and many
of them of very good design.   Around most of
them there were wine-hogsheads, waiting their
turn to be cleansed and rinsed, before receiving
the wine of the present vintage.   Passing a
doorway, Julian saw some men treading out the
grapes in a great vat with their naked feet. . . .

Among the beggars here, the loudest and
most vociferous was a crippled postilion, wearing
his uniform jacket, green, faced with red ; and
he seemed to consider himself entitled still to
get his living from travellers, as having been
disabled in the way of his profession.   I recognized his claim, and was rewarded with a courteous and grateful bow at our departure. . . . To
beggars — after my much experience both in
England and Italy — I give very little, though
I am not certain that it would not often be real
beneficence in the latter country.   There being
little or no provision for poverty and age, the
poor must often suffer.   Nothing can be more
earnest than their entreaties for aid ; nothing
seemingly more genuine than their gratitude
when they receive it.   They return you the value
of their alms in prayers, and say, " God will
accompany you."   Many of them have a professional whine, and a certain doleful twist of the

neck and turn of the head, which hardens my heart against them at once. A painter might find numerous models among them, if canvas had not already been more than sufficiently covered with their style of the picturesque. There is a certain brick-dust colored cloak worn in Viterbo, not exclusively by beggars, which, when ragged enough, is exceedingly artistic.

ROME, 68 PIAZZA POLI, *October* 17.—We left Viterbo on the 15th, and proceeded, through Monterosi, to Sette Vene. There was nothing interesting at Sette Vene, except an old Roman bridge, of a single arch, which had kept its sweep, composed of one row of stones, unbroken for two or more thousand years, and looked just as strong as ever, though gray with age, and fringed with plants that found it hard to fix themselves in its close crevices.

The next day we drove along the Cassian Way towards Rome. It was a most delightful morning, a genial atmosphere ; the more so, I suppose, because this was the Campagna, the region of pestilence and death. I had a quiet, gentle, comfortable pleasure, as if, after many wanderings, I was drawing near Rome, for, now that I have known it once, Rome certainly does draw into itself my heart, as I think even London, or even little Concord itself, or old sleepy Salem, never did and never will. Besides, we are

to stay here six months, and we had now a
house all prepared to receive us ; so that this
present approach, in the noontide of a genial
day, was most unlike our first one, when we
crept towards Rome through the wintry midnight, benumbed with cold, ill, weary, and not
knowing whither to betake ourselves. Ah !
that was a dismal time ! One thing, however,
that disturbed even my present equanimity a
little was the necessity of meeting the custom
house at the Porta del Popolo ; but my past
experience warranted me in believing that even
these ogres might be mollified by the magic touch
of a scudo ; and so it proved. We should have
escaped any examination at all, the officer whispered me, if his superior had not happened to be
present ; but, as the case stood, they took down
only one trunk from the top of the vettura, just
lifted the lid, closed it again, and gave us permission to proceed. So we came to 68 Piazza
Poli, and found ourselves at once at home, in
such a comfortable, cosy little house, as I did
not think existed in Rome.

I ought to say a word about our vetturino,
Constantino Bacci, an excellent and most favorable specimen of his class ; for his magnificent
conduct, his liberality, and all the good qualities
that ought to be imperial, Sophia called him the
Emperor. He took us to good hotels, and
feasted us with the best ; he was kind to us all,

and especially to little Rosebud, who used to run by his side, with her small white hand in his great brown one; he was cheerful in his deportment, and expressed his good spirits by the smack of his whip, which is the barometer of a vetturino's inward weather; he drove admirably, and would rumble up to the door of an albergo, and stop to a hair's breadth, just where it was most convenient for us to alight; he would hire postilions and horses, where other vetturini would take nothing better than sluggish oxen, to help us up the hilly roads, so that sometimes we had a team of seven; he did all that we could possibly require of him, and was content, and more, with a *buon mano* of five scudi, in addition to the stipulated price. Finally, I think the tears had risen almost to his eyelids when we parted with him.

Our friends, the Thompsons, through whose kindness we procured this house, called to see us soon after our arrival. In the afternoon I walked with Rosebud to the Medici Gardens, and, on our way thither, we espied our former servant, Lalla, who flung so many and such bitter curses after us, on our departure from Rome, sitting at her father's fruit stall. Thank God, they have not taken effect. After going to the Medici, we went to the Pincian Gardens, and looked over into the Borghese grounds, which, methought, were more beautiful than

ever. The same was true of the sky, and of
every object beneath it ; and as we came homeward along the Corso, I wondered at the stateliness and palatial magnificence of that noble
street. Once, I remember, I thought it narrow,
and far unworthy of its fame.

In the way of costume, the men in goatskin
breeches, whom we met on the Campagna, were
very striking, and looked like Satyrs.

October 21. — . . . I have been twice to St.
Peter's and was impressed more than at any
former visit by a sense of breadth and loftiness,
and, as it were, a visionary splendor and magnificence. I also went to the Museum of the
Capitol ; and the statues seemed to me more
beautiful than formerly, and I was not sensible
of the cold despondency with which I have so
often viewed them. Yesterday we went to the
Corsini Palace, which we had not visited before.
It stands in the Trastevere, in the Longara, and
is a stately palace, with a grand staircase, leading
to the first floor, where is situated the range of
picture-rooms. There were a good many fine
pictures, but none of them have made a memorable impression on my mind, except a portrait
by Vandyke, of a man in point lace, very grand
and very real. The room in which this picture
hung had many other portraits by Holbein,
Titian, Rembrandt, Rubens, and other famous

painters, and was wonderfully rich in this department. In another, there was a portrait of Pope Julius II., by Raphael, somewhat differing from those at the Pitti and the Uffizi galleries in Florence, and those I have seen in England and Paris ; thinner, paler, perhaps older, more severely intellectual, but at least as high a work of art as those.

The palace has some handsome old furniture, and gilded chairs, covered with leather cases, possibly relics of Queen Christina's time, who died here. I know not but the most curious object was a curule chair of marble, sculptured all out of one piece, and adorned with bas-reliefs. It is supposed to be Etruscan. It has a circular back, sweeping round, so as to afford sufficient rests for the elbows ; and, sitting down in it, I discovered that modern ingenuity has not made much real improvement on this chair of three or four thousand years ago. But some chairs are easier for the moment, yet soon betray you, and grow the more irksome.

We strolled along Longara, and found the piazza of St. Peter's full of French soldiers at their drill. . . . We went quite round the interior of the church, and perceiving the pavement loose and broken near the altar where Guido's Archangel is placed, we picked up some bits of rosso antico and gray marble to be set in brooches, as relics.

We have the snuggest little set of apartments in Rome, seven rooms, including an antechamber; and, though the stairs are exceedingly narrow, there is really a carpet on them, — a civilized comfort of which the proudest palaces in the Eternal City cannot boast. The stairs are very steep, however, and I should not wonder if some of us broke our noses down them. Narrowness of space within doors strikes us all rather ludicrously, yet not unpleasantly, after being accustomed to the wastes and deserts of the Montauto Villa. It is well thus to be put in training for the over-snugness of our cottage in Concord. Our windows here look out on a small and rather quiet piazza, with an immense palace on the left hand, and a smaller yet statelier one on the right; and just round the corner of the street, leading out of our piazza, is the Fountain of Trevi, of which I can hear the plash in the evening, when other sounds are hushed.

Looking over what I have said of Sodoma's Christ Bound, at Siena, I see that I have omitted to notice what seems to me one of its most striking characteristics, — its loneliness. You feel as if the Saviour were deserted, both in heaven and earth; the despair is in him which made him say, " My God, why hast thou forsaken me ? " Even in this extremity, however, he is still Divine, and Sodoma almost seems to have reconciled the impossibilities of combining an

omnipresent divinity with a suffering and out-
raged humanity. But this is one of the cases
in which the spectator's imagination completes
what the artist merely hints at.

Mr. ——, the sculptor, called to see us, the
other evening, and quite paid Powers off for all
his trenchant criticisms on his brother artists.
He will not allow Powers to be an artist at all,
or to know anything of the laws of art, although
acknowledging him to be a great bust-maker,
and to have put together the Greek Slave and
the Fisher Boy very ingeniously. The latter,
however (he says), is copied from the Apollino
in the Tribune of the Uffizi; and the former
is made up of beauties that had no reference to
one another; and he affirms that Powers is ready
to sell, and has actually sold, the Greek Slave,
limb by limb, dismembering it by reversing the
process of putting it together, — a head to one
purchaser, an arm or a foot to another, a hand
to a third. Powers knows nothing scientifically
of the human frame, and only succeeds in representing it, as a natural bone-doctor succeeds
in setting a dislocated limb, by a happy accident
or special providence. (The illustration was
my own, and adopted by Mr. ——.) Yet Mr.
—— seems to acknowledge that he did succeed.
I repeat these things only as another instance
how invariably every sculptor uses his chisel and
mallet to smash and deface the marble-work of

every other.   I never heard Powers speak of
Mr. ———, but can partly imagine what he would
have said.

Mr. ——— spoke of Powers's disappointment
about the twenty-five-thousand-dollar appropriation from Congress, and said that he was altogether to blame, inasmuch as he attempted to
sell to the nation for that sum a statue which,
to Mr. ———'s certain knowledge, he had already
offered to private persons for a fifth part of it.
I have not implicit faith in Mr. ———'s veracity,
and doubt nct Powers acted fairly in his own
eyes.

October 23. — I am afraid I have caught one
of the colds which the Roman air continually
affected me with last winter; at any rate, a
sirocco has taken the life out of me, and I have
no spirit to do anything.   This morning I took
a walk, however, out of the Porta Maggiore,
and looked at the tomb of the baker Eurysaces,
just outside of the gate, — a very singular ruin,
covered with symbols of the man's trade in
stone-work, and with bas-reliefs along the cornice, representing people at work making bread.
An inscription states that the ashes of his wife
are likewise reposited there, in a breadbasket.
The mausoleum is perhaps twenty feet long, in
its largest extent, and of equal height; and if
good bakers were as scarce in ancient Rome as

in the modern city, I do not wonder that they were thought worthy of stately monuments. None of the modern ones deserve any better tomb than a pile of their own sour loaves.

I walked onward a good distance beyond the gate alongside of the arches of the Claudian aqueduct, which, in this portion of it, seems to have had little repair, and to have needed little, since it was built. It looks like a long procession, striding across the Campagna towards the city, and entering the gate over one of its arches; within the gate, I saw two or three slender jets of water spurting from the crevices; this aqueduct being still in use to bring the Acqua Felice into Rome.

Returning within the walls, I walked along their inner base to the Church of St. John Lateran, into which I went, and sat down to rest myself, being languid and weary, and hot with the sun, though afraid to trust the coolness of the shade. I hate the Roman atmosphere; indeed, all my pleasure in getting back — all my home feeling — has already evaporated, and what now impresses me, as before, is the languor of Rome, — its weary pavements, its little life, pressed down by a weight of death.

Quitting St. John Lateran, I went astray, as I do nine times out of ten in these Roman intricacies, and at last, seeing the Coliseum in the vista of a street, I betook myself thither to get

314

a fresh start.   Its round of stones looked vast
and dreary, but not particularly impressive.
The interior was quite deserted ; except that a
Roman, of respectable appearance, was making
a pilgrimage at the altars, kneeling and saying
a prayer at each one.

Outside of the Coliseum, a neat-looking little
boy came and begged of me ; and I gave him a
baioccho, rather because he seemed to need it
so little than for any other reason.   I observed
that he immediately afterwards went and spoke
to a well-dressed man, and supposed that the
child was likewise begging of him.   I watched
the little boy, however, and saw that, in two or
three other instances, after begging of other individuals, he still returned to this well-dressed
man ; the fact being, no doubt, that the latter
was fishing for baiocchi through the medium of
his child, — throwing the poor little fellow out
as a bait, while he himself retained his independent respectability.   He had probably come
out for a whole day's sport ; for, by and by, he
went between the arches of the Coliseum, followed by the child, and taking with him what
looked like a bottle of wine, wrapped in a hand-
kerchief.

November 2. — The weather lately would
have suited one's ideal of an English November, except that there have been no fogs ; but of

ugly, hopeless clouds, chill, shivering winds, drizzle, and now and then pouring rain, much more than enough. An English coal fire, if we could see its honest face within doors, would compensate for all the unamiableness of the outside atmosphere; but we might ask for the sunshine of the New Jerusalem, with as much hope of getting it. It is extremely spirit-crushing, this remorseless gray, with its icy heart; and the more to depress the whole family, Una has taken what seems to be the Roman fever, by sitting down in the Palace of the Cæsars, while Mrs. S—— sketched the ruins. . . .

[During four months of the illness of his daughter, Mr. Hawthorne wrote no word of Journal. — S. H.]

February 27, 1859. — For many days past, there have been tokens of the coming Carnival in the Corso and the adjacent streets; for example, in the shops, by the display of masks of wire, pasteboard, silk, or cloth, some of beautiful features, others hideous, fantastic, currish, asinine, huge-nosed, or otherwise monstrous; some intended to cover the whole face, others concealing only the upper part, also white dominos, or robes bedizened with gold lace and theatric splendors, displayed at the windows of mercers or flaunting before the doors. Yesterday, Una and I came along the Corso, between

one and two o'clock, after a walk, and found all
these symptoms of impending merriment multi-
plied and intensified ; . . . rows of chairs, set
out along the sidewalks, elevated a foot or two
by means of planks ; great baskets, full of confetti, for sale in the nooks and recesses of the
streets ; bouquets of all qualities and prices.
The Corso was becoming pretty well thronged
with people; but, until two o'clock, nobody
dared to fling as much as a rosebud or a handful of sugar-plums.   There was a sort of holiday expression, however, on almost everybody's
face, such as I have not hitherto seen in Rome,
or in any part of Italy ; a smile gleaming out,
an aurora of mirth, which probably will not be
very exuberant in its noontide.   The day was
so sunny and bright that it made this opening
scene far more cheerful than any day of the last
year's Carnival.   As we threaded our way
through the Corso, Una kept wishing she could
plunge into the fun and uproar as Julian would ;
and for my own part, though I pretended to
take no interest in the matter, I could have
bandied confetti and nosegays as readily and as
riotously as any urchin there.   But my black
hat and grave talma would have been too good
a mark for the combatants, . . . so we went
home before a shot was fired. . . .

March 7. — I, as well as the rest of the family,

have followed up the Carnival pretty faithfully, and enjoyed it as well, or rather better, than could have been expected; principally in the street, as a mere looker-on, — which does not let one into the mystery of the fun, — and twice from a balcony, where I threw confetti, and partly understood why the young people like it so much. Certainly, there cannot well be a more picturesque spectacle in human life, than that stately, palatial avenue of the Corso, the more picturesque because so narrow, all hung with carpets and Gobelin tapestry, and the whole palace heights alive with faces ; and all the capacity of the street thronged with the most fantastic figures that either the fancies of folks alive at this day are able to contrive, or that live traditionally from year to year. . . . The Prince of Wales has fought manfully through the Carnival with confetti and bouquets and Una received several bouquets from him, on Saturday, as her carriage moved along.

March 8. — I went with Una to Mr. Motley's balcony, in the Corso, and saw the Carnival from it yesterday afternoon ; but the spectacle is strangely like a dream, in respect to the difficulty of retaining it in the mind and solidifying it into a description. I enjoyed it a good deal, and assisted in so far as to pelt all the people in cylinder hats with handsful of confetti. The

318

scene opens with a long array of cavalry, who ride through the Corso, preceded by a large band, playing loudly on their brazen instruments. . . . There were some splendid dresses, particularly contadina costumes of scarlet and gold, which seem to be actually the festal attire of that class of people, and must needs be so expensive that one must serve for a lifetime, if indeed it be not an inheritance. . . .

March 9. — I was, yesterday, an hour or so among the people on the sidewalks of the Corso, just on the edges of the fun. They appeared to be in a decorous, good-natured mood, neither entering into the merriment, nor harshly repelling; and when groups of maskers overflowed among them, they received their jokes in good part. Many women of the lower class were in the crowd of bystanders; generally broad and sturdy figures, clad evidently in their best attire, and wearing a good many ornaments; such as gold or coral beads and necklaces, combs of silver or gold, heavy ear-rings, curiously wrought brooches, perhaps cameos or mosaics, though I think they prefer purely metallic work to these. One ornament very common among them is a large bodkin, which they stick through their hair. It is usually of silver, but sometimes it looks like steel, and is made in the shape of a sword, — a long Spanish thrusting-sword, for

example. Dr. Franco told us a story of a woman of Trastevere, who was addressed rudely
at the Carnival by a gentleman ; she warned
him to desist, but, as he still persisted, she drew
the bodkin from her hair, and stabbed him to
the heart.

By and by I went to Mr. Motley's balcony
and looked down on the closing scenes of the
Carnival. Methought the merry-makers labored
harder to be mirthful, and yet were somewhat
tired of their eight play-days ; and their dresses
looked a little shabby, rumpled, and draggled ;
but the lack of sunshine — which we have had
on all the preceding days — may have produced
this effect. The wheels of some of the carriages
were wreathed round and spoked with green
foliage, making a very pretty and fanciful appearance, as did likewise the harnesses of the
horses, which were trimmed with roses. The
pervading noise and uproar of human voices is
one of the most effective points of the matter ;
but the scene is quite indescribable, and its
effect not to be conceived without both witnessing and taking part in it. If you merely look
at it, it depresses you; if you take even the
slightest share in it, you become aware that it
has a fascination, and you no longer wonder that
the young people, at least, take such delight in
plunging into this mad river of fun that goes
roaring between the narrow limits of the Corso.

As twilight came on, the moccoli commenced,
and, as it grew darker, the whole street twinkled
with lights, which would have been innumerable
if every torch-bearer had not been surrounded by
a host of enemies, who tried to extinguish his
poor little twinkle. It was a pity to lose so
much splendor as there might have been ; but yet
there was a kind of symbolism in the thought
that every one of those thousands of twinkling
lights was in charge of somebody, who was striv-
ing with all his might to keep it alive. Not
merely the street-way, but all the balconies and
hundreds of windows were lit up with these
little torches ; so that it seemed as if the stars
had crumbled into glittering fragments, and
rained down upon the Corso, some of them
lodging upon the palace fronts, some falling on
the ground. Besides this, there were gas-lights
burning with a white flame; but this illumination was not half so interesting as that of the
torches, which indicated human struggle. All
this time there were myriad voices shouting,
" SENZA MOCCOLO ! " and mingling into one long
roar. We, in our balcony, carried on a civil war
against one another's torches, as is the custom
of human beings, within even the narrowest precincts ; but after a while we grew tired, and so did
the crowd, apparently ; for the lights vanished,
one after another, till the gas-lights — which at
first were an unimportant part of the illumina-

tion — shone quietly out, overpowering the scattered twinkles of the moccoli. They were what the fixed stars are to the transitory splendors of human life.

Mr. Motley tells me that it was formerly the custom to have a mock funeral of Harlequin, who was supposed to die at the close of the Carnival, during which he had reigned supreme, and all the people, or as many as chose, bore torches at his burial. But this being considered an indecorous mockery of popish funereal customs, the present frolic of the moccoli was instituted, — in some sort, growing out of it.

All last night, or as much of it as I was awake, there was a noise of song and late revellers in the streets; but to-day we have waked up in the sad and sober season of Lent.

It is worthy of remark, that all the jollity of the Carnival is a genuine ebullition of spirit, without the aid of wine or strong drink.

March 11. — Yesterday we went to the Catacomb of St. Calixtus, the entrance to which is alongside of the Appian Way, within sight of the tomb of Cecilia Metella. We descended not a very great way under ground, by a broad flight of stone steps, and, lighting some wax tapers, with which we had provided ourselves, we followed the guide through a great many

intricate passages, which mostly were just wide
enough for me to touch the wall on each side,
while keeping my elbows close to my body ; and
as to height, they were from seven to ten feet,
and sometimes a good deal higher. . . . It was
rather picturesque, when we saw the long line of
our tapers, for another large party had joined us,
twinkling along the dark passage, and it was interesting to think of the former inhabitants of
these caverns. . . . In one or two places there
was the round mark in the stone or plaster where
a bottle had been deposited.   This was said to
have been the token of a martyr's burial place,
and to have contained his blood.   After leaving
the Catacomb, we drove onward to Cecilia Metella's tomb, which we entered and inspected.
Within the immensely massive circular substance of the tomb was a round, vacant space,
and this interior vacancy was open at the top,
and had nothing but some fallen stones and a
heap of earth at the bottom.

On our way home we entered the Church of
" Dominè, quo Vadis," and looked at the old
fragment of the Appian Way where our Saviour
met St. Peter, and left the impression of his feet
in one of the Roman paving-stones.   The stone
has been removed, and there is now only a facsimile engraved in a block of marble, occupying
the place where Jesus stood.   It is a great pity
they had not left the original stone ; for then all

ts brother stones in the pavement would have
ieemed to confirm the truth of the legend.

While we were at dinner, a gentleman called
and was shown into the parlor. We supposed
it to be Mr. May; but soon his voice grew
familiar, and my wife was sure it was General
Pierce, so I left the table, and found it to be
really he. I was rejoiced to see him, though a
little saddened to see the marks of care and
coming age, in many a whitening hair, and many
a furrow, and, still more, in something that
seemed to have passed away out of him, without leaving any trace. His voice, sometimes,
sounded strange and old, though generally it
was what it used to be. He was evidently glad
to see me, glad to see my wife, glad to see the
children, though there was something melancholy in his tone, when he remarked what a
stout boy Julian had grown. Poor fellow! he
has neither son nor daughter to keep his heart
warm. This morning I have been with him to
St. Peter's, and elsewhere about the city, and
find him less changed than he seemed to be last
night; not at all changed in heart and affections.
We talked freely about all matters that came up;
among the rest, about the project — recogniz-
able by many tokens — for bringing him again
forward as a candidate for the presidency next
year. He appears to be firmly resolved not
again to present himself to the country, and is

content to let his one administration stand, and to be judged by the public and posterity on the merits of that. No doubt, he is perfectly sincere ; no doubt, too, he would again be a candidate, if a pretty unanimous voice of the party should demand it. I retain all my faith in his administrative faculty, and should be glad, for his sake, to have it fully recognized ; but the probabilities, as far as I can see, do not indicate for him another presidential term.

March 15. — This morning I went with my wife and Miss Hoar to Miss Hosmer's studio, to see her statue of Zenobia. We found her in her premises, springing about with a bird-like action. She has a lofty room, with a skylight window ; it was pretty well warmed with a stove, and there was a small orange-tree in a pot, with the oranges growing on it, and two or three flower shrubs in bloom. She herself looked prettily, with her jaunty little velvet cap on the side of her head, whence came clustering out her short brown curls ; her face full of pleasant life and quick expression ; and though somewhat worn with thought and struggle, handsome and spirited. She told us that " her wig was growing as gray as a rat."

There were but very few things in the room ; two or three plaster busts, a headless cast of a plaster statue, and a cast of the Minerva Medica, which perhaps she had been studying as a help towards the design of her Zenobia; for, at any rate, I seemed to discern a resemblance or analogy between the two. Zenobia stood in the centre of the room, as yet unfinished in the clay, but a very noble and remarkable statue indeed, full of dignity and beauty. It is wonderful that so brisk a woman could have achieved a work so quietly impressive; and there is something in Zenobia's air that conveys the idea of music, uproar, and a great throng all about her; whilst she walks in the midst of it, self-sustained, and kept in a sort of sanctity by her native pride. The idea of motion is attained with great success; you not only perceive that she is walking, but know at just what tranquil pace she steps, amid the music of the triumph. The drapery is very fine and full; she is decked with ornaments; but the chains of her captivity hang from wrist to wrist; and her deportment — indicating a soul so much above her misfortune, yet not insensible to the weight of it — makes these chains a richer decoration than all her other jewels. I know not whether there be some magic in the present imperfect finish of the statue, or in the material of clay, as being a better medium of expression than even marble; but certainly I have seldom been more impressed by a piece of modern sculpture. Miss Hosmer showed us photo-

graphy of her Puck — which I have seen in the
marble — and likewise of the Will-o'-the-Wisp,
both very pretty and fanciful.   It indicates
much variety of power that Zenobia should be
the sister of these, which would seem the more
natural offspring of her quick and vivid character.   But Zenobia is a high, heroic ode.

. . . On my way up the Via Babuino, I met
General Pierce.   We have taken two or three
walks together, and stray among the Roman
ruins, and old scenes of history, talking of matters in which he is personally concerned, yet
which are as historic as anything around us.
He is singularly little changed ; the more I see
him, the more I get him back, just such as he
was in our youth.   This morning, his face, air,
and smile were so wonderfully like himself of
old, that at least thirty years are annihilated.

Zenobia's manacles serve as bracelets ; a very
ingenious and suggestive idea.

March 18. — I went to the sculpture-gallery
of the Capitol yesterday, and saw, among other
things, the Venus in her secret cabinet.   This
was my second view of her : the first time, I
greatly admired her ; now, she made no very
favorable impression.   There are twenty Venuses whom I like as well, or better.   On the
whole, she is a heavy, clumsy, unintellectual,
and commonplace figure ; at all events, not in

327

good looks to-day. Marble beauties seem to
suffer the same occasional eclipses as those of
flesh and blood. We looked at the Faun, the
Dying Gladiator, and other famous sculptures;
but nothing had a glory round it, perhaps because the sirocco was blowing. These halls
of the Capitol have always had a dreary and
depressing effect upon me, very different from
those of the Vatican. I know not why, except that the rooms of the Capitol have a dingy,
shabby, and neglected look, and that the statues are dusty, and all the arrangements less
magnificent than at the Vatican. The corroded
and discolored surfaces of the statues take away
from the impression of immortal youth, and
turn Apollo[1] himself into an old stone; unless
at rare intervals, when he appears transfigured
by a light gleaming from within.

March 23. — I am wearing away listlessly
these last precious days of my abode in Rome.
Una's illness is disheartening, and by confining
——, it takes away the energy and enterprise
that were the spring of all our movements. I
am weary of Rome, without having seen and
known it as I ought, and I shall be glad to get
away from it, though no doubt there will be
many yearnings to return hereafter, and many
regrets that I did not make better use of the

[1] The Lycian Apollo.

opportunities within my grasp. Still, I have
been in Rome long enough to be imbued with
its atmosphere, and this is the essential condition of knowing a place; for such knowledge
does not consist in having seen every particular
object it contains. In the state of mind in
which I now stand towards Rome, there is very
little advantage to be gained by staying here
longer.

And yet I had a pleasant stroll enough yesterday afternoon, all by myself, from the Corso
down past the Church of St. Andrea della
Valle, — the site where Cæsar was murdered,
— and thence to the Farnese Palace, the noble
court of which I entered; thence to the Piazza
Cenci, where I looked at one or two ugly old
palaces, and fixed on one of them as the residence of Beatrice's father; then past the Temple of Vesta, and skirting along the Tiber, and
beneath the Aventine, till I somewhat unexpectedly came in sight of the gray pyramid of
Caius Cestius. I went out of the city gate,
and leaned on the parapet that encloses the
pyramid, advancing its high, unbroken slope
and peak, where the great blocks of marble still
fit almost as closely to one another as when
they were first laid; though, indeed, there are
crevices just large enough for plants to root
themselves, and flaunt and trail over the face
of this great tomb; only a little verdure, how-

ever, over a vast space of marble, still white in spots, but pervadingly turned gray, by two thousand years' action of the atmosphere. Thence I came home by the Cœlian, and sat down on an ancient flight of steps under one of the arches of the Coliseum, into which the sunshine fell sidelong. It was a delightful afternoon, not precisely like any weather that I have known elsewhere ; certainly never in America, where it is always too cold or too hot. It resembles summer more than anything which we New Englanders recognize in our idea of spring, but there was an indescribable something, sweet, fresh, gentle, that does not belong to summer, and that thrilled and tickled my heart with a feeling partly sensuous, partly spiritual.

I go to the bank and read Galignani and the American newspapers ; thence I stroll to the Pincian or to the Medici Gardens ; I see a good deal of General Pierce, and we talk over his presidential life, which, I now really think, he has no latent desire nor purpose to renew. Yet he seems to have enjoyed it while it lasted, and certainly he was in his element as an administrative man ; not far-seeing, not possessed of vast stores of political wisdom in advance of his occasions, but endowed with a miraculous intuition of what ought to be done just at the time for action. His judgment of things about him is wonderful, and his Cabinet recognized it as such; for though they were men of great ability, he was evidently the master-mind among them. None of them were particularly his personal friends when he selected them; they all loved him when they parted; and he showed me a letter, signed by all, in which they expressed their feelings of respect and attachment at the close of his administration. There was a noble frankness on his part that kept the atmosphere always clear among them, and in reference to this characteristic, Governor Marcy told him that the years during which he had been connected with his Cabinet had been the happiest of his life. Speaking of Caleb Cushing, he told me that the unreliability, the fickleness, which is usually attributed to him is an actual characteristic, but that it is intellectual, not moral. He has such comprehensiveness, such mental variety and activity, that, if left to himself, he cannot keep fast hold of one view of things, and so cannot, without external help, be a consistent man. He needs the influence of a more single and stable judgment to keep him from divergency, and, on this condition, he is a most inestimable coadjutor. As regards learning and ability, he has no superior.

Pierce spoke the other day of the idea among some of his friends that his life had been planned, from a very early period, with a view

331

to the station which he ultimately reached. He
smiled at the notion, said that it was inconsist-
ent with his natural character, and that it implied foresight and dexterity beyond what any
mortal is endowed with. I think so too ; but
nevertheless, I was long and long ago aware that
he cherished a very high ambition, and that,
though he might not anticipate the highest
things, he cared very little about inferior objects.
Then as to plans, I do not think that he had any
definite ones ; but there was in him a subtle
faculty, a real instinct, that taught him what was
good for him, — that is to say, promotive of
his political success, — and made him inevitably do it. He had a magic touch, that arranged matters with a delicate potency, which
he himself hardly recognized ; and he wrought
through other minds so that neither he nor
they always knew when and how far they were
under his influence. Before his nomination
for the presidency I had a sense that it was coming, and it never seemed to me an accident. He
is a most singular character ; so frank, so true,
so immediate, so subtle, so simple, so complicated.

I passed by the tower in the Via Portoghese
to-day, and observed that the nearest shop appears to be for the sale of cotton or linen cloth.
. . . The upper window of the tower was half
open ; of course, like all, or almost all, other

Roman windows, it is divided vertically, and each half swings back on hinges. . . .

Last week a fritter establishment was opened in our piazza. It was a wooden booth erected in the open square, and covered with canvas painted red, which looked as if it had withstood much rain and sunshine. In front were three great boughs of laurel, not so much for shade, I think, as ornament. There were two men, and their apparatus for business was a sort of stove, or charcoal furnace, and a frying-pan to place over it ; they had an armful or two of dry sticks, some flour, and I suppose oil, and this seemed to be all. It was Friday, and Lent besides, and possibly there was some other peculiar propriety in the consumption of fritters just then. At all events, their fire burned merrily from morning till night, and pretty late into the evening, and they had a fine run of custom ; the commodity being simply dough, cut into squares or rhomboids, and thrown into the boiling oil, which quickly turned them to a light brown color. I sent Julian to buy some, and, tasting one, it resembled an unspeakably bad doughnut, without any sweetening. In fact, it was sour, for the Romans like their bread, and all their preparations of flour, in a state of acetous fermentation, which serves them instead of salt or other condiment. This fritter shop had grown up in a night, like Aladdin's palace, and vanished as suddenly ; for after standing through Friday, Saturday, and Sunday, it was gone on Monday morning ; and a charcoal-strewn place, on the pavement where the furnace had been, was the only memorial of it. It was curious to observe how immediately it became a lounging-place for idle people, who stood and talked all day with the fritter-friers, just as they might at any old shop in the basement of a palace, or between the half-buried pillars of the Temple of Minerva, which had been familiar to them and their remote grandfathers.

April 14. — Yesterday afternoon I drove with Mr. and Mrs. Story and Mr. Wilde to see a statue of Venus, which has just been discovered, outside of the Porta Portese, on the other side of the Tiber. A little distance beyond the gate we came to the entrance of a vineyard, with a wheel track through the midst of it ; and, following this, we soon came to a hillside, in which an excavation had been made with the purpose of building a grotto for keeping and storing wine. They had dug down into what seemed to be an ancient bathroom, or some structure of that kind, the excavation being square and cellar-like, and built round with old subterranean walls of brick and stone. Within this hollow space the statue had been found, and it was now standing against one of the walls, covered with a coarse cloth, or a canvas bag. This being removed, there appeared a headless marble figure, earth stained, of course, and with a slightly corroded surface, but wonderfully delicate and beautiful, the shape, size, and attitude, apparently, of the Venus di Medici, but, as we all thought, more beautiful than that. It is supposed to be the original from which the Venus di Medici was copied. Both arms were broken off, but the greater part of both, and nearly the whole of one hand, had been found, and these being adjusted to the figure, they took the well-known position before the bosom and the middle, as if the fragmentary woman retained her instinct of modesty to the last. There were the marks on the bosom and thigh where the fingers had touched ; whereas in the Venus di Medici, if I remember rightly, the fingers are sculptured quite free of the person. The man who showed the statue now lifted from a corner a round block of marble, which had been lying there among other fragments, and this he placed upon the shattered neck of the Venus ; and behold, it was her head and face, perfect, all but the nose ! Even in spite of this mutilation, it seemed immediately to light up and vivify the entire figure ; and, whatever I may heretofore have written about the countenance of the Venus di Medici, I here record my belief that that head has been wrongfully foisted upon the statue ; at all events, it is unspeakably inferior to this newly discovered one. This face has a breadth and front which are strangely deficient in the other. The eyes are well opened, most unlike the buttonhole lids of the Venus di Medici ; the whole head is so much larger as to entirely obviate the criticism that has always been made on the diminutive head of the Di Medici statue. If it had but a nose ! They ought to sift every handful of earth that has been thrown out of the excavation, for the nose and the missing hand and fingers must needs be there ; and, if they were found, the effect would be like the reappearance of a divinity upon earth. Mutilated as we saw her, it was strangely interesting to be present at the moment, as it were, when she had just risen from her long burial, and was shedding the unquenchable lustre around her which no eye had seen for twenty or more centuries. The earth still clung about her ; her beautiful lips were full of it, till Mr. Story took a thin chip of wood and cleared it away from between them.

The proprietor of the vineyard stood by ; a man with the most purple face and hugest and reddest nose that I ever beheld in my life. It must have taken innumerable hogsheads of his thin vintage to empurple his face in this man-

ner. He chuckled much over the statue, and,
I suppose, counts upon making his fortune by
it. He is now awaiting a bid from the papal
government, which, I believe, has the right
of preëmption whenever any relics of ancient
art are discovered. If the statue could but
be smuggled out of Italy, it might command
almost any price. There is not, I think, any
name of a sculptor on the pedestal, as on that
of the Venus di Medici. A dolphin is sculptured on the pillar against which she leans.
The statue is of Greek marble. It was first
found about eight days ago, but has been offered for inspection only a day or two, and
already the visitors come in throngs, and the
beggars gather about the entrance of the vineyard. A wine shop, too, seems to have been
opened on the premises for the accommodation
of this great concourse ; and we saw a row of
German artists sitting at a long table in the
open air, each with a glass of thin wine and
something to eat before him ; for the Ger-
mans refresh nature ten times to other persons
once.

How the whole world might be peopled with
antique beauty if the Romans would only dig!

April 19. — General Pierce leaves Rome this
morning for Venice, by way of Ancona, and
taking the steamer thence to Trieste. I had

hoped to make the journey along with him ; but Una's terrible illness has made it necessary for us to continue here another month, and we are thankful that this seems now to be the extent of our misfortune.   Never having had any trouble before that pierced into my very vitals, I did not know what comfort there might be in the manly sympathy of a friend ; but Pierce has undergone so great a sorrow of his own, and has so large and kindly a heart, and is so tender and so strong, that he really did me good, and I shall always love him the better for the recollection of his ministrations in these dark days. Thank God, the thing we dreaded did not come to pass.

Pierce is wonderfully little changed.   Indeed, now that he has won and enjoyed — if there were any enjoyment in it — the highest success that public life could give him, he seems more like what he was in his early youth than at any subsequent period.   He is evidently happier than I have ever known him since our college days ; satisfied with what he has been, and with the position in the country that remains to him, after filling such an office.   Amid all his former successes, — early as they came, and great as they were, — I always perceived that something gnawed within him, and kept him forever restless and miserable.   Nothing he won was worth the winning, except as a step gained toward the summit. I cannot tell how early he began to look towards the presidency; but I believe he would have died an unhappy man without it. And yet what infinite chances there seemed to be against his attaining it! When I look at it in one way, it strikes me as absolutely miraculous; in another, it came like an event that I had all along expected. It was due to his wonderful tact, which is of so subtle a character that he himself is but partially sensible of it.

I have found in him, here in Rome, the whole of my early friend, and even better than I used to know him; a heart as true and affectionate, a mind much widened and deepened by his experience of life. We hold just the same relation to each other as of yore, and we have passed all the turning-off places, and may hope to go on together still the same dear friends as long as we live. I do not love him one whit the less for having been President, nor for having done me the greatest good in his power; a fact that speaks eloquently in his favor, and perhaps says a little for myself. If he had been merely a benefactor, perhaps I might not have borne it so well; but each did his best for the other as friend for friend.

May 15. — Yesterday afternoon we went to the Barberini picture-gallery to take a farewell look at the Beatrice Cenci, which I have twice

visited before since our return from Florence.
I attempted a description of it at my first visit,
more than a year ago, but the picture is quite
indescribable and unaccountable in its effect, for
if you attempt to analyze it you can never succeed in getting at the secret of its fascination.
Its peculiar expression eludes a straightforward
glance, and can only be caught by side glimpses,
or when the eye falls upon it casually as it were,
and without thinking to discover anything, as
if the picture had a life and consciousness of its
own, and were resolved not to betray its secret
of grief or guilt, though it wears the full expression of it when it imagines itself unseen.   I
think no other such magical effect can ever have
been wrought by pencil.   I looked close into
its eyes, with a determination to see all that
there was in them, and could see nothing that
might not have been in any young girl's eyes;
and yet, a moment afterwards, there was the
expression — seen aside, and vanishing in a
moment — of a being unhumanized by some
terrible fate, and gazing at me out of a remote
and inaccessible region, where she was frightened
to be alone, but where no sympathy could reach
her.   The mouth is beyond measure touching;
the lips apart, looking as innocent as a baby's
after it has been crying.   The picture never can
be copied.   Guido himself could not have done
it over again.   The copyists get all sorts of

expression, gay as well as grievous; some copies have a coquettish air, a half-backward glance, thrown alluring at the spectator, but nobody ever did catch, or ever will, the vanishing charm of that sorrow. I hated to leave the picture, and yet was glad when I had taken my last glimpse, because it so perplexed and troubled me not to be able to get hold of its secret.

Thence we went to the Church of the Capuchins, and saw Guido's Archangel. I have been several times to this church, but never saw the picture before, though I am familiar with the mosaic copy at St. Peter's, and had supposed the latter to be an equivalent representation of the original. It is nearly or quite so as respects the general effect; but there is a beauty in the Archangel's face that immeasurably surpasses the copy, — the expression of heavenly severity, and a degree of pain, trouble, or disgust, at being brought in contact with sin, even for the purpose of quelling and punishing it. There is something finical in the copy, which I do not find in the original. The sandalled feet are here those of an angel; in the mosaic they are those of a celestial coxcomb, treading daintily, as if he were afraid they would be soiled by the touch of Lucifer.

After looking at the Archangel we went down under the church, guided by a fleshy monk, and saw the famous cemetery, where the dead monks of many centuries back have been laid to sleep in sacred earth from Jerusalem. . . .

HÔTEL DES COLONIES, MARSEILLES, *May* 29, *Saturday*. — Wednesday was the day fixed for our departure from Rome, and after breakfast I walked to the Pincian, and saw the garden and the city, and the Borghese grounds, and St. Peter's in an earlier sunlight than ever before. Methought they never looked so beautiful, nor the sky so bright and blue. I saw Soracte on the horizon, and I looked at everything as if for the last time; nor do I wish ever to see any of these objects again, though no place ever took so strong a hold of my being as Rome, nor ever seemed so close to me and so strangely familiar. I seem to know it better than my birthplace, and to have known it longer; and though I have been very miserable there, and languid with the effects of the atmosphere, and disgusted with a thousand things in its daily life, still I cannot say I hate it, perhaps might fairly own a love for it. But life being too short for such questionable and troublesome enjoyments, I desire never to set eyes on it again. . . .

. . . We traversed again that same weary and dreary tract of country which we passed over in a winter afternoon and night on our first arrival in Rome. It is as desolate a country as can well be imagined, but about midway of our journey we came to the seashore, and kept very near it during the rest of the way. The sight and fragrance of it were exceedingly refreshing after so long an interval, and Una revived visibly as we rushed along, while Julian chuckled and contorted himself with ineffable delight.

We reached Cività Vecchia in three or four hours, and were there subjected to various troubles. . . . All the while Miss S—— and I were bothering about the passport, the rest of the family sat in the sun on the quay, with all kinds of bustle and confusion around them; a very trying experience to Una after the long seclusion and quiet of her sick-chamber. But she did not seem to suffer from it, and we finally reached the steamer in good condition and spirits. . . .

I slept wretchedly in my short and narrow berth, more especially as there was an old gentleman who snored as if he were sounding a charge; it was terribly hot too, and I rose before four o'clock, and was on deck amply in time to watch the distant approach of sunrise. We arrived at Leghorn pretty early, and might have gone ashore and spent the day. Indeed, we had been recommended by Dr. Franco, and had fully purposed to spend a week or ten days there, in expectation of benefit to Una's health from the sea air and sea bathing, because he thought her still too feeble to make the whole voyage to Marseilles at a stretch. But she showed herself so strong that we thought she would get as much good from our three days' voyage as from the days by the seashore. Morever, . . . we all of us still felt the languor of the Roman atmosphere, and dreaded the hubbub and crazy confusion of landing at an Italian port. . . . So we lay in the harbor all day without stirring from the steamer. . . . It would have been pleasant, however, to have gone to Pisa, fifteen miles off, and seen the leaning tower; but, for my part, I have arrived at that point where it is somewhat pleasanter to sit quietly in any spot whatever than to see whatever grandest or most beautiful thing. At least this was my mood in the harbor of Leghorn. From the deck of the steamer there were many things visible that might have been interesting to describe: the boats of peculiar rig, and covered with awning; the crowded shipping; the disembarkation of horses from the French cavalry, which were lowered from steamers into gondolas or lighters, and hung motionless, like the sign of the Golden Fleece, during the transit, only kicking a little when their feet happened to graze the vessel's side. One horse plunged overboard, and narrowly escaped drowning. There was likewise a disembarkation of French soldiers in a train of boats, which rowed shoreward with sound of

344

trumpet.   The French are concentrating a considerable number of troops at this point.

Our steamer was detained by order of the
French government to take on board despatches;
so that, instead of sailing at dusk, as is customary, we lay in the harbor till seven of the next
morning.   A number of young Sardinian officers, in green uniform, came on board, and a
pale and picturesque-looking Italian, and other
worthies of less note, — English, American, and
of all races, — among them a Turk with a little
boy in Christian dress; also a Greek gentleman
with his young bride.

At the appointed time we weighed anchor for
Genoa, and had a beautiful day on the Medi-
terranean, and for the first time in my life I saw
the real dark blue of the sea. I do not remember noticing it on my outward voyage to Italy.
It is the most beautiful hue that can be imagined,
like a liquid sky ; and it retains its lustrous blue
directly under the side of the ship, where the
water of the mid-Atlantic looks greenish. . . .
We reached Genoa at seven in the afternoon. . . .
Genoa looks most picturesquely from the sea,
at the foot of a sheltering semicircle of lofty hills :
and as we lay in the harbor we saw, among other
interesting objects, the great Doria Palace, with
its gardens, and the Cathedral, and a heap and
sweep of stately edifices, with the mountains
looking down upon the city, and crowned with

fortresses. The variety of hue in the houses, white, green, pink, and orange, was very remarkable. It would have been well to go ashore here for an hour or two and see the streets, — having already seen the palaces, churches, and public buildings at our former visit, — and buy a few specimens of Genoa goldsmiths' work ; but I preferred the steamer's deck, so the evening passed pleasantly away ; the two lighthouses at the entrance of the port kindled up their fires, and at nine o'clock the evening gun thundered from the fortress, and was reverberated from the heights. We sailed away at eleven, and I was roused from my first sleep by the snortings and hissings of the vessel as she got under way.

At Genoa we took on board some more passengers, an English nobleman with his lady being of the number. These were Lord and Lady J——, and before the end of our voyage his lordship talked to me of a translation of Tasso in which he is engaged, and a stanza or two of which he repeated to me. I really liked the lines, and liked too the simplicity and frankness with which he spoke of it to me, a stranger, and the way he seemed to separate his egotism from the idea which he evidently had that he is going to make an excellent translation. I sincerely hope it may be so. He began it without any idea of publishing it, or of ever bring-

ing it to a conclusion, but merely as a solace
and occupation while in great trouble during
an illness of his wife, but he is gradually come
to find it the most absorbing occupation he ever
undertook; and as Mr. Gladstone and other high
authorities give him warm encouragement, he
now means to translate the entire poem, and to
publish it, with beautiful illustrations, and two
years hence the world may expect to see it. I do
not quite perceive how such a man as this — a
man of frank, warm, simple, kindly nature, but
surely not of a poetical temperament, or very
refined, or highly cultivated — should make a
good version of Tasso's poems; but perhaps
the dead poet's soul may take possession of
this healthy organization, and wholly turn him
to its own purposes.

The latter part of our voyage to-day lay close
along the coast of France, which was hilly and
picturesque, and as we approached Marseilles
was very bold and striking. We steered among
the rocky islands, rising abruptly out of the sea,
mere naked crags, without a trace of verdure
upon them, and with the surf breaking at their
feet. They were unusual specimens of what
hills would look like without the soil, that is to
them what flesh is to a skeleton. Their shapes
were often wonderfully fine, and the great headlands thrust themselves out, and took such hues
of light and shade that it seemed like sailing

through a picture.   In the course of the afternoon a squall came up and blackened the sky
all over in a twinkling ; our vessel pitched and
tossed, and a brig a little way from us had her
sails blown about in wild fashion.   The blue of
the sea turned as black as night, and soon the
rain began to spatter down upon us, and continued to sprinkle and drizzle a considerable time
after the wind had subsided.   It was quite calm
and pleasant when we entered the harbor of
Marseilles, which lies at the foot of very fair
hills, and is set among great cliffs of stone.   I
did not attend much to this, however, being in
dread of the difficulty of landing and passing
through the custom house, with our twelve or
fourteen trunks and numberless carpet-bags.
The trouble vanished into thin air, nevertheless, as we approached it, for not a single trunk
or bag was opened, and, moreover, our luggage
and ourselves were not only landed, but the
greater part of it conveyed to the railway without any expense.   Long live Louis Napoleon,
say I.   We established ourselves at the Hôtel
des Colonies, and then Miss S——, Julian,
and I drove hither and thither about Marseilles,
making arrangements for our journey to Avignon, where we mean to go to-day.   We might
have avoided a good deal of this annoyance ;
but travellers, like other people, are continually
getting their experience just a little too late.

It was after nine before we got back to the hotel and took our tea in peace.

Avignon, Hôtel de l'Europe, *June* 1. — I remember nothing very special to record about Marseilles; though it was really like passing from death into life, to find ourselves in busy, cheerful, effervescing France, after living so long between asleep and awake in sluggish Italy. Marseilles is a very interesting and entertaining town, with its bold surrounding heights, its wide streets, — so they seemed to us after the Roman alleys, — its squares, shady with trees, its diversified population of sailors, citizens, Orientals, and what not; but I have no spirit for description any longer; being tired of seeing things, and still more of telling myself about them. Only a young traveller can have patience to write his travels. The newest things, nowadays, have a familiarity to my eyes; whereas in their lost sense of novelty lies the charm and power of description.

On Monday (30th May), though it began with heavy rain, we set early about our preparations for departure, . . . and, at about three, we left the Hôtel des Colonies. It is a very comfortable hotel, though expensive. The Restaurant connected with it occupies the enclosed courtyard and the arcades around it; and it was a good amusement to look down from the surrounding gallery, communicating with our apartments, and see the fashion and manner of French eating, all the time going forward. In sunny weather a great awning is spread over the whole court, across from the upper stories of the house. There is a grass-plat in the middle, and a very spacious and airy dining-saloon is thus formed.

Our railroad carriage was comfortable, and we found in it, besides two other Frenchwomen, two nuns. They were very devout, and sedulously read their little books of devotion, repeated prayers under their breath, kissed the crucifixes which hung at their girdles, and told a string of beads, which they passed from one to the other. So much were they occupied with these duties, that they scarcely looked at the scenery along the road, though, probably, it is very rare for them to see anything outside of their convent walls. They never failed to mutter a prayer and kiss the crucifix whenever we plunged into a tunnel. If they glanced at their fellow passengers, it was shyly and askance, with their lips in motion all the time, like children afraid to let their eyes wander from their lesson-book. One of them, however, took occasion to pull down Rose's dress, which, in her frisky movements about the carriage, had got out of place, too high for the nun's sense of decorum. Neither of them was at all pretty,

350

nor was the black stuff dress and white muslin
cap in the least becoming; neither were their
features of an intelligent or high-bred stamp.
Their manners, however, or such little glimpses
as I could get of them, were unexceptionable;
and when I drew a curtain to protect one of
them from the sun, she made me a very courteous gesture of thanks.

We had some very good views both of sea
and hills; and a part of our way lay along the
banks of the Rhone. . . . By the bye, at the station at Marseilles, I bought the two volumes
of the Livre des Merveilles, by a certain author of my acquaintance, translated into French,
and printed and illustrated in very pretty style.
Miss S—— also bought them and, in answer
to her inquiry for other works by the same author, the bookseller observed that "she did not
think Monsieur Nathaniel had published anything else." The Christian name seems to be
the most important one in France, and still more
especially in Italy.

We arrived at Avignon, Hôtel de l'Europe,
in the dusk of the evening. . . . The lassitude
of Rome still clings to us, and I, at least, feel no
spring of life or activity, whether at morn or
eve. In the morning we found ourselves very
pleasantly situated as regards lodgings. The
gallery of our suite of rooms looks down as
usual into an enclosed court, three sides of

which are formed by the stone house and its two wings, and the third by a high wall, with a gateway of iron between two lofty stone pillars, which, for their capitals, have great stone vases, with grass growing in them, and hanging over the brim. There is a large plane-tree in one corner of the court, and creeping plants clamber up trellises ; and there are pots of flowers and bird cages, all of which give a very fresh and cheerful aspect to the enclosure. The court is paved with small round stones ; the omnibus belonging to the hotel, and all the carriages of guests, drive into it ; and the wide arch of the stable door opens under the central part of the house. Nevertheless, the scene is not in all respects that of a stable yard ; for gentlemen and ladies come from the *salle à manger* and other rooms, and stand talking in the court, or occupy chairs and seats there ; children play about ; the hostess or her daughter often appears and talks with her guests or servants ; dogs lounge, and, in short, the court might well enough be taken for the one scene of a classic play. The hotel seems to be of the first class, though such would not be indicated, either in England or America, by thus mixing up the stable with the lodgings. I have taken two or three rambles about the town, and have climbed a high rock which dominates over it, and gives a most extensive view from the broad table-land of its summit. The old church of Avignon — as old as the times of its popes, and older — stands close beside this mighty and massive crag. We went into it, and found it a dark old place, with broad, interior arches, and a singularly shaped dome; a venerable Gothic and Grecian porch, with ancient frescos in its arched spaces; some dusky pictures within; an ancient chair of stone, formerly occupied by the popes, and much else that would have been exceedingly interesting before I went to Rome. But Rome takes the charm out of all inferior antiquity, as well as the life out of human beings.

This forenoon, Julian and I have crossed the Rhone by a bridge, just the other side of one of the city gates, which is near our hotel. We walked along the river-side, and saw the ruins of an ancient bridge, which ends abruptly in the midst of the stream; two or three arches still making tremendous strides across, while the others have long ago been crumbled away by the rush of the rapid river. The bridge was originally founded by St. Benedict, who received a Divine order to undertake the work, while yet a shepherd-boy, with only three sous in his pocket; and he proved the authenticity of the mission by taking an immense stone on his shoulder, and laying it for the foundation. There is still an ancient chapel midway on the bridge, and I believe St. Benedict lies buried

353

there, in the midst of his dilapidated work. The bridge now used is considerably lower down the stream. It is a wooden suspension bridge, broader than the ancient one, and doubtless more than supplies its place; else, unquestionably, St. Benedict would think it necessary to repair his own. The view from the inner side of this ruined structure, grass-grown and weedy, and leading to such a precipitous plunge into the swift river, is very picturesque, in connection with the gray town and above it, the great, massive bulk of the cliff, the towers of the church, and of a vast old edifice, shapeless, ugly, and venerable, which the popes built and occupied as their palace, many centuries ago. . . .

After dinner, we all set out on a walk, in the course of which we called at a bookseller's shop, to show Una an enormous cat, which I had already seen. It is of the Angora breed, of a mottled yellow color, and is really a wonder; as big and broad as a tolerably sized dog, very soft and silken, and apparently of the gentlest disposition. I never imagined the like, nor felt anything so deeply soft as this great beast. Its master seems very fond and proud of it; and great a favorite as the cat is, she does not take airs upon herself, but is gently shy and timid in her demonstrations.

We ascended the great Rocher above the palace of the popes, and on our way looked into

the old church, which was so dim in the decline
of day that we could not see within the dusky
arches, through which the chapels communicated with the nave.   Thence we pursued our
way up the farther ascent, and, standing on the
edge of the precipice, — protected by a parapet
of stone, and in other places by an iron railing,
— we could look down upon the road that winds
its dusky track far below, and at the river Rhone,
which eddies close beside it.   This is indeed a
massive and lofty cliff, and it tumbles down so
precipitously that I could readily have flung myself from the bank, and alighted on my head in
the middle of the river.   The Rhone passes so
near its base that I threw stones a good way
into its current.   We talked with a man of Avignon, who leaned over the parapet near by, and
he was very kind in explaining the points of
view, and told us that the river, which winds and
doubles upon itself so as to look like at least
two rivers, is really the Rhone alone.   The
Durance joins with it within a few miles below
Avignon, but is here invisible.

Hôtel de l'Europe, *June* 2. — This morning we went again to the Duomo of the popes ;
and this time we allowed the custode, or sacristan, to show us the curiosities of it.   He led
us into a chapel apart, and showed us the old
Gothic tomb of Pope John XXII., where the

recumbent statue of the pope lies beneath one of those beautiful and venerable canopies of stone which look at once so light and so solemn. I know not how many hundred years old it is, but everything of Gothic origin has a faculty of conveying the idea of age; whereas classic forms seem to have nothing to do with time, and so lose the kind of impressiveness that arises from suggestions of decay and the past.

In the sacristy the guide opened a cupboard that contained the jewels and sacred treasures of the church, and showed a most exquisite figure of Christ in ivory, represented as on a cross of ebony; and it was executed with wonderful truth and force of expression, and with great beauty likewise. I do not see what a full-length marble statue could have had that was lacking in this little ivory figure of hardly more than a foot high. It is about two centuries old, by an unknown artist. There is another famous ivory statuette in Avignon which seems to be more celebrated than this, but can hardly be superior. I shall gladly look at it if it comes in my way.

Next to this, the prettiest thing the man showed us was a circle of emeralds, in one of the holy implements; and then he exhibited a little bit of a pope's skull; also a great old crosier, that looked as if made chiefly of silver, and partly gilt; but I saw where the plating of silver was worn away, and betrayed the copper of its actual substance. There were two or three pictures in the sacristy, by ancient and modern French artists, very unlike the productions of the Italian masters, but not without a beauty of their own.

Leaving the sacristy, we returned into the church, where Una and Julian began to draw the pope's old stone chair. There is a beast, or perhaps more than one, grotesquely sculptured upon it; the seat is high and square, the back low and pointed, and it offers no enticing promise to a weary man.

The interior of the church is massively picturesque, with its vaulted roof, and a stone gallery, heavily ornamented, running along each side of the nave. Each arch of the nave gives admittance to a chapel, in all of which there are pictures, and sculptures in most of them. One of these chapels is of the time of Charlemagne, and has a vaulted roof of admirable architecture, covered with frescos of modern date and little merit. In an adjacent chapel is the stone monument of Pope Benedict, whose statue reposes on it, like many which I have seen in the Cathedral of York and other old English churches. In another part we saw a monument, consisting of a plain slab supported on pillars; it is said to be of a Roman or very early Christian epoch. In another chapel was a figure of Christ in wax, I believe, and clothed in real drapery; a very ugly object. Also, a figure reposing under a slab, which strikes the spectator with the idea that it is really a dead person enveloped in a shroud. There are windows of painted glass in some of the chapels; and the gloom of the dimly lighted interior, especially beneath the broad, low arches, is very impressive.

While we were there some women assembled at one of the altars, and went through their acts of devotion without the help of a priest; one and another of them alternately repeating prayers, to which the rest responded. The murmur of their voices took a musical tone, which was reverberated by the vaulted arches.

Una and I now came out; and, under the porch, we found an old woman selling rosaries, little religious books, and other holy things. We bought two little medals of the Immaculate Virgin, one purporting to be of silver, the other of gold; but as both together cost only two or three sous, the genuineness of the material may well be doubted. We sat down on the steps of a crucifix which is placed in front of the church, and the children began to draw the porch, of which I hardly know whether to call the architecture classic or Gothic (as I said before); at all events it has a venerable aspect, and there are frescos within its arches by Simone Memmi. . . . The popes' palace is contiguous to

the church, and just below it, on the hillside.
It is now occupied as barracks by some regiments of soldiers, a number of whom were
lounging before the entrance; but we passed
the sentinel without being challenged, and addressed ourselves to the concierge, who readily
assented to our request to be shown through
the edifice. A French gentleman and lady,
likewise, came with similar purpose, and went
the rounds along with us. The palace is such a
confused heap and conglomeration of buildings,
that it is impossible to get within any sort of a
regular description. It is a huge, shapeless mass
of architecture; and if it ever had any pretence
to a plan, it has lost it in the modern alterations.
For instance, an immense and lofty chapel, or
rather church, has had two floors, one above
the other, laid at different stages of its height;
and the upper one of these floors, which extends just where the arches of the vaulted roof
begin to spring from the pillars, is ranged round
with the beds of one of the regiments of soldiers. They are small iron bedsteads, each with
its narrow mattress, and covered with a dark
blanket. On some of them lay or lounged a
soldier; other soldiers were cleaning their ac-
coutrements; elsewhere we saw parties of them
playing cards. So it was wherever we went
among those large, dingy, gloomy halls and
chambers, which, no doubt, were once stately

and sumptuous, with pictures, with tapestry, and all sorts of adornment that the Middle Ages knew how to use. The windows threw a sombre light through embrasures at least two feet thick. There were staircases of magnificent breadth. We were shown into two small chapels, in different parts of the building, both containing the remains of old frescos woefully defaced. In one of them was a light, spiral staircase of iron, built in the centre of the room as a means of contemplating the frescos, which were said to be the work of our old friend Giotto. . . . Finally, we climbed a long, long, narrow stair, built in the thickness of the wall, and thus gained access to the top of one of the towers, whence we saw the noblest landscapes, mountains, plains, and the Rhone, broad and bright, winding hither and thither, as if it had lost its way.

Beneath our feet was the gray, ugly old palace, and its many courts, just as void of system and as inconceivable as when we were burrowing through its bewildering passages. No end of historical romances might be made out of this castle of the popes; and there ought to be a ghost in every room, and droves of them in some of the rooms; for there have been murders here in the gross and in detail, as well hundreds of years ago, as no longer back than the French Revolution, when there was a great massacre in one of the courts. Traces of this bloody business were visible in actual stains on the wall only a few years ago.

Returning to the room of the concierge, who, being a little stiff with age, had sent an attendant round with us, instead of accompanying us in person, he showed us a picture of Rienzi, the last of the Roman tribunes, who was once a prisoner here. On a table, beneath the picture, stood a little vase of earthenware containing some silver coin. We took it as a hint, in the customary style of French elegance, that a fee should be deposited here, instead of being put into the hand of the concierge; so the French gentleman deposited half a franc, and I, in my magnificence, twice as much.

HÔTEL DE L'EUROPE, *June* 6. — We are still here. . . . I have been daily to the Rocher des Doms, and have grown familiar with the old church on its declivity. I think I might become attached to it by seeing it often. A sombre old interior, with its heavy arches, and its roof vaulted like the top of a trunk; its stone gallery, with ponderous adornments, running round three sides. I observe that it is a daily custom of the old women to say their prayers in concert, sometimes making a pilgrimage, as it were, from chapel to chapel. The voice of one of them is heard running through the series of petitions, and at intervals the voices of the others join and swell into a chorus, so that it is like a river connecting a series of lakes; or, not to use so gigantic a simile, the one voice is like a thread, on which the beads of a rosary are strung.

One day two priests came and sat down beside these prayerful women, and joined in their petitions. I am inclined to hope that there is something genuine in the devotion of these old women.

The view from the top of the Rocher des Doms (a contraction of Dominès) grows upon me, and is truly magnificent; a vast mountain-girdled plain, illuminated by the far windings and reaches of the Rhone. The river is here almost as turbid as the Tiber itself; but, I remember, in the upper part of its course the waters are beautifully transparent. A powerful rush is indicated by the swirls and eddies of its broad surface.

Yesterday was a race day at Avignon, and apparently almost the whole population and a great many strangers streamed out of the city gate nearest our hotel, on their way to the race-course. There were many noticeable figures that might come well into a French picture or description; but only one remains in my memory,— a young man with a wooden leg, setting off for the course — a walk of several miles, I believe — with prodigious courage and alacrity, flourishing his wooden leg with an air and grace that seemed to render it positively flexible. The crowd returned towards sunset, and almost all night long the streets and the whole air of the old town were full of song and merriment. There was a ball in a temporary structure, covered with an awning, in the Place d'Horloge, and a showman has erected his tent and spread forth his great painted canvases, announcing an anaconda and a sea-tiger to be seen. Julian paid four sous for admittance, and found that the sea-tiger was nothing but a large seal, and the anaconda altogether a myth.

I have rambled a good deal about the town. Its streets are crooked and perplexing, and paved with round pebbles for the most part, which afford more uncomfortable pedestrianism than the pavement of Rome itself. It is an ancient-looking place, with some large old mansions, but few that are individually impressive; though here and there one sees an antique entrance, a corner tower, or other bit of antiquity, that throws a venerable effect over the gray commonplace of past centuries. The town is not overclean, and often there is a kennel of unhappy odor. There appear to have been many more churches and devotional establishments under the ancient dominion of the popes than have been kept intact in subsequent ages;

the tower and façade of a church, for instance,
form the front of a carpenter's shop, or some
such plebeian place. The church where Laura
lay has quite disappeared, and her tomb along
with it. The town reminds me of Chester,
though it does not in the least resemble it, and
is not nearly so picturesque. Like Chester, it
is entirely surrounded by a wall; and that of
Avignon — though it has no delightful promenade on its top, as the wall of Chester has — is
the more perfectly preserved in its mediæval
form, and the more picturesque of the two.
Julian and I have once or twice walked nearly
round it, commencing from the gate of Ouelle,
which is very near our hotel. From this point
it stretches for a considerable distance along by
the river, and here there is a broad promenade,
with trees, and blocks of stone for seats; on one
side "the arrowy Rhone," generally carrying a
cooling breeze along with it; on the other, the
gray wall, with its battlements and machicolations, impending over what was once the moat,
but which is now full of careless and untrained
shrubbery. At intervals there are round towers swelling out from the wall, and rising a little
above it. After about half a mile along the
river-side the wall turns at nearly right angles,
and still there is a wide road, a shaded walk, a
boulevard; and at short distances are cafés, with
their little round tables before the door, or

small shady nooks of shrubbery. So numerous
are these retreats and pleasaunces that I do not
see how the little old town can support them all,
especially as there are a great many cafés within
the walls. I do not remember seeing any soldiers on guard at the numerous city gates, but
there is an office in the side of each gate for
levying the *octroi*, and old women are sometimes on guard there.

This morning, after breakfast, Julian and I
crossed the suspension bridge close by the gate
nearest our hotel, and walked to the ancient
town of Villeneuve, on the other side of the
Rhone. The first bridge leads to an island,
from the farther side of which another very
long one, with a timber foundation, accom-
plishes the passage of the other branch of the
Rhone. There was a good breeze on the river,
but after crossing it we found the rest of the
walk excessively hot. This town of Villeneuve
is of very ancient origin, and owes its existence,
it is said, to the famous holiness of a female
saint, which gathered round her abode and burial place a great many habitations of people who
reverenced her. She was the daughter of the
King of Saragossa, and I presume she chose this
site because it was so rocky and desolate. Afterwards it had a long mediæval history; and in
the time of the Avignon popes, the cardinals,
regretful of their abandoned Roman villas, built

pleasure houses here, so that the town was called
Villa Nuova.   After they had done their best,
it must have seemed to these poor cardinals but
a rude and sad exchange for the Borghese, the
Albani, the Pamfili Doria, and those other per-
fectest results of man's luxurious art.   And
probably the tradition of the Roman villas had
really been kept alive, and extant examples of
them all the way downward from the times of
the empire.   But this Villeneuve is the stoni-
est, roughest town that can be imagined.   There
are a few large old houses, to be sure, but built
on a line with shabby village dwellings and
barns, and so presenting little but samples of
magnificent shabbiness.   Perhaps I might have
found traces of old splendor if I had sought for
them ; but, not having the history of the place
in my mind, I passed through its scrambling
streets without imagining that Princes of the
Church had once made their abode here.   The
inhabitants now are peasants, or chiefly such ;
though, for aught I know, some of the French
noblesse may burrow in these palaces that look
so like hovels.

A large church, with a massive tower, stands
near the centre of the town ; and, of course, I
did not fail to enter its arched door, — a pointed
arch, with many frames and mouldings, one
within another.   An old woman was at her devotions, and several others came in and knelt

during my stay there.   It was quite an interesting interior; a long nave, with six pointed
arches on each side, beneath which were as
many chapels.   The walls were rich with pictures, not only in the chapels, but up and down
the nave, above the arches.   There were gilded
virgins, too, and much other quaint device that
produced an effect that I rather liked than otherwise.   At the end of the church, farthest from
the high altar, there were four columns of exceedingly rich marble, and a good deal more
of such precious material was wrought into the
chapels and altars.   There was an old stone
seat, also, of some former pope or prelate.   The
church was dim enough to cause the lamps in
the shrines to become points of vivid light, and,
looking from end to end, it was a long, venerable, tarnished, Old World vista, not at all tam-
pered with by modern taste.

We now went on our way through the village,
and, emerging from a gate, went clambering towards the castle of St. André, which stands,
perhaps, a quarter of a mile beyond it.   This
castle was built by Philip le Bel, as a restraint
to the people of Avignon in extending their
power on this side of the Rhone.   We happened not to take the most direct way, and so
approached the castle on the farther side, and
were obliged to go nearly round the hill on
which it stands, before striking into the path

which leads to its gate. It crowns a very bold and difficult hill, directly above the Rhone, opposite to Avignon, — which is so far off that objects are not minutely distinguishable, — and looking down upon the long, straggling town of Villeneuve. It must have been a place of mighty strength in its day. Its ramparts seem still almost entire, as looked upon from without, and when, at length, we climbed the rough, rocky pathway to the entrance, we found the two vast round towers, with their battlemented summits and arched gateway between them, just as perfect as they could have been five hundred or more years ago. Some external defences are now, however, in a state of ruin ; and there are only the remains of a tower, that once arose between the two round towers, and was apparently much more elevated than they. A little in front of the gate was a monumental cross of stone ; and in the arch, between the two round towers, were two little boys at play ; and an old woman soon showed herself, but took no notice of us. Casting our eyes within the gateway, we saw what looked a rough village street, betwixt old houses built ponderously of stone, but having far more the aspect of huts than of castle halls. They were evidently the dwellings of peasantry, and people engaged in rustic labor ; and no doubt they have burrowed into the primitive structures of the castle, and, as they found

convenient, have taken their crumbling materials
to build barns and farmhouses. There was space
and accommodation for a very considerable population ; but the men were probably at work in
the fields, and the only persons visible were the
children aforesaid, and one or two old women
bearing bundles of twigs on their backs. They
showed no curiosity respecting us, and though
the wide space included within the castle rampart seemed almost full of habitations ruinous
or otherwise, I never found such a solitude in
any ruin before. It contrasts very favorably
in this particular with English castles, where,
though you do not find rustic villages within
the warlike enclosure, there is always a pad-
locked gate, always a guide, and generally half
a dozen idle tourists. But here was only antiquity, with merely the natural growth of fun-
gous human life upon it.

We went to the end of the castle court and
sat down, for lack of other shade, among some
inhospitable nettles that grew close to the wall.
Close by us was a great gap in the ramparts, —
it may have been a breach which was once
stormed through ; and it now afforded us an
airy and sunny glimpse of distant hills. . . .
Julian sketched part of the broken wall, which,
by the bye, did not seem to me nearly so thick
as the walls of English castles. Then we returned through the gate, and I stopped, rather

impatiently, under the hot sun, while Julian drew the outline of the two round towers. This done, we resumed our way homeward, after drinking from a very deep well close by the square tower of Philip le Bel. Thence we went melting through the sunshine, which beat upward as pitilessly from the white road as it blazed downwards from the sky. . . .

GENEVA, HÔTEL D'ANGLETERRE, *June* 11.— We left Avignon on Tuesday, 7th, and took the rail to Valence, where we arrived between four and five, and put up at the Hôtel de la Poste, an ancient house, with dirty floors and dirt generally, but otherwise comfortable enough. . . . Valence is a stately old town, full of tall houses and irregular streets. We found a Cathedral there, not very large, but with a high and venerable interior, a nave supported by tall pillars, from the height of which spring arches. This loftiness is characteristic of French churches, as distinguished from those of Italy. . . . We likewise saw, close by the Cathedral, a large monument with four arched entrances meeting beneath a vaulted roof; but, on inquiry of an old priest and other persons, we could get no account of it, except that it was a tomb, and of unknown antiquity. The architecture seemed classic, and yet it had some Gothic peculiarities, and it was a reverend and beautiful object.

Had I written up my Journal while the town was fresh in my remembrance, I might have found much to describe; but a succession of other objects have obliterated most of the impressions I have received here. Our railway ride to Valence was intolerably hot. I have felt nothing like it since leaving America, and that is so long ago that the terrible discomfort was just as good as new. . . .

We left Valence at four, and came that afternoon to Lyons, still along the Rhone. Either the waters of this river assume a transparency in winter which they lose in summer, or I was mistaken in thinking them transparent on our former journey. They are now turbid; but the hue does not suggest the idea of a running mud puddle, as the water of the Tiber does. No streams, however, are so beautiful in the quality of their waters as the clear, brown rivers of New England. The scenery along this part of the Rhone, as we have found all the way from Marseilles, is very fine and impressive; old villages, rocky cliffs, castellated steeps, quaint châteaux, and a thousand other interesting objects.

We arrived at Lyons at five o'clock, and went to the Hôtel de l'Universe, to which we had been recommended by our good hostess at Avignon. The day had become showery, but Julian and I strolled about a little before nightfall, and saw the general characteristics of the place. Lyons is a city of very stately aspect, hardly inferior to Paris ; for it has regular streets of lofty houses, and immense squares planted with trees, and adorned with statues and fountains. New edifices of great splendor are in process of erection ; and on the opposite side of the Rhone, where the site rises steep and high, there are structures of older date, that have an exceedingly picturesque effect, looking down upon the narrow town.

The next morning I went out with Julian in quest of my bankers, and of the Amercian Consul ; and as I had forgotten the directions of the waiter of the hotel, I of course went astray, and saw a good deal more of Lyons than I intended. In my wanderings I crossed the Rhone, and found myself in a portion of the city evidently much older than that with which I had previously made acquaintance ; narrow, crooked, irregular, and rudely paved streets, full of dingy business and bustle, — the city, in short, as it existed a century ago, and how much earlier I know not. Above rises that lofty elevation of ground which I before noticed ; and the glimpses of its stately old buildings through the openings of the street were very picturesque. Unless it be Edinburgh, I have not seen any other city that has such striking features. Altogether unawares, immediately after crossing the bridge, we came upon the Cathedral; and the grand, time-blackened Gothic front, with its deeply arched entrances, seemed to me as good as anything I ever saw, — unexpectedly more impressive than all the ruins of Rome. I could but merely glance at its interior; so that its noble height and venerable space, filled with the dim, consecrated light of pictured windows, recur to me as a vision. And it did me good to enjoy the awfulness and sanctity of Gothic architecture again, after so long shivering in classic porticos. . . .

We now recrossed the river. . . . The Frank methods and arrangements in matters of business seem to be excellent, so far as effecting the proposed object is concerned; but there is such an inexorable succession of steel-wrought forms, that life is not long enough for so much accuracy. The stranger, too, goes blindfold through all these processes, not knowing what is to turn up next, till, when quite in despair, he suddenly finds his business mysteriously accomplished. . . .

We left Lyons at four o'clock, taking the railway for Geneva. The scenery was very striking throughout the journey; but I allowed the hills, deep valleys, high impending cliffs, and whatever else I saw along the road, to pass from me without an ink blot. We reached Geneva at nearly ten o'clock. . . . It is situated partly on low, flat ground, bordering the lake, and behind this level space it rises by steep, painfully paved streets, some of which can hardly be accessible by wheeled carriages. The prosperity of the town is indicated by a good many new and splendid edifices, for commercial and other purposes, in the vicinity of the lake ; but intermixed with these there are many quaint buildings of a stern gray color, and in a style of architecture that I prefer a thousand times to the monotony of Italian streets. Immensely high, red roofs, with windows in them, produce an effect that delights me. They are as ugly, perhaps, as can well be conceived, but very striking and individual. At each corner of these ancient houses frequently is a tower, the roof of which rises in a square pyramidal form, or, if the tower be round, in a round pyramidal form. Arched passages, gloomy and grimy, pass from one street to another. The lower town creeps with busy life, and swarms like an ant-hill ; but if you climb the half-precipitous streets, you find yourself among ancient and stately mansions, high roofed, with a strange aspect of grandeur about them, looking as if they might still be tenanted by such old magnates as dwelt in them centuries ago. There is also a Cathedral, the older portion exceedingly fine ; but it has been adorned at some modern epoch with a Grecian portico, — good in itself, but absurdly out of keeping with the edifice which it prefaces. This being a Protestant country, the doors were all shut,— an inhospitality that made me half a Catholic. It is funny enough that a stranger generally profits by all that is worst for the inhabitants of the country where he himself is merely a visitor. Despotism makes things all the pleasanter for the stranger. Catholicism lends itself admirably to his purposes.

There are public gardens (one, at least) in Geneva. . . . Nothing struck me so much, I think, as the color of the Rhone, as it flows under the bridges in the lower town. It is absolutely miraculous, and, beautiful as it is, suggests the idea that the tubs of a thousand dyers have emptied their liquid indigo into the stream. When once you have conquered and thrust out this idea, it is an inexpressible delight to look down into this intense, brightly transparent blue, that hurries beneath you with the speed of a race-horse.

The shops of Geneva are very tempting to a traveller, being full of such little knickknacks as he would be glad to carry away in memory of the place : wonderful carvings in wood and ivory, done with exquisite taste and skill ; jewelry that seems very cheap, but is doubtless dear enough, if you estimate it by the solid gold that goes into its manufacture ; watches, above all things else, for a third or a quarter of the price that one pays in England, looking just as well, too, and probably performing the whole of a watch's duty as uncriticisably. The Swiss people are frugal and inexpensive in their own habits, I believe, plain and simple, and careless of ornament ; but they seem to reckon on other people's spending a great deal of money for gewgaws. We bought some of their wooden trumpery, and likewise a watch for Una. . . . Next to watches, jewelry, and wood-carving, I should say that cigars were one of the principal articles of commerce in Geneva. Cigar shops present themselves at every step or two, and at a reasonable rate, there being no duties, I believe, on imported goods. There was no examination of our trunks on arrival, nor any questions asked on that score.

VILLENEUVE, HÔTEL DE BYRON, *June* 12. — Yesterday afternoon we left Geneva by a steamer, starting from the quay at only a short distance from our hotel. The forenoon had been showery ; but the sun now came out very pleasantly, although there were still clouds and mist enough to give infinite variety to the mountain scenery. At the commencement of our voyage the scenery of the lake was not incomparably superior to that of other lakes on which I have sailed, as Lake Windermere, for instance, or Loch Lomond, or our own Lake Champlain. It certainly grew more grand and beautiful, however,

till at length I felt that I had never seen anything worthy to be put beside it.   The southern shore has the grandest scenery ; the great
hills on that side appearing close to the water's
edge, and after descending, with headlong slope,
directly from their rocky and snow-streaked
summits down into the blue water.   Our course
lay nearer to the northern shore, and all our
stopping-places were on that side.   The first
was Coppet, where Madame de Staël or her
father, or both, were either born or resided or
died, I know not which, and care very little.   It
is a picturesque village, with an old church, and
old, high-roofed, red-tiled houses, the whole
looking as if nothing in it had been changed for
many, many years.   All these villages, at several
of which we stopped momentarily, look delightfully unmodified by recent fashions.   There is
the church, with its tower crowned by a pyramidal roof, like an extinguisher ; then the château
of the former lord, half-castle and half-dwel-
ling-house, with a round tower at each corner,
pyramid topped ; then, perhaps, the ancient
town house, or Hôtel de Ville, in an open paved
square ; and perhaps the largest mansion in the
whole village will have been turned into a modern inn, but retaining all its venerable characteristics of a high, steep sloping roof, and anti-
quated windows.   Scatter a delightful shade of
trees among the houses, throw in a time-worn

monument of one kind or another, swell out
the delicious blue of the lake in front, and the
delicious green of the sunny hillside sloping up
and around this closely congregated neighborhood of old, comfortable houses, and I do not
know what more I can add to this sketch.
Often there was an insulated house or cottage,
embowered in shade, and each seeming like
the one only spot in the wide world where two
people that had good consciences and loved
each other could spend a happy life.   Half-
ruined towers, old historic castles, these, too,
we saw.   And all the while, on the other side
of the lake, were the high hills, sometimes dim,
sometimes black, sometimes green, with gray
precipices of stone, and often snow patches, right
above the warm sunny lake whereon we were
sailing.

We passed Lausanne, which stands upward,
on the slope of the hill, the tower of its Cathedral forming a conspicuous object.   We mean
to visit this to-morrow ; so I may pretermit further mention of it here.   We passed Vevay, and
Clarens, which, methought, was particularly picturesque ; for now the hills had approached
close to the water on the northern side also, and
steep heights rose directly above the little gray
church and village ; and especially I remember
a rocky cliff which ascends into a rounded pyramid, insulated from all other peaks and ridges.

But if I could perform the absolute impossibility of getting one single outline of the scene
into words, there would be all the color wanting,
the light, the haze, which spiritualizes it, and
moreover makes a thousand and a thousand
scenes out of that single one.   Clarens, however, has still another interest for me ; for I
found myself more affected by it, as the scene
of the love of St. Preux and Julia, than I have
often been by scenes of poetry and romance.
I read Rousseau's romance with great sympathy, when I was hardly more than a boy ; ten
years ago, or thereabouts, I tried to read it
again without success ; but I think, from my
feeling of yesterday, that it still retains its hold
upon my imagination.

Farther onward, we saw a white, ancient-looking group of towers, beneath a mountain, which
was so high, and rushed so precipitately down
upon this pile of building as quite to dwarf it ;
besides which, its dingy whiteness had not a
very picturesque effect.   Nevertheless, this was
the Castle of Chillon.   It appears to sit right
upon the water, and does not rise very loftily
above it.   I was disappointed in its aspect, having imagined this famous castle as situated upon
a rock, a hundred, or, for aught I know, a thousand feet above the surface of the lake ; but it
is quite as impressive a fact — supposing it to
be true — that the water is eight hundred feet

deep at its base. By this time, the mountains
had taken the beautiful lake into their deepest
heart; they girdled it quite round with their
grandeur and beauty, and, being able to do no
more for it, they here withheld it from extending any farther; and here our voyage came to
an end. I have never beheld any scene so
exquisite; nor do I ask of Heaven to show
me any lovelier or nobler one, but only to give
me such depth and breadth of sympathy with
nature, that I may worthily enjoy this. It is
beauty more than enough for poor, perishable
mortals. If this be earth, what must heaven be!

It was nearly eight o'clock when we arrived;
and then we had a walk of at least a mile to the
Hôtel Byron. . . . I forgot to mention that
in the latter part of our voyage there was a
shower in some part of the sky, and though
none of it fell upon us, we had the benefit of
those gentle tears in a rainbow, which arched
itself across the lake from mountain to mountain, so that our track lay directly under this
triumphal arch. We took it as a good omen,
nor were we discouraged, though, after the rainbow had vanished, a few sprinkles of the shower
came down.

We found the Hôtel Byron very grand indeed, and a good one too. There was a beautiful moonlight on the lake and hills, but we
contented ourselves with looking out of our

The Castle of Chillon

lofty window, whence, likewise, we had a side-long glance at the white battlements of Chillon, not more than a mile off, on the water's edge. The castle is woefully in need of a pedestal. If its site were elevated to a height equal to its own, it would make a far better appearance. As it now is, it looks, to speak profanely of what poetry has consecrated, when seen from the water, or along the shore of the lake, very like an old whitewashed factory or mill.

This morning I walked to the Castle of Chillon with Julian, who sketches everything he sees, from a wild flower or a carved chair to a castle or a range of mountains. The morning had sunshine thinly scattered through it; but, nevertheless, there was a continual sprinkle, sometimes scarcely perceptible, and then again amounting to a decided drizzle. The road, which is built along on a little elevation above the lake shore, led us past the Castle of Chillon ; and we took a side path, which passes still nearer the castle gate. The castle stands on an isthmus of gravel, permanently connecting it with the mainland. A wooden bridge, covered with a roof, passes from the shore to the arched entrance ; and beneath this shelter, which has wooden walls as well as roof and floor, we saw a soldier or gendarme who seemed to act as warder. As it sprinkled rather more freely than at first, I thought of appealing to his hos-

pitality for shelter from the rain, but concluded
to pass on.

The castle makes a far better appearance on
a nearer view, and from the land, than when
seen at a distance, and from the water. It is
built of stone, and seems to have been anciently
covered with plaster, which imparts the whiteness to which Byron does much more than justice, when he speaks of " Chillon's snow-white
battlements." There is a lofty external wall,
with a cluster of round towers about it, each
crowned with its pyramidal roof of tiles, and
from the central portion of the castle rises a
square tower, also crowned with its own pyramid to a considerably greater height than the
circumjacent ones. The whole are in a close
cluster, and make a fine picture of ancient
strength when seen at a proper proximity ; for
I do not think that distance adds anything to
the effect. There are hardly any windows, or
few, and very small ones, except the loopholes
for arrows and for the garrison of the castle to
peep from on the sides towards the water ; indeed, there are larger windows, at least in the
upper apartments ; but in that direction, no
doubt, the castle was considered impregnable.
Trees here and there on the land side grow up
against the castle wall, on one part of which,
moreover, there was a green curtain of ivy
spreading from base to battlement. The walls

retain their machicolations, and I should judge that nothing had been [altered], nor any more work been done upon the old fortress than to keep it in singularly good repair. It was formerly a castle of the Duke of Savoy, and since his sway over the country ceased (three hundred years at least), it has been in the hands of the Swiss government, who still keep some arms and ammunition there.

We passed on, and found the view of it better, as we thought, from a farther point along the road. The raindrops began to spatter down faster, and we took shelter under an impending precipice, where the ledge of rock had been blasted and hewn away to form the road. Our refuge was not a very convenient and comfortable one, so we took advantage of the partial cessation of the shower to turn homeward, but had not gone far when we met mamma and all her train. As we were close by the castle entrance, we thought it advisable to seek admission, though rather doubtful whether the Swiss gendarme might not deem it a sin to let us into the castle on Sunday. But he very readily admitted us under his covered drawbridge, and called an old man from within the fortress to show us whatever was to be seen. This latter personage was a staid, rather grim, and Calvinistic-looking old worthy ; but he received us without scruple, and forthwith proceeded to

usher us into a range of most dismal dungeons,
extending along the basement of the castle, on
a level with the surface of the lake. First, if I
remember aright, we came to what he said had
been a chapel, and which, at all events, looked
like an aisle of one, or rather such a crypt as I
have seen beneath a cathedral, being a succession of massive pillars supporting groined arches,
— a very admirable piece of gloomy Gothic
architecture. Next, we came to a very dark
compartment of the same dungeon range, where
he pointed to a sort of bed, or what might serve
for a bed, hewn in the solid rock, and this, our
guide said, had been the last sleeping-place of
condemned prisoners on the night before their
execution. The next compartment was still
duskier and dismaller than the last, and he bade
us cast our eyes up into the obscurity and see
a beam, where the condemned ones used to be
hanged. I looked and looked, and closed my
eyes so as to see the clearer in this horrible
duskiness on opening them again. Finally, I
thought I discerned the accursed beam, and the
rest of the party were certain that they saw it.
Next beyond this, I think, was a stone staircase, steep, rudely cut, and narrow, down which
the condemned were brought to death ; and beyond this, still on the same basement range of
the castle, a low and narrow [corridor] through
which we passed, and saw a row of seven mas

sive pillars, supporting two parallel series of groined arches, like those in the chapel which we first entered. This was Bonnivard's prison, and the scene of Byron's poem.

The arches are dimly lighted by narrow loopholes, pierced through the immensely thick wall, but at such a height above the floor that we could catch no glimpse of land or water, or scarcely of the sky. The prisoner of Chillon could not possibly have seen the island to which Byron alludes, and which is a little way from the shore, exactly opposite the town of Villeneuve. There was light enough in this long, gray, vaulted room, to show us that all the pillars were inscribed with the names of visitors, among which I saw no interesting one, except that of Byron himself, which is cut, in letters an inch long or more, into one of the pillars next to that to which Bonnivard was chained. The letters are deep enough to remain in the pillar as long as the castle stands. Byron seems to have had a fancy for recording his name in this and similar ways ; as witness the record which I saw on a tree of Newstead Abbey. In Bonnivard's pillar there still remains an iron ring, at the height of perhaps three feet from the ground. His chain was fastened to this ring, and his only freedom was to walk round this pillar, about which he is said to have worn a path in the stone pavement

of the dungeon ; but as the floor is now covered with earth or gravel, I could not satisfy
myself whether this be true. Certainly six years,
with nothing else to do in them save to walk
round the pillar, might well suffice to wear away
the rock, even with naked feet. This column,
and all the columns, were cut and hewn in a
good style of architecture, and the dungeon
arches are not without a certain gloomy beauty.
On Bonnivard's pillar, as well as on all the rest,
were many names inscribed ; but I thought
better of Byron's delicacy and sensitiveness for
not cutting his name into that very pillar. Perhaps, knowing nothing of Bonnivard's story, he
did not know to which column he was chained.

Emerging from the dungeon vaults, our guide
led us through other parts of the castle, showing us the Duke of Savoy's kitchen, with a
fireplace at least twelve feet long ; also the judgment hall, or some such place, hung round
with the coats of arms of some officers or other,
and having at one end a wooden post, reaching
from floor to ceiling, and having upon it the
marks of fire. By means of this post, contu-
macious prisoners were put to a dreadful torture, being drawn up by cords and pulleys,
while their limbs were scorched by a fire underneath. We also saw a chapel or two, one of
which is still in good and sanctified condition,
and was to be used this very day, our guide

told us, for religious purposes. We saw, moreover, the duke's private chamber, with a part of the bedstead on which he used to sleep, and be haunted with horrible dreams, no doubt, and the ghosts of wretches whom he had tortured and hanged ; likewise the bedchamber of his duchess, that had in its window two stone seats, where, directly over the head of Bonnivard, the ducal pair might look out on the beautiful scene of lake and mountains, and feel the warmth of the blessed sun. Under this window, the guide said, the water of the lake is eight hundred feet in depth ; an immense profundity, indeed, for an inland lake, but it is not very difficult to believe that the mountain at the foot of which Chillon stands may descend so far beneath the water. In other parts of the lake and not distant, more than nine hundred feet have been sounded. I looked out of the duchess's window, and could certainly see no appearance of a bottom in the light blue water.

The last thing that the guide showed us was a trapdoor, or opening, beneath a crazy old floor. Looking down into this aperture, we saw three stone steps, which we should have taken to be the beginning of a flight of stairs that descended into a dungeon, or series of dungeons, such as we had already seen. But inspecting them more closely, we saw that the third step terminated the flight, and beyond was a dark vacancy. Three steps a person would grope down, planting his uncertain foot on a dimly seen stone ; the fourth step would be in the empty air. The guide told us that it used to be the practice to bring prisoners hither, under pretence of committing them to a dungeon, and make them go down the three steps, and that fourth fatal one, and they would nevermore be heard of; but at the bottom of the pit there would be a dead body, and in due time a mouldy skeleton, which would rattle beneath the body of the next prisoner that fell. I do not believe that it was anything more than a secret dungeon for state prisoners whom it was out of the question either to set at liberty or bring to public trial. The depth of the pit was about forty-five feet. Gazing intently down, I saw a faint gleam of light at the bottom, apparently coming from some other aperture than the trapdoor over which we were bending, so that it must have been contemplated to supply it with light and air in such degree as to support human life. Una declared she saw a skeleton at the bottom ; Miss S—— thought she saw a hand ; but I saw only the dim gleam of light.

There are two or three courts in the castle, but of no great size. We were now led across one of them, and dismissed out of the arched entrance by which we had come in. We found

388

the gendarme still keeping watch on his roofed
drawbridge, and as there was the same gentle
shower that had been effusing itself all the
morning, we availed ourselves of the shelter,
more especially as there were some curiosities
to examine.   These consisted chiefly of wood-
carvings, — such as little figures in the national
costume, boxes with wreaths of foliage upon
them, paper knives, the chamois goat admirably well represented.   We at first hesitated to
make any advances towards trade with the gendarme because it was Sunday, and we fancied
there might be a Calvinistic scruple on his part
about turning a penny on the Sabbath ; but
from the little I know of the Swiss character, I
suppose they would be as ready as any other
men to sell not only such matters, but even
their own souls, or any smaller — or shall we
say greater — thing on Sunday, or at any other
time.   So we began to ask the prices of the
articles, and met with no difficulty in purchasing
a salad spoon and fork, with pretty bas-reliefs
carved on the handles, and a napkin ring.   For
Rosebud's and our amusement, the gendarme
now set a musical box a-going ; and as it played,
a pasteboard figure of a dentist began to pull
the tooth of a pasteboard patient, lifting the
wretched simulacrum entirely from the ground,
and keeping him in this horrible torture for
half an hour.   Meanwhile, mamma, Miss Shep-

ard, Una, and Julian sat down all in a row on a bench and sketched the mountains; and as the shower did not cease, though the sun most of the time shone brightly, we were kept actual prisoners of Chillon much longer than we wished to stay.

We took advantage of the first cessation, — though still the drops came dimpling into the water that rippled against the pebbles beneath the bridge,— of the first partial cessation of the shower, to escape, and returned towards the hotel, with this kindliest of summer rains falling upon us most of the way. . . . In the afternoon the rain entirely ceased, and the weather grew delightfully radiant, and warmer than could well be borne in the sunshine. Una and I walked to the village of Villeneuve, — a mile from the hotel, — and found a very commonplace little old town of one or two streets, standing on a level, and as uninteresting as if there were not a hill within a hundred miles. It is strange what prosaic lines men thrust in amid the poetry of nature. . . .

GENEVA, HÔTEL DE L'ANGLETERRE, *June* 14. — Yesterday morning was very fine, and we had a pretty early breakfast at Hôtel Byron, preparatory to leaving it. This hotel is on a magnificent scale of height and breadth, its staircases and corridors being the most spacious I have seen ; but there is a kind of meagreness in the life there, and a certain lack of heartiness, that prevented us from feeling at home. We were glad to get away, and took the steamer, on our return voyage, in excellent spirits. Apparently it had been a cold night in the upper regions, for a great deal more snow was visible on some of the mountains than we had before observed ; especially a mountain called " Diableries " presented a silver summit, and broad sheets and fields of snow. Nothing ever can have been more beautiful than those groups of mighty hills as we saw them then, with the gray rocks, the green slopes, the white snow patches and crests, all to be seen at one glance, and the mists and fleecy clouds tumbling, rolling, hovering about their summits, filling their lofty valleys, and coming down far towards the lower world, making the skyey aspects so intimate with the earthly ones, that we hardly knew whether we were sojourning in the material or spiritual world. It was like sailing through the sky, moreover, to be borne along on such water as that of Lake Leman, — the bluest, brightest, and profoundest element, the most radiant eye that the dull earth ever opened to see heaven withal. I am writing nonsense, but it is because no sense within my mind will answer the purpose.

Some of these mountains, that looked at no

such mighty distance, were at least forty or fifty miles off, and appeared as if they were near neighbors and friends of other mountains, from which they were really still farther removed. The relations into which distant points are brought, in a view of mountain scenery, symbolize the truth, which we can never judge within our partial scope of vision, of the relations which we bear to our fellow creatures and human circumstances. These mighty mountains think that they have nothing to do with one another, each seems itself its own centre, and existing for itself alone ; and yet, to an eye that can take them all in, they are evidently portions of one grand and beautiful idea, which could not be consummated without the lowest and the loftiest of them. I do not express this satisfactorily, but have a genuine meaning in it nevertheless.

We passed again by Chillon, and gazed at it as long as it was distinctly visible, though the water view does no justice to its real picturesqueness, there being no towers nor projections on the side towards the lake, nothing but a wall of dingy white, with an indentation that looks something like a gateway. About an hour and a half brought us to Ouchy, the point where passengers land to take the omnibus to Lausanne. The ascent from Ouchy to Lausanne is a mile and a half, which it took the omnibus nearly half an hour to accomplish. We left our shawls and carpet-bags in the *salle à manger* of the Hôtel Faucon, and set forth to find the Cathedral, the pinnacled tower of which is visible for a long distance up and down the lake. Prominent as it is, however, it is by no means very easy to find it while rambling through the intricate streets and declivities of the town itself, for Lausanne is the town, I should fancy, in all the world the most difficult to go directly from one point to another. It is built on the declivity of a hill, adown which run several valleys or ravines, and over these the contiguity of houses extends, so that the communication is kept up by means of steep streets and sometimes long weary stairs, which must be surmounted and descended again in accomplishing a very moderate distance. In some inscrutable way we at last arrived at the Cathedral, which stands on a higher site than any other in Lausanne. It has a very venerable exterior, with all the Gothic grandeur which arched mullioned windows, deep portals, buttresses, towers, and pinnacles, gray with a thousand years, can give to architecture. After waiting awhile, we obtained entrance by means of an old woman, who acted the part of sacristan, and was then showing the church to some other visitors.

The interior disappointed us; not but what it was very beautiful, but I think the excellent

repair that it was in, and the puritanic neatness
with which it is kept, does much towards effa-
cing the majesty and mystery that belong to an
old church.   Every inch of wall and column,
and all the mouldings and tracery, and every
scrap of grotesque carving, had been washed
with a drab mixture.   There were likewise seats
all up and down the nave, made of pine wood,
and looking very new and neat, just such seats
as I shall see in a hundred meeting-houses (if
ever I go into so many) in America.   Whatever
might be the reason, the stately nave, with its
high-groined roof, the clustered columns and
lofty pillars, the intersecting arches of the side
aisles, the choir, the armorial and knightly
tombs that surround what was once the high
altar, all produced far less effect than I could
have thought beforehand.

As it happened, we had more ample time
and freedom to inspect this Cathedral than any
other that we have visited, for the old woman
consented to go away and leave us there, locking
the door behind her.   The others, except Rosebud, sat down to sketch such portions as struck
their fancy ; and for myself, I looked at the
monuments, of which some, being those of old
knights, ladies, bishops, and a king, were curious from their antiquity ; and others are interesting as bearing memorials of English people,
who have died at Lausanne in comparatively

recent years. Then I went up into the pulpit, and tried, without success, to get into the stone gallery that runs all round the nave ; and I explored my way into various side apartments of the Cathedral, which I found fitted up with seats for Sabbath schools, perhaps, or possibly for meetings of elders of the Church. I opened the great Bible of the church, and found it to be a French version, printed at Lille some fifty years ago. There was also a liturgy, adapted, probably, to the Lutheran form of worship. In one of the side apartments I found a strong-box, heavily clamped with iron, and having a contrivance, like the hopper of a mill, by which money could be turned into the top, while a double lock prevented its being abstracted again. This was to receive the avails of contributions made in the church ; and there were likewise boxes, stuck on the ends of long poles, wherewith the deacons could go round among the worshippers, conveniently extending the begging-box to the remotest curmudgeon among them all. From the arrangement of the seats in the nave, and the labels pasted or painted on them, I judged that the women sat on one side and the men on the other, and the seats for various orders of magistrates, and for ecclesiastical and collegiate people, were likewise marked out.

I soon grew weary of these investigations, and so did Rosebud and Julian, who essayed to amuse themselves with running races together over the horizontal tombstones in the pavement of the choir, treading remorselessly over the noseless effigies of old dignitaries, who never expected to be so irreverently treated. I put a stop to their sport, and banished them to different parts of the Cathedral; and, by and by, the old woman appeared again, and released us from durance. . . .

While waiting for our *déjeuner*, we saw the people dining at the regular *table d'hôte* of the hotel, and the idea was strongly borne in upon me, that the professional mystery of a male waiter is a very unmanly one. It is so absurd to see the solemn attentiveness with which they stand behind the chairs, the earnestness of their watch for any crisis that may demand their interposition, the gravity of their manner in performing some little office that the guest might better do for himself, their decorous and soft steps; in short, as I sat and gazed at them, they seemed to me not real men, but creatures with a clerical aspect, engendered out of a very artificial state of society. When they are waiting on myself, they do not appear so absurd; it is necessary to stand apart in order to see them properly.

We left Lausanne — which was to us a tedious and weary place — before four o'clock. I should have liked well enough to see the house of Gibbon, and the garden in which he walked, after finishing The Decline and Fall; but it could not be done without some trouble and inquiry, and as the house did not come to see me, I determined not to go and see the house. There was, indeed, a mansion of somewhat antique respectability, near our hotel, having a garden and a shaded terrace behind it, which would have answered accurately enough to the idea of Gibbon's residence. Perhaps it was so: far more probably not.

Our former voyages had been taken in the Hirondelle; we now, after broiling for some time in the sunshine by the lakeside, got on board of the Aigle, No. 2. There were a good many passengers, the larger proportion of whom seemed to be English and American, and among the latter a large party of talkative ladies, old and young. The voyage was pleasant while we were protected from the sun by the awning overhead, but became scarcely agreeable when the sun had descended so low as to shine in our faces or on our backs. We looked earnestly for Mont Blanc, which ought to have been visible during a large part of our course; but the clouds gathered themselves hopelessly over the portion of the sky where the great mountain lifted his white peak; and we did not see it, and probably never shall. As to the meaner mountains, there were enough of them, and beautiful enough ; but we were a little weary, and feverish with the heat. . . . I think I had a headache, though it is so unusual a complaint with me that I hardly know it when it comes. We were none of us sorry, therefore, when the Eagle brought us to the quay of Geneva, only a short distance from our hotel. . . .

To-day I wrote to Mr. Wilding, requesting him to secure passages for us from Liverpool on the 15th of next month, or 1st of August. It makes my heart thrill, half pleasantly, half otherwise ; so much nearer does this step seem to bring that home whence I have now been absent six years, and which, when I see it again, may turn out to be not my home any longer. I likewise wrote to Bennoch, though I know not his present address ; but I should deeply grieve to leave England without seeing him. He and Henry Bright are the only two men in England to whom I shall be much grieved to bid farewell ; but to the island itself I cannot bear to say that word, as a finality. I shall dreamily hope to come back again at some indefinite time ; rather foolishly, perhaps, for it will tend to take the substance out of my life in my own land. But this, I suspect, is apt to be the penalty of those who stay abroad, and stay too long.

HAVRE, HÔTEL WHEELER, *June* 22. — We arrived at this hotel last evening from Paris, and

find ourselves on the borders of the Petit Quay
Notre Dame, with steamers and boats right
under our windows, and all sorts of dock business going on briskly. There are barrels, bales,
and crates of goods; there are old iron cannon
for posts; in short, all that belongs to the
Wapping of a great seaport. . . . The American partialities of the guests [of this hotel] are
consulted by the decorations of the parlor, in
which hang two lithographs and colored views
of New York, from Brooklyn and from Wee-
hawken. The fashion of the house is a sort of
nondescript mixture of Frank, English, and
American, and is not disagreeable to us after
our weary experience of Continental life. The
abundance of the food is very acceptable, in
comparison with the meagreness of French and
Italian meals; and last evening we supped
nobly on cold roast beef and ham, set generously before us, in the mass, instead of being
doled out in slices few and thin. The waiter has
a kindly sort of manner, and resembles the steward of a vessel rather than a landsman; and, in
short, everything here has undergone a change,
which might admit of very effective description.
I may now as well give up all attempts at journalizing. So I shall say nothing of our journey
across France from Geneva. . . . To-night we
shall take our departure in a steamer for South-
ampton, whence we shall go to London ; thence,

in a week or two, to Liverpool; thence to Boston and Concord, there to enjoy — if enjoyment it prove — a little rest and a sense that we are at home.

[More than four months were now taken up in writing The Marble Faun, in great part at the seaside town of Redcar, Yorkshire, Mr. Hawthorne having concluded to remain another year in England, chiefly to accomplish that romance. In Redcar, where he remained till September or October, he wrote no journal, but only the book. He then went to Leamington, where he finished The Marble Faun in March, and there is a little journalizing soon after leaving Redcar. — S. H.]

LEAMINGTON, *November* 14, 1859. — Julian and I walked to Lillington the other day. Its little church was undergoing renovation when we were here two years ago, and now seems to be quite renewed, with the exception of its square, gray battlemented tower, which has still the aspect of unadulterated antiquity. On Saturday Julian and I walked to Warwick by the old road, passing over the bridge of the Avon, within view of the castle. It is as fine a piece of English scenery as exists anywhere, — the quiet little river shadowed with drooping trees, and, in its vista, the gray towers and long line of windows of the lordly castle, with a picturesquely

varied outline ; ancient strength, a little softened
by decay. . . .

The town of Warwick, I think, has been considerably modernized since I first saw it.   The
whole of the central portion of the principal
street now looks modern, with its stuccoed or
brick fronts of houses, and, in many cases, handsome shop windows.   Leicester Hospital and
its adjoining chapel still look venerably antique ;
and so does a gateway that half bestrides the
street.   Beyond these two points on either side
it has a much older aspect.   The modern signs
heighten the antique impression.

February 5, 1860. — Mr. and Mrs. Bennoch
are staying for a little while at Mr. B——'s, at
Coventry, and Mr. B—— called upon us the
other day, with Mr. Bennoch, and invited us to
go and see the lions of Coventry ; so yesterday
Una and I went.   It was not my first visit,
therefore I have little or nothing to record, unless it were to describe a ribbon factory into
which Mr. B—— took us.   But I have no com-
prehension of machinery, and have only a confused recollection of an edifice of four or five
stories, on each floor of which were rows of huge
machines, all busy with their iron hands and
joints in turning out delicate ribbons.   It was
very curious and unintelligible to me to observe
how they caused different colored patterns *to*

appear, and even flowers to blossom, on the plain surface of a ribbon. Some of the designs were pretty, and I was told that one manufacturer pays £500 annually to French artists (or artisans, for I do not know whether they have a connection with higher art) merely for new patterns of ribbons. The English find it impossible to supply themselves with tasteful productions of this sort, merely from the resources of English fancy. If an Englishman possessed the artistic faculty to the degree requisite to produce such things, he would doubtless think himself a great artist, and scorn to devote himself to these humble purposes. Every Frenchman is probably more of an artist than one Englishman in a thousand.

We ascended to the very roof of the factory, and gazed thence over smoky Coventry, which is now a town of very considerable size, and rapidly on the increase. The three famous spires rise out of the midst, that of St. Michael being the tallest, and very beautiful. Had the day been clear, we should have had a wide view on all sides ; for Warwickshire is well laid out for distant prospects, if you can only gain a little elevation from which to see them.

Descending from the roof, we next went to see Trinity Church, which has just come through an entire process of renovation, whereby much of its pristine beauty has doubtless been re-

stored ; but its venerable awfulness is greatly
impaired.   We went into three churches, and
found that they had all been subjected to the
same process.   It would be nonsense to regret
it, because the very existence of these old edifices is involved in their being renewed ; but it
certainly does deprive them of a great part of
their charm, and puts one in mind of wigs,
padding, and all such devices for giving de-
crepitude the aspect of youth.   In the pavement
of the nave and aisles there are worn tombstones,
with defaced inscriptions, and discolored marbles affixed against the wall ; monuments, too,
where a mediæval man and wife sleep side by
side on a marble slab ; and other tombs so old
that the inscriptions are quite gone.   Over an
arch, in one of the churches, there was a fresco,
so old, dark, faded, and blackened, that I found
it impossible to make out a single figure or the
slightest hint of the design.   On the whole, after
seeing the churches of Italy, I was not greatly
impressed with these attempts to renew the ancient beauty of old English minsters ; it would
be better to preserve as sedulously as possible
their aspect of decay, in which consists the principal charm. . . .

On our way to Mr. B———'s house, we looked
into the quadrangle of a charity school and old
men's hospital, and afterwards stepped into a
large Roman Catholic church, erected within

these few years past, and closely imitating the mediæval architecture and arrangements. It is strange what a plaything, a trifle, an unserious affair, this imitative spirit makes of a huge, ponderous edifice, which if it had really been built five hundred years ago would have been worthy of all respect. I think the time must soon come when this sort of thing will be held in utmost scorn, until the lapse of time shall give it a claim to respect. But, methinks, we had better strike out any kind of architecture, so it be our own, however wretched, than thus tread back upon the past.

Mr. B—— now conducted us to his residence, which stands a little beyond the outskirts of the city, on the declivity of a hill, and in so windy a spot that, as he assured me, the very plants are blown out of the ground. He pointed to two maimed trees whose tops were blown off by a gale two or three years since ; but the foliage still covers their shortened summits in summer, so that he does not think it desirable to cut them down.

In America, a man of Mr. B——'s property would take upon himself the state and dignity of a millionaire. It is a blessed thing in England, that money gives a man no pretensions to rank, and does not bring the responsibilities of a great position.

We found three or four gentlemen to meet

us at dinner, — a Mr. D—— and a Mr. B——, an author, having written a book called The Philosophy of Necessity, and is acquainted with Emerson, who spent two or three days at his house when last in England. He was very kindly appreciative of my own productions, as was also his wife, next to whom I sat at dinner. She talked to me about the author of Adam Bede, whom she has known intimately all her life. . . . Miss Evans (who wrote Adam Bede) was the daughter of a steward, and gained her exact knowledge of English rural life by the connection which this origin brought her with the farmers. She was entirely self-educated, and has made herself an admirable scholar in classical as well as in modern languages. Those who knew her had always recognized her wonderful endowments, and only watched to see in what way they would develop themselves. She is a person of the simplest manner and character, amiable and unpretending, and Mrs. B—— spoke of her with great affection and respect. . . . Mr. B——, our host, is an extremely sensible man ; and it is remarkable how many sensible men there are in England, — men who have read and thought, and can develop very good ideas, not exactly original, yet so much the product of their own minds that they can fairly call them their own. . . .

405

February 18. — . . . This present month has been somewhat less dismal than the preceding ones; there have been some sunny and breezy days when there was life in the air, affording something like enjoyment in a walk, especially when the ground was frozen. It is agreeable to see the fields still green through a partial covering of snow; the trunks and branches of the leafless trees, moreover, have a verdant aspect, very unlike that of American trees in winter, for they are covered with a delicate green moss, which is not so observable in summer. Often, too, there is a twine of green ivy up and down the trunk. The other day, as Julian and I were walking to Whitnash, an elm was felled right across our path, and I was much struck by this verdant coating of moss over all its surface, — the moss plants too minute to be seen individually, but making the whole tree green. It has a pleasant effect here, where it is the natural aspect of trees in general; but in America a mossy tree trunk is not a pleasant object, because it is associated with damp, low, unwholesome situations. The lack of foliage gives many new peeps and vistas, hereabouts, which I never saw in summer.

March 17. — Julian and I walked to Warwick yesterday forenoon, and went into St. Mary's Church, to see the Beauchamp chapel. . . . On one side of it were some worn steps ascending to a confessional, where the priest used to sit, while the penitent, in the body of the church, poured his sins through a perforated auricle into this unseen receptacle. The sexton showed us, too, a very old chest which had been found in the burial vault, with some ancient armor stored away in it. Three or four helmets of rusty iron, one of them barred, the last with visors, and all intolerably weighty, were ranged in a row. What heads those must have been that could bear such massiveness ! On one of the helmets was a wooden crest — some bird or other — that of itself weighed several pounds. . . .

BATH, *April* 23. — We have been here several weeks. . . . Had I seen Bath earlier in my English life, I might have written many pages about it, for it is really a picturesque and interesting city. It is completely sheltered in the lap of hills, the sides of the valley rising steep and high from the level spot on which it stands, and through which runs the muddy little stream of the Avon. The older part of the town is on the level, and the more modern growth — the growth of more than a hundred years — climbs higher and higher up the hillside, till the upper streets are very airy and lofty. The houses are built almost entirely of Bath stone, which in time loses its original buff

color, and is darkened by age and coal smoke
into a dusky gray ; but still the city looks clean
and pure as compared with most other English
towns.   In its architecture it has somewhat of
a Parisian aspect, the houses having roofs rising
steep from their high fronts, which are often
adorned with pillars, pilasters, and other good
devices so that you see it to be a town built
with some general idea of beauty, and not for
business.   There are Circuses, Crescents, Terraces, Parades, and all such fine names as we
have become familiar with at Leamington, and
other watering-places.   The declivity of most
of the streets keeps them remarkably clean, and
they are paved in a very comfortable way, with
large blocks of stone, so that the middle of the
street is generally practicable to walk upon, although the sidewalks leave no temptation so to
do, being of generous width.   In many alleys,
and round about the Abbey and other edifices,
the pavement is of square flags, like those of
Florence, and as smooth as a palace floor.   On
the whole, I suppose there is no place in England where a retired man, with a moderate in-
come, could live so tolerably as at Bath ; it being almost a city in size and social advantages ;
quite so, indeed, if eighty thousand people
make a city, — and yet having no annoyance of
business nor spirit of worldly struggle.   All
modes of enjoyment that English people like

may be had here ; and even the climate is said
to be milder than elsewhere in England. How
this may be, I know not; but we have had rain
or passing showers almost every day since we
arrived, and I suspect the surrounding hills
are just about of that inconvenient height, that
keeps catching clouds, and compelling them to
squeeze out their moisture upon the included
valley.   The air, however, certainly is preferable to that of Leamington. . . .

There are no antiquities except the Abbey,
which has not the interest of many other English churches and cathedrals.   In the midst of
the old part of the town stands the house which
was formerly Beau Nash's residence, but which
is now part of the establishment of an ale mer-
chant.   The edifice is a tall, but rather mean-
looking, stone building, with the entrance from
a little side court, which is so cumbered with
empty beer barrels as hardly to afford a passage.
The doorway has some architectural pretensions, being pillared and with some sculptured
devices — whether lions or winged heraldic
monstrosities I forget — on the pediment.
Within there is a small entry, not large enough
to be termed a hall, and a staircase, with carved
balustrade, ascending by angular turns and
square landing-places.   For a long course of
years, ending a little more than a century ago,
princes, nobles, and all the great and beautiful

people of old times, used to go up that staircase, to pay their respects to the King of Bath.
On the side of the house there is a marble slab
inserted, recording that here he resided, and that
here he died in 1767, between eighty and ninety
years of age.   My first acquaintance with him
was in Smollett's Roderick Random, and I
have met him in a hundred other novels.

His marble statue is in a niche at one end of
the great pump-room, in wig, square-skirted
coat, flapped waistcoat, and all the queer costume of the period, still looking ghost-like upon
the scene where he used to be an autocrat.
Marble is not a good material for Beau Nash,
however; or, if so, it requires color to set him
off adequately. . . .

It is usual in Bath to see the old sign of the
checker-board on the doorposts of taverns.   It
was originally a token that the game might be
played there, and is now merely a tavern sign.

LONDON, 31 HERTFORD STREET, MAYFAIR,
May 16, 1860. — I came hither from Bath on
the 14th, and am staying with my friends, Mr.
and Mrs. Motley.   I would gladly journalize
some of my proceedings, and describe things and
people; but I find the same coldness and stiffness
in my pen as always since our return to England.
I dined with the Motleys at Lord Dufferin's,
on Monday evening, and there met, among a

few other notable people, the Honorable Mrs. Norton, a dark, comely woman; who doubtless was once most charming, and still has charms, at above fifty years of age. In fact, I should not have taken her to be greatly above thirty, though she seems to use no art to make herself look younger, and talks about her time of life without any squeamishness. Her voice is very agreeable, having a sort of muffled quality, which is excellent in woman. She is of a very cheerful temperament, and so has borne a great many troubles without being destroyed by them. But I can get no color into my sketch, so shall leave it here.

LONDON, *May* 17. [From a letter.] — Affairs succeed each other so fast, that I have really forgotten what I did yesterday. I remember seeing my dear friend, Henry Bright, and listening to him, as we strolled in the Park, and along the Strand. To-day I met at breakfast Mr. Field Talfourd, who promises to send you the photograph of his portrait of Mr. Browning. He was very agreeable, and seemed delighted to see me again. At lunch, we had Lord Dufferin, the Honorable Mrs. Norton, and Mr. Sterling (author of the Cloister Life of Charles V.), with whom we are to dine on Sunday.

You would be stricken dumb, to see how

quietly I accept a whole string of invitations, and what is more, perform my engagements without a murmur.

A German artist has come to me with a letter of introduction, and a request that I will sit to him for a portrait in bas-relief. To this, likewise, I have assented! subject to the condition that I shall have my leisure.

The stir of this London life, somehow or other, has done me a wonderful deal of good, and I feel better than for months past. This is strange, for if I had my choice, I should leave undone almost all the things I do.

I have had time to see Bennoch only once.

[This closes the European Journal. After Mr. Hawthorne's return to America, he published Our Old Home, and began a new romance, of which two chapters appeared in the Atlantic Monthly. But the breaking out of the war stopped all imaginative work with him, and all journalizing, until 1862, when he went to Maine for a little excursion, and began another journal, from which I take one paragraph, giving a slight note of his state of mind at an interesting period of his country's history. — S. H.]

WEST GOULDSBOROUGH, *August* 15, 1862. — It is a week ago, Saturday, since Julian and I reached this place, . . . Mr. Barney S. Hill's.

At Hallowell, and subsequently all along the
route, the country was astir with volunteers, and
the war is all that seems to be alive, and even
that doubtfully so.   Nevertheless, the country
certainly shows a good spirit, the towns offering everywhere most liberal bounties, and every
able-bodied man feels an immense pull and
pressure upon him to go to the war.   I doubt
whether any people was ever actuated by a more
genuine and disinterested public spirit; though,
of course, it is not unalloyed with baser motives
and tendencies.   We met a train of cars with a
regiment or two just starting for the South, and
apparently in high spirits.   Everywhere some
insignia of soldiership were to be seen, — bright
buttons, a red stripe down the trousers, a military cap, and sometimes a round-shouldered
bumpkin in the entire uniform.   They require
a great deal to give them the aspect of soldiers;
indeed, it seems as if they needed to have a good
deal taken away and added, like the rough clay
of a sculptor as it grows to be a model.   The
whole talk of the bar-rooms and every other
place of intercourse was about enlisting and the
war, this being the very crisis of trial, when the
voluntary system is drawing to an end, and the
draft almost immediately to commence.

413

INDEX TO NOTES OF TRAVEL

INDEX TO NOTES OF TRAVEL

416

INDEX TO NOTES OF TRAVEL

417

INDEX TO NOTES OF TRAVEL

INDEX TO NOTES OF TRAVEL

INDEX TO NOTES OF TRAVEL

INDEX TO NOTES OF TRAVEL

INDEX TO NOTES OF TRAVEL

431

INDEX TO NOTES OF TRAVEL

INDEX TO NOTES OF TRAVEL

Lincoln's Inn Hall, iii. 97.
Lincolnshire, ii. 332.
Lind, Jenny, ii. 96, 198, 199, 200.
Linlithgow, ii. 418.
Linlithgow Church, ii. 418.
Linlithgow Palace, ii. 419, 425; iii. 192.
Linnell, John, the younger, iii. 43.
Lion Hotel, i. 323, 326.
Lions, ii. 201.
Lippi, Filippo, iv. 60, 169.
Lisbon, i. 417, 422, 424.
Literary Fund, ii. 58.
"Little John," iii. 52.
Liverpool, i. 2, 11, 12; ii. 156; iii. 61; history of, 39.
Livre des Merveilles, iv. 351.
Lizards, iii. 282.
Llandudno, i. 139.
Lloyd, Mayor, i. 158.
Lloyd, Mrs., i. 158.
Locanda, a, iii. 397.
Lodgings, i. 135, 213; ii. 258; iii. 18, 37, 53, 54, 389; at Oxford, ii. 233, 237.
Lodore, i. 274, 276.
Loggie, iii. 316, 321; iv. 181.
Lomond, Ben, ii. 113, 117, 384, 411.
Lomond, Loch, ii. 113, 114, 389, 396.
London, i. 332; ii. 37, 81; iii. 70; iv. 410; bridge, i. 335; fog, iii. 77, 97, 111, 115; by night, i. 386; wall, ii. 52; weariness of, iii. 120.
London Stone, ii. 53.
Long, Loch, ii. 115.
Longara, iv. 309, 310.
Longfellow, H. W., i. 157; ii. 91, 97, 241, 320; Poems, ii. 223.
Longsword, Earl of Salisbury, ii. 171.
Lonsdale, Earl of, ii. 375.
Lopez, Narcisso, i. 203.
Lord Mayor, the, ii. 202.
Lough, John Graham, i. 279.
Louis IX., Saint, iii. 140.
Louis XIV., statue, iii. 167.

Louis XVI., iii. 153.
Louis XVII., iii. 153.
Louis le Grand, Place de, iii. 167.
Louvre, the, iii. 137, 139, 148.
Louvre, Hôtel de, iii. 126, 134, 163.
Lovat, Lord, i. 356.
Lovel, Robert, i. 281.
Lovelaces, the, ii. 356.
Lover, Samuel, ii. 200, 202.
"Lover's Leap," ii. 383.
Lovers, Italian, iv. 111.
Lowell, James Russell, i. 370; ii. 91.
Lowwood Hotel, i. 239, 241, 244, 296.
Luce, Captain, i. 165.
Lucifer, iii. 237.
Ludovisi, Villa, iii. 295.
Luly's hand, iv. 88.
Lunatic Asylum, a, i. 44, 56.
Luncheon, i. 220.
Lung' Arno, iv. 59.
Lupus, Hugh, i. 129.
Lyndoch, Lady, iii. 266.
Lyons, iii. 164, 166; iv. 371.
Lyons, Cathedral of, iv. 373.
Lyulph's Tower, i. 269.

M——, Miss, iii. 229, 266.
Macchiavelli, Nicholas, iv. 130, 137.
Macaulay, Thomas Babington, ii. 212, 213.
Madeleine, Church of the, iii. 143.
Macclesfield Hundred, i. 71.
Macdonald, James, ii. 290.
Macdonald, John, ii. 290.
Macgregor, Mr. (of Arroquhar), ii. 116.
Mackay, Dr., ii. 107, 198.
Mackay, Mrs., ii. 107.
Madeira, the ship, ii. 3.
Madonnas, iii. 252, 266; iv. 90, 95, 139, 150, 164, 172, 203, 265, 269, 283; della Seggiola, iv. 77.
Madness, i. 170, 180.
Malaria, iii. 330; iv. 296, 297.
Magdalen College Chapel, ii. 234.

433

INDEX TO NOTES OF TRAVEL

INDEX TO NOTES OF TRAVEL

INDEX TO NOTES OF TRAVEL

INDEX TO NOTES OF TRAVEL

447

INDEX TO NOTES OF TRAVEL

Webster, Daniel, iv. 98, 241.

Webster family, the, ii. 75, 78.

Webster, Lady, ii. 74.

Weddings, i. 57, 386; ii. 319; iii. 41; iv. 171.

Wellesley, Marquis of, ii. 245.

Wellington, Duke of, i. 286; ii. 46; statues, iii. 76, 122.

Wellington Hotel, ii. 185.

Wells, iv. 26, 156, 261.

Welsh, i. 115, 148, 150.

Wept of the Wish-ton-Wish, the, iii. 304.

Wessyngtons, De, the, ii. 148.

West, Benjamin, ii. 45; iv. 260.

Westmacott, Richard, iii. 61.

Westminster Abbey, i. 350, 351, 367, 386, 397, 412, 413, 422; ii. 52, 151, 226, 335; ii. 78, 121. *See* Poets' Corner.

Westminster Bridge, i. 416.

Westminster Hall, i. 410.

Westminster, Marquis of, i. 67.

Westmoreland, i. 262, 289.

Weston, Misses, iii. 287, 346.

Wharfe, the river, ii. 300.

Whealby, Thomas, i. 222.

Wheatley (American volunteer), ii. 277.

Wheeler, Hotel, iv. 398.

White, Blanco, i. 89.

White, Thomas, ii. 291, 292.

Whitechapel, i. 334.

Whitehall, i. 334, 350.

Whitnash, iii. 69.

Whitsuntide, i. 204; ii. 357, 365.

Whooping-cough, i. 109.

Wickham, William of, ii. 241.

Widower's ring, a, iii. 361.

Wigan, i. 68.

Wigs, i. 123.

Wilde, Mr., iii. 343; iv. 334.

Wilding, Mr. (Vice-Consul), i. 80, 106, 196; ii. 13, 16, 58, 345; iii. 38; iv. 398.

Wildman, Colonel, ii. 348, 349, 356.

Wilkie, Sir David, i. 158; ii. 229; iii. 26.

Wilkinson, Dr., iii. 123.

Will-o'-the-Wisp, iv. 327.

William I., the Conqueror, ii. 76.

William III., ii. 46, 127, 379.

William of Deloraine, iii. 3.

Williams, Miss Anna, i. 180.

Williams, Sir William, ii. 204.

Winckelmann, John, iii. 370.

Windermere, i. 226, 239, 252, 290, 297; ii. 114.

Wine, iv. 29, 231, 304. *See* Grapes and Vines.

Wine-shops, iv. 32, 337.

Wine-vaults of the London Docks, ii. 196.

Winter, i. 173; ii. 19; iii. 126, 128, 388.

Wolfe, General, i. 355; ii. 399.

Wolsey, Cardinal, ii. 41, 255; iii. 23, 219.

Wolverhampton, ii. 184.

Women, ii. 98, 307; carrying burdens, i. 15; at the Carnival, iv. 319; at confession, iv. 271; English and American compared, i. 5, 28; French, iv. 358, 362; health of, ii. 200; Italian, iii. 401, 402; iv. 29–31, 169, 217, 268; literary, i. 23; at the Louvre, iii. 150; of the lowest classes, i. 207; at Marseilles, iii. 175; at Rome, iii. 231, 280, 326, 351, 396; iv. 25; Scotch, ii. 134.

Wood, Anthony-à-, ii. 249.

Wood's *Narrative of the Campaign*, ii. 27.

Woolner, Thomas, iii. 34.

Wooton, ii. 68.

Worcester, ii. 4; Cathedral, 6; Natural History Society, 8.

Wordsworth, William, house, i. 249; grave, 255, 282, 289; monument, 260, 262, 264, 266, 281, 304; portrait, 399; statue, ii. 226, 303.

Wordsworth, Mrs. William, i. 249, 253.

Workhouses. *See* Almshouses.

449

INDEX TO NOTES OF TRAVEL

INDEX TO THE TITLES

OF

NATHANIEL HAWTHORNE'S WORKS

AS ARRANGED IN THIS EDITION

INDEX TO THE TITLES

OF

NATHANIEL HAWTHORNE'S WORKS

The titles in small capitals are those of the separate volumes or of principal divisions; those in Roman small letters are single short pieces.

INDEX TO THE TITLES

OF HAWTHORNE'S WORKS

INDEX TO THE TITLES

OF HAWTHORNE'S WORKS

INDEX TO THE TITLES

OF HAWTHORNE'S WORKS

459